Scottish Verse

1851 – 1951

Selected for the general reader
by

Douglas Young

With Foreword, Notes and Glossary

Thomas Nelson and Sons Ltd
London Edinburgh Paris Melbourne
Toronto and New York

THOMAS NELSON AND SONS LTD
Parkside Works Edinburgh 9
3 Henrietta Street London WC2
312 Flinders Street Melbourne C1
5 Parker's Buildings Burg Street Cape Town

THOMAS NELSON AND SONS (CANADA) LTD
91–93 Wellington Street West Toronto 1

THOMAS NELSON AND SONS
19 East 47th Street New York 17

SOCIÉTÉ FRANÇAISE D'EDITIONS NELSON
25 rue Henri Barbusse Paris V^e

First published 1952

B220552

The text of this book is set in
11 on 12 Bembo

Til the memorie o my faither
STEPHEN YOUNG
(1878–1945)
and the lave o my forebearers
Lallan or Hielant
frae baith sides o the Tay
and aa the airts o Scotland
that fine wad likeit
this outwale

CONTENTS

FOREWORD   xvii

ACKNOWLEDGMENTS   xxxi

CHARLES GRAY	from *Epistle to Mr David Sillar*	1
DAVID SHAW	*Tammie Treddlefeet*	2
DAVID VEDDER	*Auld Freends*	3
THOMAS LYLE	*Smile through thy tears . . .*	5
HEW AINSLIE	*The Hint o' Hairst*	6
JOHN GIBSON LOCKHART	*When youthful faith . . .*	7
JANET HAMILTON	from *The Sunday Rail*	8
	Oor Location	9
THOMAS CARLYLE	*To-day*	10
ALEXANDER SMART	*Election Lyric*	10
WILLIAM KENNEDY	*The Friend*	12
LORD MACAULAY	*A Jacobite's Epitaph*	13
JAMES NICOL	*The Apostle Paul*	14
LORD NEAVES	*A Lyric for Saturday Night*	14
ANON.	from *The Barnyards o Delgaty*	16
EDWARD L. SLOAN	*The Weaver's Triumph*	17
THOMAS AIRD	*St Mary's Well*	19
GEORGE OUTRAM	*The Annuity*	19
WILLIAM LIVINGSTONE	*Eirinn ag Gul. Ireland Greitan*	24
WILLIAM MILLER	*Wee Willie Winkie*	25
	Lines to Victor Hugo	26
THOMAS TOD STODDART	*Song: 'A Rosary of Stars . . .'*	27
LADY JOHN SCOTT	*Durrisdeer*	27
W. E. AYTOUN	*The Massacre of the Macpherson*	28
JAMES HEDDERWICK	from *The Villa by the Sea*	30
JOHN MITCHELL	from *The St Rollox Lum's Address to his Brethren*	31
JOHN CRAWFORD	*Causey Courtship*	33
HUGH MACDONALD	*My Ain Hearthstane*	34
GEORGE MURRAY	*The Auld Kirk o' Scotland*	36
SIR JOSEPH NOEL PATON	*Timor Mortis conturbat me*	37
DOROTHEA MARIA OGILVY	*The Weary Spinnin O't*	37
GEORGE MACDONALD	*The Lord is my Shepherd*	39
	That Holy Thing	39
	A Sang o Zion	39

vii

CONTENTS

WALTER CHALMERS SMITH	*Miss Penelope Leith*	40
ALEXANDER NICOLSON	*Skye*	43
ALEXANDER SMITH	*Glasgow*	46
WILLIAM McGONAGALL	*Lines in Praise of Professor Blackie*	50
JAMES MACFARLAN	from *The Lords of Labour*	51
J. B. SELKIRK	from *Death in Yarrow*	51
	Second-Sight	53
JAMES EASSON	*The Factory Girl*	54
ADAM LINDSAY GORDON	from *Gordon's Valedictory Poem*	55
JAMES THOMSON	from *The City of Dreadful Night*	56
'MOSES PEERIE, D.D.'	from *The Goodly Ironmaster*	62
ELLEN JOHNSTON	*The Last Sark*	65
DAVID GRAY	*Sonnet*	65
THOMAS DAVIDSON	*And there will I be buried*	66
ROBERT BUCHANAN	from *The Wedding of Shon Maclean*	67
ANDREW LANG	*To Robert Louis Stevenson*	67
	from *Clevedon Church*	68
	In Ithaca	69
	Matrimony	70
ALEXANDER ANDERSON	from *The Spirit of the Times*	71
JOHN YOUNG GRAY	*My Loonie*	72
HUGH HALIBURTON	*On the Decadence of the Scots Language, Manners and Customs*	73
ROBERT LOUIS STEVENSON	*Singing*	75
	It is not yours, O Mother . . .	76
	A Portrait	77
	The Maker to Posterity	78
	My Conscience	79
	Youth and Love, I	81
	In the Highlands	81
	To S. R. Crockett	82
JAMES YOUNG GEDDES	from *Glendale & Co.*	83
THOMAS GIVEN	*A Song for February*	87
ROGER QUIN	*To a Skylark*	88
ADAM WILSON	from *The Brotherhood of Man*	89
SIR DONALD MACALISTER	*The Twa Traivlers*	90
ROB WANLOCK	*Gloaming*	91
RONALD CAMPBELL MACFIE	*A Moral*	91
	Man in Evolution	92
W. A. MACKENZIE	*Shon Campbell*	92

CONTENTS

JAMES KEIR HARDIE	*Evening Prayer*	93
JAMES PITTENDRIGH MACGILLIVRAY	*Glances*	94
	Abasshyd	95
JOHN DAVIDSON	from *A Ballad in Blank Verse of the Making of a Poet*	96
	Thirty Bob a Week	103
	Decadents	106
WALLACE MARTIN LINDSAY	*A Song of Putting*	107
DUGALD SUTHERLAND MACCOLL	*What are We Fighting for—Scotland*	109
BASIL RAMSAY ANDERSON	*A Cry from the Poor*	110
	Fragment to His Mother	111
DAVID RORIE	*The Pawky Duke*	111
J. J. HALDANE BURGESS	from *Dokkins*	114
ROBERT FULLER MURRAY	Ἀιὲν Ἀριστεύειν	114
MARY SYMON	*The Glen's Muster-Roll*	115
VIOLET JACOB	*Jock to the First Army*	118
	The Field by the Lirk o' the Hill	119
	Tam i' the Kirk	120
	Baltic Street	120
	Pride	122
NEIL MUNRO	from *Bannocks o Barley*	123
	Lament for Macleod of Raasay	124
CHARLES MURRAY	*The Hint o' Hairst*	125
	Gin I was God	126
JOHN FERGUS	*Blin'*	126
WALTER WINGATE	*Conscience*	127
	After	128
RUDYARD KIPLING	from *McAndrew's Hymn*	129
DOUGLAS GRANT DUFF AINSLIE	*Memory* (for S.G.)	133
	Serenade (from the Sanskrit)	133
JOHN GRAY	*Ad Matrem*	134
	A Prelate	134
	Ettrickdale	135
MARION ANGUS	*The Wild Lass*	136
	Alas! Poor Queen	136
SIR WILLIAM CRAIGIE	from *Autumn in Denmark* (1892)	138
GEORGE DOUGLAS BROWN	*Covenanter's Deathbed*	138

ix

CONTENTS

ROBERT MURRAY	*The Bairn*	139
M. C. SMITH	*The Boy in the Train*	140
G. K. MENZIES	*Poaching in Excelsis*	141
WILL H. OGILVIE	*The Blades of Harden*	142
LORD ALFRED DOUGLAS	from *The City of the Soul*	143
	Lighten our Darkness	144
JOHN FERGUSON	*Sonnet No. III* from *Thyrea*	144
	Ad majorem Dei gloriam	145
HAMISH HENDRY	*Saunders MacSiccar*	146
LEWIS SPENCE	*The Prows o' Reekie*	148
	The Queen's Bath-house, Holyrood	149
	Portrait of Mary Stuart, Holyrood	149
	The Pavone	150
	The Carse	150
JOHN BUCHAN	*Home Thoughts from Abroad*	151
NANNIE K. WELLS	*A Prayer*	153
RACHEL ANNAND TAYLOR	*The Princess of Scotland*	154
	The Doubles	155
	The Doubt	156
ROBERT CRAWFORD	*Darkness Visible*	156
A. W. MAIR	*The Prayer of the Lover*	157
	Epitaph	158
JOSEPH LEE	*The Bullet*	158
	German Prisoners	158
J. M. CAIE	*Sair Wark's Nae Easy*	159
HAROLD MONRO	*Week-End*	160
JOHN MACDOUGALL HAY	*Celtic Melancholy*	161
WILLIAM MOIR CALDER	*Moray Sang*	162
	An Epitaph	163
W. D. COCKER	*The Deluge*	163
SIR ALEXANDER GRAY	*Scotland*	166
	Grief	168
IVO MACNAUGHTON CLARK	*Ascensioun*	168
ANDREW YOUNG	*Field-Glasses*	169
A. M. DAVIDSON	*Auld Fowk*	170
HELEN BURNESS CRUICKSHANK	*Overdue*	170
	Comfort in Puirtith	171
	The Stranger	171
	Sae Lang has Sorrow	172

CONTENTS

	The Ponnage	172
	Glenskenno Wood	173
	Ealasaid	174
	Spring in the Mearns	175
W. H. HAMILTON	Armistice Day	177
EDWIN MUIR	Scotland's Winter	177
	The Transmutation	178
	The Stronghold	179
	The Return	180
	Song	181
	The Rider Victory	182
	The Castle	183
	The Swimmer's Death	184
	Epitaph	184
	Variations on a Time Theme, VII	185
	Merlin	185
	from The Journey Back	186
ANON.	The Station-Master's Dochter	187
JAMES BRIDIE	Martha's Prayer to St. Eloi	188
	The Three Tykes	189
WALTER ELLIOT	Sestette to Fish	190
ISOBEL WYLIE HUTCHISON	Advent Sunday at Umanak	191
BESSIE J. B. MACARTHUR	The Collady-Stane	192
	Last Leave	193
G. BRUCE THOMSON	McFarlane o' the Sprots o' Burnie-boozie	193
GEORGE BUCHANAN-SMITH	Fragment	195
WILLA MUIR	Speerin'	195
WILLIAM OGILVIE	There's Nane o' My Ain to Care	196
IVOR BROWN	Never Go Back	196
NEIL M. GUNN	The Serpent	197
MARGARET WINEFRIDE SIMPSON	Villanelle	198
FREDERICK VICTOR BRANFORD	Ardgay	198
	Secret Treaties, II	199
	To D. C. B.	199
	The Iron Flower	200
HUGH MACDIARMID (C. M. Grieve)	Cophetua	200
	The Watergaw	201

CONTENTS

	O Jesu Parvule	201
	The Eemis-stane	201
	Empty Vessel	202
	At My Father's Grave	202
	Milk-wort and Bog-cotton	203
	Water Music	203
	With a Lifting of the Head	205
	The Skeleton of the Future	206
	The Parrot Cry	206
	On Reading Professor Ifor Williams's 'Canu Aneirin' . . .	209
	The Seamless Garment	212
	The Little White Rose	215
EWART ALAN MACKINTOSH	*In Memoriam Private D. Sutherland . . .*	215
NAN SHEPHERD	*Above Loch Avon*	217
	In the Cairngorms, XVIII	217
WILLIAM JEFFREY	*John Knox in the Galleys (1547-49)*	217
CHARLES HAMILTON SORLEY	*The Song of the Ungirt Runners*	221
	To Germany	221
JAMES PEACOCK	from *Desideria* (a Sonnet Sequence)	222
ALAN FLEMING McGLASHAN	*Anaesthesia*	223
ANON.	*The Dundonian at Bonn*	223
RODERICK WATSON KERR	*The Grave-digger*	225
GABRIEL RIVERS	*Last Lullaby*	225
	True Wedlock	225
NAOMI MITCHISON	*Lament*	226
	Westminster	226
WILLIAM SOUTAR	*The Bairn*	227
	The Tryst	227
	The Lanely Müne	228
	The Sea-shell	228
	The Makar	229
	Content	229
	Riddle on a Library	230
	The Auld House	230
	The Earth Abides	231
	The Unicorn	232
	Reality	232
	Healing Moment	233
	For a Sundial	233

CONTENTS

	The Permanence of the Young Men	233
	Song	234
ROBERT RENDALL	Cragsman's Widow	234
	Orkney Crofter	235
ERIC LINKLATER	from Seven Years	235
	Soldiers and Guns	236
	Teheran	236
ALICE V. STUART	The Clock in the Sick-room	236
JOE CORRIE	The Image o God	237
	When Bess was Badly	238
HAMISH MACLAREN	Little Sea House	238
	Island Rose	239
MARION LOCHHEAD	Knight and Lady	239
	Fiddler's Bidding	240
ADAM DRINAN	from The Ghosts of the Strath	240
HUNTER DIACK	Talk	241
ALBERT D. MACKIE	Sea Strain	242
	What's Aheid o's ?	242
	Thunder Sky	243
	A New Spring	243
WILLIAM MONTGOMERIE	Glasgow Street	244
	from The Castle on the Hill	244
DOROTHY MARGARET PAULIN	Said the Spaewife	245
	Prayer on Good Friday	246
	Sodger's Lass	246
	Breaking Covert	247
ARCHIE LAMONT	The White Rose	248
ROBERT MACLELLAN	Sang	248
ROBERT KEMP	Last Judgment	249
LAVINIA DERWENT	Traitor	250
JANET MARY SMITH	The Fairm Quean to her Birl Pleugh	250
GEORGE BRUCE	The Fisherman	252
ROBERT GARIOCH	Embro tae the Ploy	253
JOHN KINCAID	Citie	256
NORMAN MCCAIG	I Remember You	257
	So Many Make One	258
	The Last Week of the Year	258
	Instrument and Agent	259
	No Time, No Time	259
GEORGE SCOTT-MONCRIEFF	The Toad	260

CONTENTS

STUART HOOD	*Du Rote Fahn'*	260
T. S. LAW	*Lynes Scryveit til Henry P. Cameron*	261
	Epitaph	262
BERNARD FERGUSSON	*The Tryst*	262
SOMHAIRLE MACLEAN	*Bu tu camhanaich*	264
	[*Ye Were the Dawn*]	265
	Cha do chuir de bhuaireadh	264
	[*I never kent sic glawmerie*]	265
	Ban-Ghaidheal	266
	[*Hielant Woman*]	267
	bho *An Cuilthionn*	268
	[Finale of *The Coolin*]	269
	Coin is Madaidhean-allaidh	270
	[*Dogs and Wolves*]	271
	Am Trom-Laighe	272
	[*The Widdreme*]	273
	Calbharaigh	272
	[*My een are nae on Calvary*]	273
J. F. HENDRY	from *The Orchestral Mountain*	274
DOUGLAS YOUNG	*Last Lauch*	274
	Love	275
	For the Old Highlands	275
	For a Wife in Jizzen	276
	Winter Homily on the Calton Hill	276
	Simplon Tunnel	277
G. S. FRASER	*Lean Street*	278
	Meditation of a Patriot	279
ANN SCOTT-MONCRIEFF	*A Night in the Country*	280
ALEXANDER GALLOWAY	*The Ploughman*	280
R. CROMBIE SAUNDERS	*The Panthers*	281
	Sonnet	281
DAVID MARTIN	*Lament for the Gordons*	282
DERICK THOMSON	*An Loch-a-Tuath*	284
	[*The Loch o the North*]	285
GEORGE CAMPBELL HAY	*Grunnd na Mara*	284
	[*The Grund o the Sea*]	285
	Aonarain na Cille	286
	[*The Solitaries*]	287

CONTENTS

	To a Certain Loch Fyne Fisherman	288
	The Three Brothers	288
JOHN SINGER	Smooth on the Aftermath	290
SYDNEY GOODSIR SMITH	The Mither's Lament	291
	Largo	291
	Sahara	292
	Ye Mongers aye Need Masks for Cheatrie	292
	For my Newborn Son	293
	from The Eildon Tree, VIII	293
	The Moment	294
ALEX DOW	from The New-rigged Ship	295
W. S. GRAHAM	from The First Journey	296
	Fourth Sonnet (1940)	296
ANTONY ROSS	Christ ran stumbling	297
	To love, and more to love	297
TOM SCOTT	To X	298
MAURICE LINDSAY	Hurlygush	299
	The Tunnel	299
	John Knox	300
THURSO BERWICK	Brig o Giants	300
HAMISH HENDERSON	from The Highlanders at Alamein	302
ALEXANDER SCOTT	Calvinist Sang	304
	Coronach	304
R. L. COOK	Bothwell at Malmo (1578)	305
	Thocht on a Winter E'en	306
GEORGE KAY	Rome	306
	Exile	307
A. H. EMSLIE-SMITH	Scottish Renaissance	308
NOTES		309
GLOSSARY		337
ALPHABETICAL LIST OF AUTHORS		353
ALPHABETICAL INDEX OF FIRST LINES		357

FOREWORD BY DOUGLAS YOUNG

THIS selection is of verse produced by Scots—or by persons writing in some Scottish tradition—living at some time during the period 1851–1951. A century is not a long time in the history of the Scottish Nation or of the Scottish Muse, but the past century happens to be the most influential progenitor of our present, and may repay attention on that account. No doubt the main forces of the Scottish consciousness have been directed into channels other than Poetry : into Science, Capitalism and Socialism, for example. But the compatriots of Burns, Drummond of Hawthornden and Alasdair MacMhaighstir Alasdair have not wholly neglected the craft of verse in the various tongues used north of Tweed, and it has seemed to me worth while to examine the aspirations and the achievements of the past four generations.

The year 1851 was almost a nadir, and 1951 is by no means a zenith, but the various luminaries composing the Scottish poetic constellation seem to have been in the ascendant during the century. Scots writing in the official King's dialect of English are flying higher and more surely today than in 1851, Edwin Muir above all. Those who employ the most peculiarly Scottish linguistic medium, that used by Barbour, Dunbar, Fergusson, Burns, Lady Nairne, whether you affect to call it Braid Scots, Broad Scotch, Lallans, Lawlant, Doric, Plastic, Vernacular, the northern dialect of Anglo-Saxon or the western dialect of Frisian or of Jutish—those who employ this language, speech, dialect or amalgam, have raised their sights from the miniature range of 1851, and some are even in the *avant-garde* of Atomic Age poetry, swept round in the

2

vortex of Hugh MacDiarmid. As for Gaelic, our oldest and most beautiful tongue, with the longest tradition, and perhaps the fullest capacity for high poetry, of any medium yet used by Scots, though the colloquial use of its dialects in the West Highlands and Isles and in Eastern Canada has dwindled till only about 150,000 people habitually speak it, a wealth of versification continues, mostly for song and satire, and two major poets have lately appeared, whom good judges think better than any for a couple of centuries—Somhairle Maclean and George Campbell Hay.

There is a certain interpenetration of the languages current in Scotland, and literary interanimation. Scots or Gaelic words and idioms and rhythms crop up even in the English of the most Anglicised. More fundamental, there is a common underlying national consciousness whose expression in superficially very diverse media may sometimes be sensed. One thinks of an old long-rooted stock imparting some autochthonous sap to various scions engrafted on it. The outward and visible signs of this inward and spiritual grace are not classifiable otherwise than by the term ' Scottish,' which I use in its widest extension. ' Scots ' or ' Scotch ' are forms of the word often used more narrowly, to refer to the kindly *mither tongue* used by Burns and the rest ; but to avoid confusion I have followed Robert Burns, Robert Louis Stevenson and Edwin Muir in using the term *Lallans* for that part of Scottish verse which is expressed in what the English often call Broad Scotch. Lallans in colloquial use has become increasingly mixed up with King's English, especially since the advent of compulsory universal schooling and the invention of radio and cinema ; as a reaction there has been a purist movement, like the Greek *katharevousa*, to establish a full canon of vocabulary and usage, with a better spelling, founded on the main literary tradition in the language. That tradition comes down from Barbour's *Brus* in the fourteenth century, through the Court Scots of the fifteenth- and sixteenth-century Makars and the palace, law-courts and parliament; it was popularised by the sixteenth- and seventeenth-century Ballads and was revived for literature in the eighteenth century by Ramsay, Fergusson and Burns. The Scottish spirit abhors standardisation; regional, parochial and personal idiosyncrasies flourish even in the works of those most conversant with the Lallans literary tradition; and I have not modified authors' spellings beyond what seemed to me the minimum needed to help the reader—least of all in the few Norn pieces included from Orkney and Shetland.

This anthology endeavours to gather representative blossoms from the cultivation of Scottish poetry and verse during four generations in three languages. Very few of the cultivators are poets in the higher sense—probably no more than six—chronologically, John Davidson, Edwin Muir, Hugh Mac-Diarmid, Somhairle Maclean, Sydney Goodsir Smith, George Campbell Hay. There are rather more good minor poets: James Thomson, Robert Louis Stevenson, Uilleam MacDhun-Leibhe, Violet Jacob, William Soutar, to give examples only from the dead. Some accomplished versifiers, like George Outram, Andrew Lang and myself. Then a great swarm of minimal poets and practitioners of verse, not without a certain interest or even value.

What have been my principles of selection? With the major poets, few though they are, I have been unable, for lack of space, to give more than what I hope are representative samples of the main aspects of their output. I have not tried to present their best achievements in order of merit. Not only would the effort have been presumptuous, but also the method of sampling better suits the aim of the anthology. With the Gaelic poets my choice was restricted by the need to print a Lallans or English metrical version—many good representative pieces have not yet been translated. With minor and minimal poets, and with accomplished or less accomplished versifiers, I make no claim to have produced anything approaching a comprehensive, scholarly or definitive selection. Comprehensiveness will not be possible till the National Library of Scotland possesses and has available all the relevant sources of material. Though I have looked over hundreds of volumes at odd moments in the past twenty years, and of magazines, there must be hundreds that have eluded me, including a few of considerable merit. I am sure also that much good verse never gets printed.

Though we Scots are a polyglot and world-dispersed nation, like the Jews, I have not used pieces in languages other than Gaelic, Lallans and English, and have taken little from outside our official territory. John Hewitt was anxious that I should indicate the participation of Ulster in the Lallans literary tradition a century ago, by including pieces from Edward L. Sloan, Thomas Given, Sir Samuel Fergusson, Cecil Frances Alexander (who wrote not only ' There is a green hill ' but also the ' Legend of Stumpie's Brae ') and others ; and I have been able to do a little in this line. There is also a fair amount of minor stuff by Scots scattered in Australia, like Adam Lindsay Gordon, and other Dominions, and in the U.S.A. I like to think of Roy Campbell from South Africa as a Scot in more than name. The alleged Scots descent of Robert Browning perhaps gets some corroboration from his ' Grammarian's Funeral.' The fact that Rudyard Kipling's maternal grandfather was a Macdonald and a man of religion is no doubt a partial explanation of ' McAndrew's Hymn.' Had Mr Winston Churchill versified I should have thought him eligible, because he appears to be not very much less Scots than English by pedigree. Some politicians who versified have been included, also some novelists and others for whom verse is a minor activity ; because an able mind often makes more interesting verse at an odd moment than the would-be high-flying poet who essays a flutter every day and night.

In the matter of scholarship, it is known that not even the most respectable editions of such a poet as Stevenson conform to strict editorial requirements, and I suspect the case is much worse with others.* The spelling and punctuation even of most collections issued under the author's supervision leave much to be desired (as I know from my own issues). I have usually taken a few liberties with orthography, in the hope of easing the general reader's perusal, but if anyone notes errors of more substance the publishers and I will be gratified to be informed, that they may be corrected in due course.

Regarding definitiveness, where poetic value has been small, that is to say with ninety per cent of the authors perused, I have often been influenced in my choice by theme, technique, language or merely by personality ; sometimes by the preference for brevity, or by the wish to avoid familiar pieces where another almost as good might be as representative of the writer. There are dozens of authors, and hundreds of pieces, omitted, though just as good as many that are included. It is not to be supposed that every point that has sometimes interested me will always interest everyone else, but there is some likelihood that most of the writers and pieces chosen will have some appeal or interest for the intelligent general reader, whether specially concerned with Scotland or merely interested in verse.

Were I to attempt to discuss tendencies in the Scottish verse-production of the past century, and to support my contentions by reference to this anthology, I should in some

---

* My generalisation does not apply to Janet Adam Smith's collected poems of Stevenson, which appeared while this preface was going to press.

quarters be accused of having made a tendentious selection to grind an axe for myself or some clique of my friends. The only axes I have to grind are two propositions : first, that the Lallans and Gaelic languages, like the English language, have expressive potentialities peculiar to themselves ; second, that sometimes some people can better express themselves in Lallans or in Gaelic than in other languages, and should not be discouraged from doing so. It cannot be proved from my selection, nor from any selection, that any one language or style is paramount for poetic purposes, any more than in a garden or in an orchestra one would prove that any particular flower or instrument is paramount and should supersede all the others. I feel bound to stress the second proposition, because for much of the past century there has been a widespread view that serious expression in verse should be in King's English, even when the writer was a Scot accustomed to Gaelic or Lallans in speech and literature. This view has tended to restrict the range of both Gaelic and Lallans to song and satire. Gaelic has been helped by the fact that it has remained a language for extended discourse, in sermons and prose ; but, owing to the accidents that an English Bible became current before a Lallan translation was completed and printed, and that when the English ran short of a monarch the Scot who inherited their throne went off to occupy it instead of sending a viceroy, Lallans has now for over three centuries been excluded from Kirk and State, and has ceased to be a complete all-purpose language of discourse. The relatively atrophied development of prose and drama has caused an ill-balanced development also in verse, and this has been accentuated by the dominance of a great poet, Burns, whose range of expression was itself circumscribed partly by the immediate tradition in which he worked and partly by personal factors. Burns was strong in personal lyric, strong in satire, strong in the epistle, the *genre* piece ; but, through dying untimely and never having had adequate leisure and means, he failed to develop drama or prose, and the other types of verse in which he might have achieved something. So popular were his successes in his own types of verse that the public and the versifiers after him thought of little else but singable ditties and humorous *genre* pieces. Verse designed to be sung or declaimed before a sociable gathering in a mood of relaxation will seldom aim at the exalted or the recondite effect. It will tend to employ only words and phrases immediately intelligible and acceptable ; in fact we find by 1851 little but sentimental *cliché*, some of it amusing enough, as preserved in the *Whistle Binkie* volumes, but usually too rambling to quote. Apart from songs and satires there persisted a taste for ballads, complete with fairies and devils in the style of James Hogg, but never as good. Even the best of these I have excluded on grounds of space. I confess also that I get quickly bored with fairies and devils and literary *eeriness* generally. Perhaps I have offered too little of those who specialise in this potentiality of Lallans, its eerie power, with Marion Angus for example.

Indeed, the reader ought to be warned that my tastes run in quite other directions. If I cannot have good poetry—and most writers cannot produce that—then, in the way of verse, I like deftness, wit and social awareness. My favourite contemporaries among English versifiers are Sagittarius and John Betjeman, which no doubt explains my choice of many pieces neglected by previous anthologists. The relevance of particular pieces to the anthology is often indicated by my comment *ad locum* at the end of this volume. Meantime I point out that the first three or four dozen items merely set the stage for the movement that in fact develops a generation after 1851, the movement *towards* a Scottish Renaissance.

As a self-conscious and self-critical movement this starts I am not sure where, but I rather believe Robert Louis Stevenson has a good deal to do with it. I find my suspicion corroborated by a knowledgeable authority, J. M. Bulloch, in his introduction to John Mitchell's *Bydand* (Aberdeen, 1918), where he discusses 'verse in the vernacular,' and states : 'As a literary and successful venture it did not reach the outside world till Stevenson took it in hand ; since when it has been cultivated to good purpose by many men.' You will find here Stevenson's Lallan verses, 'The Maker to Posterity,' as showing his attitude ; I regret that space does not allow me to give all the note to 'Underwoods' (1887), in which he defends his practice of what came to be called 'Synthetic Scots,' that is to say, the adoption of words from all the land's dialects on to a Lothian and traditional literary basis.

Stevenson and George Macdonald, both best-selling novelists in English, did something to purify Lallans as a medium for verse, and vitality in this purer medium was soon forthcoming, chiefly from the north-east, with the poetesses Violet Jacob, Marion Angus, Mary Symon, Helen Cruickshank, and the poets Charles Murray, Pittendrigh MacGillivray and Lewis Spence. Sir Alexander Gray, from the same region, added an international element, during the First World War, with his admirable translations from Heine and other German and Danish works. Concurrently, the outpouring of Scots blood on the Western Front, for the independence of Serbia and Belgium, caused a certain stirring of the national subconsciousness. Here too J. M. Bulloch confirms my belief (*op. cit.*, p. vi) : 'Just as the Great War has excited the admiration of all spectators for the fighting qualities of the Scot, so it has reawakened ourselves to a new perception of the value of our vernacular for expressing the profound emotions called forth by the conflict.' To me, as to many

others, Violet Jacob succeeded best in conveying these profound emotions, and did so in Lallans, though her habitual
language was English. *Née* Erskine of Dun, Mrs Jacob
belonged to a famous and cosmopolitan county family, nearly
related to the Royal House of Great Britain ; she had spent
much of her life abroad. In these circumstances it is surely a
strong evidence of national collective subconsciousness, of
la voix du sang, that the stresses of the South African War, in
which her husband's regiment was badly cut up, and of the
First World War, should have moved her to powerful
utterance in an ancestral tongue which had by her time
descended from the metropolitan, sophisticated, curial, literary
level almost into a rustic and proletarian patois.

So far I have noted a tendency in Lallans, but something
had been happening in the Scottish use of English also. In
the eighteenth century English in Scotland was like French in
Germany, a courtly intellectual language, zealously written
and nervously spoken. Its impact in verse was mainly through
the doggerel versions of the Psalms of David and certain
passages of Scripture paraphrased, which were used to aid the
worship of the Established Church and other Presbyterian
bodies. If you look at my early selections in English you will
see that the cultivated advocate John Gibson Lockhart, Sir
Walter Scott's son-in-law, and the intellectual *homme d'affaires*,
William Kennedy, secretary to Lord Durham's commission
in the Canadas, show the metrical Psalm influence hardly less
blatantly than a poor religious weaver, James Nicol. Pursuing
our English-writing Scots we note the Celtic assonantal
influence in Thomas Aird's blank verse (a passage pointed
out to me by that admirable critic, John Hewitt), and the
comic pseudo-Celtic influence in Aytoun's ' Massacre of
Macpherson ' (one of a considerable class of compositions
representing the nearest Scotland got in the nineteenth century

to the inter-influence which in Ireland produced a far finer
product, Synge and Yeats). There is an influence of Poe on
Thomson, and of Keats on poor David Gray, popular as
' The Poet of " The Luggie." ' Thomas Hood, Tennyson,
Whitman, were all influences. Then we come to John
Davidson, the first major figure in our gallery, and one who,
writing in English, achieves a distinctive Scottish style ;
rather as Thomas Carlyle did in English prose. If Davidson
is not a product of Scotland and of the contemporary world,
the *Zeitgeist*, the main influences to which he responds
are to be sought rather in Germany than in England, in
Nietzsche perhaps. One thinks also of Ibsen and Strindberg.
But I stress the specifically West Lowland Scottish development of Calvinism in the general Nordic Protestant ambiency,
and refer to his ' Ballad in Blank Verse,' of which I quote
enough to be revealing.

John Davidson, like his hunted stag, drowned himself in the
English Channel, in 1909, an event that made a tremendous
impression on Christopher Murray Grieve, then a seventeen-
year-old journalist from the Scottish Frontier at Langholm,
educated at Edinburgh by George Ogilvie, a sympathetic
teacher devoted to Scottish literature. Davidson was an
avant-garde poet, who sought to cope with new ideas through
the medium of English, but who failed, and, in frustration
like his hunted stag, drowned himself in the English Channel.
No drowning in an English channel for C. M. Grieve, but a
gallant stand at bay on his native heath, sprouting fresh tines
at every angle and bellowing to quell the pack. The psycho-
logical and poetic development of Grieve (Hugh MacDiarmid
is his chief pseudonym) cannot be here appraised, but the aims
of his propaganda for a Scottish Renaissance can be stated.
They are : first, the extended use of the distinctive national
languages, Lallans and Gaelic, not only for verse but also for

drama and prose and all the purposes of discourse ; second, the renewal of international contacts, occluded since the cessation of the Auld Alliance with France and the many special connections with the Low Countries, Scandinavia and elsewhere, after the Union under insular England in 1707 ; third, the raising of the intellectual level of Scottish literature in all its languages, and of Scottish living, to place Scotland in the vanguard of Humanity. The few hundred lines allowable to one writer in a general anthology naturally cannot display adequately even MacDiarmid's own achievement in poetry, still less give any idea of the fertilising influence his work has had on his contemporaries, even those with whom he quarrels most persistently, or on younger Scots writers, or on writers in Wales, Ireland, England and elsewhere. I have given a few of his early lyrics, but could not give the musical settings by Francis George Scott, which complete them. I can give no idea of his major success, ' A Drunk Man Looks at the Thistle,' which handles in a full canon of Lallans, with no less emotional depth than Violet Jacob's, no less felicity in translation than Sir Alexander Gray's, and hardly less refinement of language than Lewis Spence achieved, an *avant-garde* theme such as those that engaged John Davidson in his prime. Nor can I give any idea of his more recent prose-poem tracts, whose enormousness exceeds the resources of publishers, and of which we have so far been favoured with glimpses hardly more revealing than those vouchsafed by the Loch Ness monster.

Regarding the aims of the Renaissance movement, there is a good deal of evidence of progress in all three. An interesting volume could be made of translations into Lallans and Gaelic from a dozen languages, but I lack room here. This selection shows a little of the extension in the use of our national languages, and the inquiring reader can consult the volumes and group publications of the writers concerned. None of the Lallan Makars approaches the quality of MacDiarmid, except Sydney Goodsir Smith. Of the Gaelic poets Somhairle Maclean in some ways excels MacDiarmid, so far as my acquaintance with Gaelic allows me to judge. Touching the third aim of the movement, raising the intellectual level of Scottish literature, I am inclined to think that so far this has occurred rather in English than in Gaelic or Lallans ; but up to now there is nothing in any language to write abroad about, except perhaps Edwin Muir, whose reputation as a critic is already international, and the quality of whose imagination is altogether unique, in Scotland or anywhere else.

In the temerarious business of selecting from the outpourings of my contemporaries, most of whom are as dud as the general run of verse-producers in England or France or Denmark, I have been as much interested in tendency as in achievement. It is surely a sign of something fermenting in Scotland when a young man from Fife, employed by the Glasgow Education Authority to teach English literature and British history, takes the name Thurso Berwick from the two burghs at the extremes of Scotland's Continent-facing coast, and inscribes to Goodsir Smith and Mayakovsky a poem linking the Forth Bridge, the Eiffel Tower and the Dnyepr Dam, and containing such lines as

> Tovarisch Scotland !—Vodka richt awa !
> Ah'm proud ti tak yuir haun, an hou's the Clyde ?

In 1851 Scottish verse-making was mainly backward-looking and sentimental and sociable, with hankerings for rusticity and childhood. Yet already then an industrial revolution had taken place which had turned the Scotland of Burns and Alasdair MacMhaighstir Alasdair, a country of peasants and small burgesses, into a megalopolitan hive, with four-fifths of the people living crowded in four big cities and a few large burghs. The Lallans-speaking handloom-weaver of the Lowland villages and the Gaelic-speaking crofter had been huddled together in slums, among the factory chimneys of manufacturers who always knew how to combine against the people and the steeples of churches which continually kept the people divided. The ancient community of Scotland was deeply disintegrated, and there is no doubt that this national psychosis was inimical to literature. Small indications of that are the tendency of Scots writers to use pseudonyms (Stevenson, for instance, published *Jekyll and Hyde* pseudonymously—a striking fact), and to commit suicide. Edwin Muir, an Orkneyman from the periphery, speaks of every Scot carrying, deep inside, ' the broken image of the lost Kingdom.' Today there is a wide-spreading groping to recover that lost Kingdom and to restore the broken image, to redintegrate the Community of Scotland. It may be that a synthesis is impending : that in our megalopolitan culture there will be a syncretism of the superficially diverse elements represented by Lallans, Gaelic and English, and that another century hence an anthologist will be choosing items of Scottish provenance in some national interlingua emerging from the various tendencies displayed towards the end of this collection. Whatever the medium may be of Scottish verse in 2051, it is at any rate worth noting that, as compared with 1851, we are today forward-looking rather than nostalgic, analytic rather than sentimental, socialist rather than sociable, more addicted to urbanity than to rusticity, and wondering how to grow up further.

Levels of appreciation of verse vary, and this selection offers things to be enjoyed on various levels : something for the poet and the aesthete ; much for the lover of wit-writing and declamation ; plenty for the sociologist and the literary historian. It contains nothing, I trust, to harm the spirit of a child, and nothing beyond the comprehension of the intelligent general reader. It is the hope of the editor and of the publishers that, like its predecessor and companion, John Buchan's *The Northern Muse*, this volume will revive or stimulate in a wide public the knowledge and pursuit of Scottish Poetry.

ACKNOWLEDGMENTS

THE living poets represented in this volume are warmly thanked for their copyright material, and especially those who have taken a personal interest in the selection—by sending manuscripts and otherwise—of whom I mention particularly : Thurso Berwick, (the late) James Bridie, Ivor Brown, Professor W. M. Calder, W. D. Cocker, Lieut. R. L. Cook, R.N., Joe Corrie, Sir William Craigie, Helen Cruickshank, Alex Dow, Colonel Walter Elliot, Robert Garioch, Sir Alexander Gray, Neil Gunn, Dr W. H. Hamilton, George Campbell Hay, Hamish Henderson, Dr Isobel Wylie Hutchison, George Kay, Robert Kemp, John Kincaid, T. S. Law, Maurice Lindsay, Eric Linklater, Marion Lochhead, Naomi Mitchison, William Montgomerie, Edwin and Willa Muir, Bessie MacArthur, Norman McCaig, Hugh MacDiarmid, Albert Mackie, Somhairle Maclean, Robert Maclellan, Dorothy Paulin, Robert Rendall, Father Antony Ross, Crombie Saunders, Alexander Scott, George Scott-Moncrieff, Sydney Goodsir Smith, Dr Janet Smith, Lewis Spence, Alice V. Stuart, Rachel Annand Taylor, Derick Thomson, Nannie K. Wells.

Other private owners of copyright to whom I am indebted are : Col. A. D. Buchanan-Smith for the fragment by his brother ; Mrs (J. M.) Caie ; Mr E. Colman for Lord Alfred Douglas's poems ; Mr A. M. Davidson ; Brigadier Bernard Fergusson ; Mr Alexander Galloway ; Mr Wm. O. Given, of Cullybackey, grandson of Thomas Given ; Mrs MacDougall Hay ; Mr Emrys Hughes, M.P., son-in-law of Keir Hardie ; Mr A. Fraser Innes for Mary Symon's poem ; Mrs (William) Jeffrey ; Mrs (Joseph) Lee ; Mr R. M. Linklater for two poems by the late J. B. Selkirk (James B. Brown) ; Mr C. G. R. Mair, son of A. W. Mair ; the executors of the late W. E. Martyn for Robert Buchanan's poem ; Mrs (Harold) Monro ; the trustees of the late Dr Neil Munro ; Dr Stark Murray, son of Robert Murray ; the executors of the late George Macdonald for two poems from *George Macdonald's Poetical Works* ; Miss E. M. P. Macgillivray, daughter of Pittendrigh Macgillivray ; Mr Hamish Maclaren ; Mr Will H. Ogilvie ; Gabriel Rivers ; Mr J. M. Russell for a version from S. Maclean ; Mrs M. C. Smith ; Mrs Ina Stark for Wm. Ogilvie's poem ; Mr G. Bruce Thomson. It has in some cases been impossible to trace authors or executors, especially in respect of pieces that were taken from periodicals now defunct. I beg to be excused by all concerned, both for unauthorised insertions and for any omissions or errors in the acknowledgments of copyright : if such are communicated to the Editor, correction will be made in any subsequent reprint.

Acknowledgment is gratefully made to the following publishing houses for permission to reprint items from works listed after their names : Allen & Unwin, for Lewis Spence, *Plumes of Time* (1926) ; Blackie & Son, for Isobel Wylie Hutchison, *Lyrics from Greenland* (1935) ; Basil Blackwell, for Dorothy Paulin, *The Wan Water* (1939), and Robert Crawford, *Poems* (1924) ; Wm. Blackwood & Sons, for Hugh Haliburton, *Horace in Homespun* (1925), ' Moses Peerie ', *Nugae Ecclesiasticae* (1884), Neil Munro, *The Poetry of Neil Munro* (1931), Hugh MacDiarmid, *Sangschaw* (1925), *Pennywheep* (1926), *To Circumjack Cencrastus* (1930) ; Boriswood, for William Montgomerie, *Via* (1933) ; Brown Son & Ferguson, for W. D. Cocker, *Poems, Scots & English* ; The Caledonian Press, for Alexander Scott, *The Latest in Elegies* (1949) ; The Cambridge University Press for C. H. Sorley, *Marlborough* (1916) ; Jonathan Cape, for Eric Linklater, *A Dragon Laughed* (1930), and Andrew Young, *Collected Poems* ; Chatto & Windus, for Robert Buchanan, *Poetical Works* (1884), George Macdonald, and Harold Monro, *Twentieth Century Poetry* (1929) ; Christophers, for F. V. Branford, *Titans and Gods*, and *The White Stallion* (1924) ; R. & R. Clark, for J. B. Selkirk, *Poems* (1905) ; Constable, for David Rorie, *The Pawky Duke*, Charles Murray, and James Bridie, *Tedious and Brief* (1945) ; *Country Life*, for Violet Jacob, *Jock to the First Army* and *The Field by the Lirk o' the Hill* ; Curtis Brown Ltd, for Edwin Muir, *Variations on a Time Theme* (1934) ; Andrew Dakers, for William Soutar, *Collected Poems* (1948) ; J. M. Dent & Sons, for Walter C. Smith, *Poetical Works* (1902), and Edwin Muir, *Journeys and Places* (1937) ; Editions Poetry London, Ltd, for G. S. Fraser, *Home Town Elegy* (1944) ; The Ettrick Press, for A. H. Emslie-Smith, *Scottish Student Verse*, 1937–47 ; Faber & Faber, for Marion Angus, *The Turn of the Day* and *Sun and Candlelight*, Sir Alexander Gray, *Gossip*, and Edwin Muir, *The Narrow Place* (1943), *The Voyage* (1946) and *The Labyrinth* (1949) ; Mr Adam Drinan, for *The Ghosts of the Strath*, and Mr Maurice Lindsay, for *No Crown for Laughter* (1943), published by The Fortune Press ; Alex. Gardner, for Sir Donald Macalister's poem in Dugald Mitchell, *The Book of Highland Verse* (1912) ; Victor Gollancz, for Hugh MacDiarmid, *Stony Limits* (1934), and Hamish MacLaren, *Sailor with Banjo* (1929) ; Gowans and Gray's representatives, for Dr John Fergus, *The Sodger* (1915), Walter Wingate, *Poems* (1919), Hamish Hendry, *A Scots Dominie* (1924), Gabriel Rivers, *The Passion-flower* (1935), Marion Lochhead, *Poems* (1928) ; The Hogarth Press, for Douglas Ainslie, *Chosen Poems* (1926) ; J. Johnston (Aberdeen), for W. A. Mackenzie,

ACKNOWLEDGMENTS

Poems (1893) ; John Lane, for R. C. Macfie, *New Poems* (1904), D. S. MacColl, *Bull* (1919), E. A. Mackintosh, *A Highland Regiment*, R. W. Kerr, *War Daubs*, John Davidson, *Ballads & Songs* (1895) ; the representatives of the late Andrew Lang, and Longmans Green & Co Ltd, for *Poetical Works of Andrew Lang* ; Andrew Melrose (1927), for John Ferguson, *Thyrea* ; Mrs George Bambridge, Methuen & Co Ltd and The Macmillan Company of Canada, for Rudyard Kipling, *The Seven Seas* ; Methuen & Co Ltd, for George Scott-Moncrieff, *A Book of Uncommon Prayer* (1937) ; The Moray Press, for Robert Murray, *The Deil and John Knox* (1936), Margaret Winefride Simpson, *Aisles of Song* (1937), Nan Shepherd, *In the Cairngorms* (1934) ; John Murray, for R. C. Macfie, *War* (1918), Joseph Lee, *Workaday Warriors* and *Ballads of Battle* ; Violet Jacob, *Songs of Angus* (1916) and *Bonnie Joann* (1921) ; Eneas Mackay, for Hugh MacDiarmid, *Scots Unbound* (1932) ; William Maclellan, for Somhairle Maclean, *Dain do Eimhir* (1943), George Bruce, *Sea Talk*, Douglas Young, *Auntran Blads* (1943) and *A Braird o Thristles* (1947), George Campbell Hay, *Fuaran Sleibh*, David Martin, *Battlefields and Girls*, Sydney Goodsir Smith, *The Deevil's Waltz*, W. S. Graham, *The Seven Journeys* ; the Trustees of the late Lord Tweedsmuir, and Thomas Nelson & Sons Ltd, for John Buchan, *Poems Scots and English* ; New Alliance Publications Ltd, for Maurice Lindsay, *Ode for St Andrew's Night and Other Poems* ; Oliver & Boyd, for A. W. Mair, *Poems* (1929), Bessie J. B. MacArthur, *Scots Poems* (1938) and *Last Leave* (1943), Marion Lochhead, *Fiddler's Bidding* (1939), Dr A. Lamont, *Patria Deserta* (1943), and Sydney Goodsir Smith, *The Wanderer* (1943) ; The Richards Press, for John Davidson, *Earl Lavender*, and Rachel Annand Taylor, *The End of Fiammetta* ; Routledge and Kegan Paul Ltd, for J. F. Hendry, *The Orchestral Mountain* ; Selwyn & Blount, for W. H. Hamilton, *The Desire of the Moth* (1925), and A. F. McGlashan, *St George & the Dragon* (1931) ; The Serif Books, for Maurice Lindsay, *Hurlygush* (1948), and Sydney Goodsir Smith, *Under the Eildon Tree* (1948) ; Sheed & Ward, for John Gray, *Poems* (1931) ; Simpkin Marshall, for Alex. Anderson, *Songs of the Rail* (1877), and R. F. Murray, *The Scarlet Gown* (1893) ; Williams & Norgate, for A. V. Stuart, *The Far Calling* (1944) ; D. Wyllie & Son (Aberdeen), for J. M. Caie, *The Kindly North* (1934).

PERIODICALS to whose proprietors and editors I am indebted for items from their columns are : *Ayr Advertiser*—G. D. Brown ; *College Echoes* —Sir William Craigie, W. M. Lindsay ; *Evening Times* (Glasgow)— Lavinia Derwent ; *Evening Dispatch* (Edinburgh)—L. Spence ; *Glasgow University Magazine*—W. Elliot ; *The Modern Scot* (per James Whyte)— Edwin Muir, W. Jeffrey, Stuart Hood, Neil Gunn ; *The New Alliance*

ACKNOWLEDGMENTS

and Scots Review—H. Henderson ; *Outlook*—Hunter Diack ; *The People's Friend*—Anon. ; *Poetry Scotland*—R. Maclellan, Tom Scott, Derick Thomson ; *The Scotsman*—W. M. Calder, I. M. Clark ; *The Shetlander*—Haldane Burgess ; *Tribune*—Naomi Mitchison ; *The Voice of Scotland*—W. Soutar. G. K. Menzies, 'Poaching in Excelsis' and Ivor Brown, 'Never Go Back' are reproduced by permission of the Proprietors of *Punch*.

CHARLES GRAY 1782–1851

from *Epistle to Mr David Sillar,*
Burns' Irvine friend

[from H.M. Ship *Unité*, Adriatic, 31 December 1808,
in the blockade of Venice]

Will *Burns'* late frien' and bosom cronie
List to my lays, tho far frae bonnie ?
Will he, wha strays 'mang hills and woods
List to a Rhymer on the floods,
Whar *Adria* pours her foamin tides
And swift the stately vessel glides,
Near rough rude mountains theek'd wi snaw,
That simmer suns can hardly thaw,
Whar savage beasts prowl for their prey,
And men almost as wild as they ?

Yet sometimes am I wafted o'er,
Near famed *Italia's* flowery shore,
Where all the Muses sung of yore ;
But fient a ane e'er visits me ;
Aiblins they dinna like the sea !
And hark ye, lad, (tho' dinna tell,)
They like it nae waur than mysel !
For, gin I culd but better do,
Saut water ne'er suld weet my shoe.
But, Davie, if, in twa-three year,
Peace suld return ilk hert to cheer,
Back to auld *Scotia* quick I'll flie,
Her cakes and Usquebae to prie ;
The auld thack house I'll cleed aince mair,
And whiten weel the outer stair,
And mak the inside snug and bien,

I

For weel I like to see things clean ;
And nae attention sall be spared
To cultivate the green kailyaird ;
I'll plant my cabbage and potatoes,
And be anither *Cincinnatus* !

DAVID SHAW

1786–1856

Tammie Treddlefeet

My name is Tammie Treddlefeet,
  I live in Shuttle Ha' ;
And I hae been a weaver lad
  This twenty year and twa :
Wi waft and warp, and shears sae sharp,
  My rubbin bane, my reed and heddles,
Sae nimbly as my shuttle flees,
  While up and doon I tramp my treddles.

We weaver lads were merry blades
  When Osnaburgs sellt weel,
And when the price o ilka piece
  Did pey a bow o meal.
The fowk got sale for beef and veal,
  For cash was rife wi everybody ;
And ilka ale-hoose had the smell
  O roas'en pies and reekin toddy.

But fegs, sic sport was unco short,
  Thae times hae crept awa,
And left us noo wi scarce a shoe
  Or ony hose ava.
And troth I fear when meal's sae dear

There's some fowk hardly get their sairin,
And gin the price again sud rise
    We'd a' be stairved as deid's a herrin.

Gin times wad come like times that's gane
    We sud be merry a' ;
We'll jump and prance and lowp and dance
    Till we be like to fa'.
And syne you see we'll happy be,
    And ilka wab we'll hae a drink on ;
We'll lauch and sing ' God save the King,'
    And a' the sangs that we can think on.

DAVID VEDDER   1790–1854

Auld Freends

My word ! but ye seem nae sheep-shank ;
I like your visage free and frank ;
That ye're a man o walth and rank
    I suldna wonder,
Wi credit in Sir Willie's Bank
    For twa-three hunder ;

Forbye a sclated house to bide in,
A powny cairt to tak a ride in ;
Sax guid milk-kye ye'll hae a pride in,
    A mare and filly.
This comes o thrift and frugal guidin,
    Auld muirland Willie.

And when ye gae to tryst and fair,
Gin ye hae little time to spare,

3

Ye'll trot the cannie auld gray mare
  Through dubs and plashes,
Your legs happed in a cosie pair
  O splatterdashes.

Nae dout, but ye hae struggled sair
Through fifty year to gather gear ;
Your manly brow wi lines o care
  Is sair indentit,
But *truth* and *honesty* are there
  As deep imprentit.

The parish kens that ye maintained
Through life a character unstained ;
The eldership ye'll hae attained,
  As is richt meet ;—
Or, if ye binna yet ordained,
  Ye're on the leet.

When neebours cam to altercation,
Aspersion and recrimination,
And naething for't but Courts o Session
  And Judge and Jury,
Your mild and richteous arbitration
  Aye laid their fury.

When tailor Tam brak yard and shears,
And listit wi the Fusiliers,
His widowed mither, bathed in tears,
  Mourned owre the staff
And stay o her declining years,—
  Ye bought him aff.

Besides, it's kent that ye can len'
Sma sums to puir but honest men ;

But, a' unlike ' my uncle ' Ben
  O Borrowstoun,
Ye never seek a pledge again,
  But shools it doun.

I'se wad ye hae ane ample store
O solid theologic lore,
Frae Baillie, Boston, Brown, and More,
  And weel can quote them ;
And ither worthies, half a score,
  Though I've forgot them.

I see ye've trotted owre the green
To meet your valued early freen' ;
He's sittin on an auld gray stane
  Quite at his leisure ;
The verra twinkle o his een
  Denotes his pleasure.

Ah ! had we mony mae like thee
To prop the State's auld randle-tree
And drink the stream o Libertie
  In moderation,
In spite o grumblers we wad be
  A happy nation.

THOMAS LYLE   1792–1859

Smile Through thy Tears

Smile through thy tears, like the blush moss-rose,
  When the warm rains fall around it ;
Thy fond heart now may seek repose
  From the rankling griefs that wound it.

5

For a parent's loss the eye may fill
    And weep till the heart runs over ;
But the pang is longer and deeper still
    That wails o'er the grave of a lover.

Smile through thy tears, like the pale primrose
    When the zephyrs play around it ;
In me let thy trembling heart repose ;
    I will ward the sorrows that wound it.
Ah ! vain were the wish, such love to crave
    As warmed thy maiden bosom
Ere Henry slept, where the alders wave
    O'er the night-shade's drooping blossom.

HEW AINSLIE   1792–1878

The Hint o' Hairst

It's dowie in the hint o' hairst,
    At the wa-gang o' the swallow,
When the wind grows cauld, and the burns grow bauld,
    And the wuds are hingin' yellow ;
But oh, it's dowier far to see
The wa-gang o' her the hert gangs wi',
The deid-set o' a shinin' e'e—
That darkens the weary world on thee.

There was mickle love atween us twa—
    Oh, twa could ne'er been fonder ;
And the thing on yird was never made,
    That could ha'e gart us sunder.
But the way of Heaven's abune a' ken,
And we maun bear what it likes to sen'—
It's comfort, though, to weary men,
That the warst o' this warld's waes maun en'.

6

There's mony things that come and gae,
   Just kent, and syne forgotten ;
And the flowers that busk a bonnie brae,
   Gin anither year lie rotten.
But the last look o' that lovely e'e,
And the dying grip she ga'e to me,
They're settled like eternitie—
Oh, Mary ! that I were wi' thee.

JOHN GIBSON LOCKHART   1794–1854

When youthful faith hath fled,
   Of loving take thy leave ;
Be constant to the dead—
   The dead cannot deceive.

Sweet modest flowers of spring,
   How fleet your balmy day !
And man's brief year can bring
   No secondary May,
No earthly burst again
   Of gladness out of gloom,
Fond hope and vision vain,
   Ungrateful to the tomb.

But 'tis an old belief
   That on some solemn shore,
Beyond the sphere of grief,
   Dear friends shall meet once more,
Beyond the sphere of time,
   And Sin and Fate's control,
Serene in endless prime
   Of body and of soul.

7

That creed I fain would keep,
That hope I'll not forgo ;
Eternal be the sleep
Unless to waken so.

JANET HAMILTON   1795-1873

from *The Sunday Rail*

(On the first running of Sunday trains on the North British Railway)

Now range up the carriages, feed up the fires !
To the rail, to the rail, now the pent-up desires
Of the pale toiling million find gracious reply,
On the pinions of steam they shall fly, they shall fly,
The beauties of nature and art to explore,
To ramble the woodlands and roam by the shore.
The city spark here with his smart smirking lass,
All peg-topped and crinolined, squat on the grass,
While with quips and with cranks and soft-wreathed smiles,
Each nymph with her swain the dull Sabbath beguiles.
Here mater and paterfamilias will come
With their rollicking brood from their close city home.
How they scramble and scream, how they scamper and run,
While pa and mamma are enjoying the fun !
And the urchins bawl out, ' Oh, how funny and jolly,
Dear ma, it is thus to keep Sabbath-day holy.'

Now for pipe and cigar and the snug pocket-flask,
What's the rail on a Sunday without them, we ask ?
What the sweet-scented heather and rich clover-blooms
To the breath of the weed as it smoulders and fumes ?
So in courting and sporting, in drinking and smoking,
Walking and talking, in laughter and joking,
They while the dull hours of the Sabbath away.
What a Sabbath it is !   Who is Lord of the day ?

Oor Location

A hunner funnels bleezin, reekin,
Coal and airnstane, charrin, smeekin ;
Navvies, miners, keepers, fillers,
Puddlers, rollers, airn-millers ;
Reestit, reekit, raggit laddies,
Firemen, enginemen, and Paddies ;
Boatmen, banksmen, rogh and rattlin,
About the wecht wi colliers battlin ;
Sweitin, sweirin, fechtin, drinkin,
Change-hoose bells and gill-stowps clinkin ;
Police—ready men and willin—
Aye at hand when stowps are fillin ;
Clerks, and counter-lowpers plenty,
Wi trim moustache and whiskers dainty—
Chaps that winna staund at trifles,
Mind ye they can handle rifles.

About the wives in oor location,
And the lasses' botheration,
Some are decent, some are dandies,
And a gey wheen drucken randies,
Aye to neebors' hooses sailin,
Greetin bairns ahint them trailin,
Gaun for nouther breid nor butter,
Jist to drink and rin the cutter.
Oh, the dreidfu curse o drinkin !
Men are ill, but tae my thinkin,
Luikin through the drucken fock,
There's a Jenny for ilk Jock.

THOMAS CARLYLE 1795-1881

To-day

So here hath been dawning
Another blue Day ;
Think, wilt thou let it
Slip useless away ?

Out of Eternity
This new Day is born ;
Into Eternity
At night will return.

Behold it aforetime
No eye ever did :
So soon it for ever
From all eyes is hid.

Here hath been dawning
Another blue Day ;
Think, wilt thou let it
Slip useless away ?

ALEXANDER SMART 1798-1866

Election Lyric

Arouse ! all ye true-hearted Scots,
    The Tories are now in high feather ;
They come to solicit your votes,
    So lay all your noddles together.
O'er the length and the breadth of the land
    They muster and rally their forces,

Determined that few shall withstand
  Their power or the length of their purses.
                  Sing tol de rol lol etc.

The tenant that boggles to sell
  His vote for a mess of their pottage,
His politics soon may bewail,
  When they bundle him out of his cottage.
The farmer must bow to the laird,
  Or he'll soon be a poor humble cottar ;
While ' Jemmy that delved i the yaird '
  May rise to the rank of a voter.

The tradesman that votes for a Whig
  May shut up his shop when he pleases.
The grocer—a Radical prig !—
  They'll purchase no more of his cheeses.
Ye tailors or cobblers who dare
  To oppose the ' Conservative ' faction,
The Tories have pennies to spare,
  But ye'll never finger a fraction.

Then hey for the cause of Reform,
  And hey for the bonny Scots Thistle,
And ' the pilots that weathered the storm,'
  Grey, Brougham, Jeffrey, Althorp, and Russell.
Reformers are wonderful rife,
  But put not your trust in a *new* one.
The man who has fought all his life
  Against you, can ne'er prove a *true* one.
                  Sing tol de rol lol etc.

WILLIAM KENNEDY 1799–1871

The Friend

I have a friend,—a faithful friend,—
  His truth hath long been tried ;
He moves, where'er my footsteps wend,
  A shadow by my side.
The loved of early years are gone—
  The one, of all, most dear—
Yet fly who may, he lingers on,
  My last companion here.

He greets me from his hiding-place,
  In eyes that lightly roll ;
I call the wine, and lo ! his face
  Is mirrored in the bowl.
It recks not where, by sea or shore,
  On banned or holy ground,
I rest ; he pauses not before
  My presence he hath found.

But most his ever-watchful love
  Attends me in the night,
When tempests shake the spheres above,
  And stars send forth no light :
When broods, upon a troubled brow,
  The dread of coming ill,
Then—then—I doubly feel, as now,
  That with me he is still.

Recording devil ! how he glares
  Upon me in that time,
And stamps, in burning characters,
  Each perpetrated crime ;—

And spits abasement on my cheek,
    And turns my soul from prayer,
In utter hopelessness, to seek
    A refuge in despair.

THOMAS BABINGTON, LORD MACAULAY

1800–59

A Jacobite's Epitaph

To my true king I offer'd free from stain
Courage and faith ; vain faith, and courage vain.
For him I threw lands, honours, wealth, away,
And one dear hope, that was more prized than they.
For him I languish'd in a foreign clime,
Gray-hair'd with sorrow in my manhood's prime ;
Heard on Lavernia Scargill's whispering trees,
And pined by Arno for my lovelier Tees ;
Beheld each night my home in fever'd sleep,
Each morning started from the dream to weep ;
Till God, who saw me tried too sorely, gave
The resting-place I ask'd, an early grave.
O thou, whom chance leads to this nameless stone,
From that proud country which was once mine own,
By those white cliffs I never more must see,
By that dear language which I spake like thee,
Forget all feuds, and shed one English tear
O'er English dust. A broken heart lies here.

JAMES NICOL 1800-60

The Apostle Paul

Among the twelve Apostles whom
  The Lord Himself did call,
Not one of them in usefulness
  Was equal unto Paul.

Sprung from the tribe of Benjamin,
  His parents Hebrews were,
And he a Roman freeman, in
  The nation everywhere.

In Tarsus he was born, as he
  Did oftentimes declare ;
And Saul appeared to be the name
  His parents gave him there.

When young, he studied under that
  Great learned pedagogue,
Gamaliel by name, to get
  All learning then in vogue.

CHARLES, LORD NEAVES 1800-76

A Lyric for Saturday Night

We zealots made up of stiff clay,
  The sour-looking children of sorrow,
While not over jolly today,
  Resolve to be wretched tomorrow.

We can't for a certainty tell
    What mirth may molest us on Monday ;
But, at least, to begin the week well,
    Let us all be unhappy on Sunday.

That day, the calm season of rest,
    Shall come to us freezing and frigid ;
A gloom all our thoughts shall invest,
    Such as Calvin would call over-rigid,
With sermons from morning to night,
    We'll strive to be decent and dreary :
To preachers a praise and delight,
    Who ne'er think that sermons can weary.

All tradesmen cry up their own wares ;
    In this they agree well together :
The Mason by stone and lime swears ;
    The Tanner is always for leather ;
The Smith still for iron would go ;
    The Schoolmaster stands up for teaching ;
And the Parson would have you to know,
    There's nothing on earth like his preaching.

The face of kind Nature is fair ;
    But our system obscures its effulgence :
How sweet is a breath of fresh air !
    But our rules don't allow the indulgence.
These gardens, their walks and green bowers,
    Might be free to the poor man for one day ;
But no, the glad plants and gay flowers
    Mustn't bloom or smell sweetly on Sunday.

What though a good precept we strain
    Till hateful and hurtful we make it !
What though, in thus pulling the rein,
    We may draw it as tight as to break it !

Abroad we forbid folks to roam,
    For fear they get social or frisky ;
But of course they can sit still at home,
    And get dismally drunk upon whisky.

Then, though we can't certainly tell
    How mirth may molest us on Monday ;
At least, to begin the week well,
    Let us all be unhappy on Sunday.

ANON.   *c.* 1 8 5 0

from *The Barnyards o Delgaty*

As I cam in by Netherdale
    At Turra market for to fee,
I fell in wi a farmer chiel
    Frae the Barnyards o Delgaty.

He promised me the ae best pair
    I ever set my een upon :
When I gaed hame to Barnyards
    There was naething there but skin and bone.

The auld black horse sat on his dowp,
    The auld white meer lay on her wime,
And aa that I could hup and crack
    They wadna rise at yokin-time.

Meg Macpherson maks my brose,
    And her and me we canna gree ;
First a mote and syne a knot
    And aye the ither jilp o bree.

When I gae to the kirk on Sunday
    Mony's the bonny lass I see,
Prim, sittin by her daddy's side,
    And winkin owre the pews at me.

I can drink and nae be drunk,
    I can fecht and nae be slain,
I can court anither's lass
    And aye be welcome tae my ain.

Linten adie toorin adie,
Linten adie toorin ae,
Linten, lourin, lourin, lourin,
Linten lourin lourin lee.

EDWARD L. SLOAN   *c.* 1800–60

The Weaver's Triumph

It was but yestreen I had oot my bit claith, man,
    Tuk it under my arm, doun tae Balford I went,
Untee the Braid Square, tae wee cockit Rab's warehoose—
    For a trifle o cash, man, it was my intent.
My noddle bein' reemin wi stowps o guid liquor,
    I marched in fu' stately and throwed the dud doun,
Whan a cock-o-the-north o a foreman, ca'd Hudson,
    Whispered tae his employer—' We'll gie him a croon.'
My wee bit o labour bein' thrown on the counter,
    Wi butterfly's een tae examine't he goes ;
He hemmed and he ha'd, and he swore it was shameless,
    Syne oot wi his snoot-cloot and dighted his nose.
He swore that the warp would been better by double—
    For their penny collars 'twas nae use ava ;
Though the price o my labour was just half-a-guinea,
    He would gie me a shilling and let me awa.

17

I glowered at the ape wi twa een like red cinders,
    While wee cockit Rab at his knavery did wink ;
Quo I, ' Honest foreman, ye hae turned a barber,
    Tae shave simple weavers sae neatly, I think ;
But haud ye a jiffey, my potstick-legged callan—
    For my nine-and-sixpence I'll gie ye some fun :
I'll ca' doun your betters tae think on your capers,
    And see if you'll rob me, you half-stocked gun.'

Noo, twa honest neebors together convened,
    And examined it weel, frae beginnin tae end ;
And the verdict they gien was ' Return him his money,
    Or before Parson Wilkins you'll hae tae attend.'
My money I pouched wi a rollickin smirk—
    Oh ! what was the look that his foremanship gien !
Quo I, ' Honest foreman, act somewhat mair justly :
    You see arbitration's but seldom your frien'.'

Noo, some o my neebors mayna ken this same foreman,
    But I'll draw you his portrait as weel as I can,
Though it's nae easy job for a puir simple weaver,
    As I would wrang him greatly tae ca' him a man :
His face—it's the texture and shape o a monkey's ;
    Each cheek would hold neatly a shilling o pence ;
A' the wit that he has in his weel-theekit noddle's
    What our neebor Tam ca's a ' guid gripin sense.'

He's like, but why need I attempt tae describe him—
    The pen o a Buffon would soon be tae blame ;
Some day, whan auld Nature has been busy workin,
    She has tossed by the gruns—made him oot o' the same.
Farewell tae you, Robin ; adieu tae your foreman—
    A pair o sweet rascals you are, I declare ;
It's a pity tae waste pen and ink on sic creatures—
    Guid-bye tae you, neebors, I'll noo say nae mair.

THOMAS AIRD   1802-76

St Mary's Well

Homeward by other paths, Frank never fails,
With hat in hand, and reverence as of love,
To drink and rest at sweet St Mary's Well.
Cold, still, and glassy deep, a grassy brow
O'ershading it, here lies the virgin well.
Frost never films it, ne'er the Dog-Star drinks
Its liquid brimming lower.   Self-relieved,
By soft green dimples in its yielding lip,
The trembling fulness breaks, and slipping o'er,
Cold bubbles through the grass ; the infant spilth
Assumes a voice, and, gathering as it goes,
A runnel makes : how beautiful the green
Translucent lymph, crisp curling, purling o'er
The floating duckweed, lapsingly away !

GEORGE OUTRAM   1805-56

The Annuity

I gaed to spend a week in Fife—
    An unco week it proved to be—
For there I met a waesome wife
    Lamentin' her viduity.
Her grief brak out sae fierce and fell,
I thought her heart wad burst the shell ;
And—I was sae left tae mysel—
    I sell't her an annuity.

The bargain lookit fair eneugh—
　　　She just was turned o' saxty-three ;
I couldna guessed she'd prove sae teugh,
　　　By human ingenuity.
But years have come, and years have gane,
And there she's yet as stieve's a stane—
The limmer's growin' young again,
　　　Since she got her annuity.

She's crined awa' to bane and skin,
　　　But that it seems is nought to me ;
She's like to live—although she's in
　　　The last stage o' tenuity.
She munches wi' her wizened gums,
An' stumps about on legs o' thrums,
But comes—as sure as Christmas comes—
　　　To ca' for her annuity.

She jokes her joke, an' cracks her crack,
　　　As spunkie as a growin' flea—
An' there she sits upon my back,
　　　A livin' perpetuity.
She hurkles by her ingle side,
An' toasts an' tans her wrunkled hide—
Lord kens how lang she yet may bide
　　　To ca' for her annuity !

I read the tables drawn wi' care
　　　For an Insurance Company ;
Her chance o' life was stated there,
　　　Wi' perfect perspicuity.
But tables here or tables there,
She's lived ten years beyond her share,
An's like to live a dizzen mair,
　　　To ca' for her annuity.

I gat the loun that drew the deed—
    We spelled it o'er right carefully ;—
In vain he yerked his souple heid,
    To find an ambiguity :
It's dated—tested—a' complete—
The proper stamp—nae word delete—
And diligence, as on decreet,
    May pass for her annuity.

Last Yule she had a fearfu' hoast—
    I thought a kink might set me free ;
I led her out, 'mang snaw and frost,
    Wi' constant assiduity.
But Deil ma' care—the blast gaed by,
And missed the auld anatomy ;
It's just cost me a tooth, forbye
    Discharging her annuity.

I thought that grief might gar her quit—
    Her only son was lost at sea—
But aff her wits behoved to flit,
    An' leave her in fatuity !
She threeps, an' threeps, he's livin' yet,
For a' the tellin' she can get ;
But catch the doited runt forget
    To ca' for her annuity !

If there's a sough o' cholera
    Or typhus—wha sae gleg as she ?
She buys up baths, an' drugs, an a',
    In siccan superfluity !
She doesna need—she's fever-proof—
The pest gaed owre her very roof ;
She tauld me sae—an' then her loof
    Held out for her annuity.

21

Ae day she fell—her arm she brak,—
    A compound fracture as could be ;
Nae leech the cure wad undertak,
    Whate'er was the gratuity.
It's cured !   She handles't like a flail—
It does as weel in bits as hale ;
But I'm a broken man mysel'
    Wi' her and her annuity.

Her broozled flesh and broken banes,
    Are weel as flesh an' banes can be,
She beats the tades that live in stanes,
    An' fatten in vacuity !
They die when they're exposed to air—
They canna thole the atmosphere ;
But her ! expose her onywhere—
    She lives for her annuity.

If mortal means could nick her threid,
    Sma' crime it wad appear to me ;
Ca't murder—or ca't homicide—
    I'd justify't—an' do it tae.
But how to fell a withered wife
That's carved out o' the tree o' life—
The timmer limmer daurs the knife
    To settle her annuity.

I'd try a shot.—But whar's the mark ?—
    Her vital parts are hid frae me ;
Her back-bane wanders through her sark
    In an unken'd corkscrewity.
She's palsified—an' shaks her head
Sae fast about, ye scarce can see't ;
It's past the power o' steel or lead
    To settle her annuity.

She might be drouned ;—but go she'll not
    Within a mile o' loch or sea ;—
Or hanged—if cord could grip a throat
    O' siccan exiguity.
It's fitter far to hang the rope—
It draws out like a telescope ;
'Twad take a dreadfu' length o' drop
    To settle her annuity.

Will pushion do't ?—It has been tried ;
    But, be't in hash or fricassee,
That's just the dish she can't abide,
    Whatever kind o' *goût* it hae.
It's needless to assail her doubts,—
She gangs by instinct—like the brutes—
An' only eats an' drinks what suits
    Hersel an' her annuity.

The Bible says the age o' man
    Threescore an' ten perchance may be ;
She's ninety-four ;—let them wha can
    Explain the incongruity.
She suld hae lived afore the Flood—
She's come o' Patriarchal blood—
She's some auld Pagan, mummified
    Alive for her annuity.

She's been embalmed inside and out—
    She's sauted to the last degree—
There's pickle in her very snout
    Sae caper-like an' cruety ;
Lot's wife was fresh compared to her ;
They've kyanised the useless knir—
She canna decompose—nae mair
    Than her accursed annuity.

23

The water-drap wears out the rock
    As this eternal jad wears me ;
I could withstand the single shock,
    But no the continuity.
It's pay me here—an' pay me there—
An' pay me, pay me, evermair ;
I'll gang demented wi' despair—
    I'm *charged* for her annuity !

WILLIAM LIVINGSTONE   1808–70

Eirinn Ag Gul. Ireland Greitan

Uttermost isle of Europe,
    loveliest land under sky,
often I saw your coastline
    beyond ocean's bellowing cry.
With the south-east blowing gently
    and in heaven no mist or cloud
the Gaels in the Rhinns of Islay
    admired your beauty aloud.
Your pastures grassy and goodly,
    Magh Aoidh, smooth Lagan Rotha,
your wooded dells where the winged
    singers sheltering go.
Pure springs bubbling freshly,
    strong herds thronging your glens,
woods, hills, and meadow-scenery,
    and you green from end to end.
In boyhood's innocent morning
    I heard talk of ancient days
by the hearths of Clan Donald in Islay
    before exiling of the Gaels.

We thought they were true, as bairnies,
    the tales that the old folk had ;
we believed you were always merry,
    as we'd heard, exulting and glad.
Today as of old I descry still
    your sky-line over the swell
from Islay's southern wave-beach,
    but your state is mournful to tell.
Sad tale of eviction, oppression,
    dearth, injustice, woe ;
and no way of abating your burden,
    since you struck your own strength the blow.
Where is the three Hughs' ardour,—
    the valiant O'Donnell, O'Neill,
Maguire among foemen steadfast
    to death, not yielding on his feet ?
And where is the breed of the brave ones
    at Dun-a-bheire shunned not fight,
like a moorland torrent charging
    with targe-rims speckled bright ?
The rocks reply with an echo
    to the yell of the battle-sound ;
breathless the foxes are tumbled,
    their blood purling on the ground.

               [*trans.* Douglas Young]

WILLIAM MILLER   1 8 1 0 – 7 2

Wee Willie Winkie

Wee Willie Winkie rins through the toon,
Up stairs an' doon stairs in his nicht-goun,
Tirlin' at the window, crying at the lock,
' Are the weans in their bed, for it's now ten o'clock ? '

' Hey Willie Winkie, are ye comin' ben ?
The cat's singin' grey thrums to the sleepin' hen,
The dog's speldert on the floor and disna gie a cheep,
But here's a waukrife laddie, that *wunna fa' asleep.*'

Onything but sleep, you rogue, glow'rin' like the moon,
Rattlin' in an airn jug wi' an airn spoon,
Rumblin', tumblin' roon about, crawin' like a cock,
Skirlin like a kenna-what, waukenin' sleepin' fock.

' Hey Willie Winkie, the wean's in a creel,
Wamblin' aff a bodie's knee like a verra eel,
Ruggin' at the cat's lug and ravelin' a' her thrums—
Hey Willie Winkie—see there he comes.'

Wearit is the mither that has a stoorie wean,
A wee, stumpie stousie, that canna rin his lane,
That has a battle aye wi' sleep afore he'll close an e'e—
But a kiss frae aff his rosy lips gies strength anew to me.

Lines to Victor Hugo

(On reading of his great grief for the death of his grandson,
Victor Hugo, aged one year)

I ken the ploys that ye had planned,
The summer days' sweet lingering journeys,
To pu' the gowans, or to sit
By thymey brim o muirland burnies ;
Or sing him sangs that he wad ken
The meanin o when he grew aulder ;
And as thy voice rose wi the strain
Note that his braid brent brou luiked baulder.

I hae an oe, a lassie wean,—
A wee ma'msel, as ye wad ca' her ;

I luik at her, then think o thee.
What wad I dae did aught befa' her ?
Your grief has grieved me, and I feel
Man's closely linked wi ane anither ;
Thy darlin grandchild's made me know
My grandpa's but my bigger brither !

THOMAS TOD STODDART   1810–80

Song (from Chimera II of *The Death Wake*)

A rosary of stars, love ! we'll count them as we go
Upon the laughing waters, that are wandering below,
And we'll o'er the pearly moonbeam, as it lieth in the sea,
In beauty and in glory, like a shadowing of thee !
A rosary of stars, love ! a prayer as we glide,
And a whisper in the wind, and a murmur on the tide !
And we'll say a fair adieu to the flowers that are seen,
With shells of silver sown in radiancy between.
A rosary of stars, love ! the purest they shall be,
Like spirits of pale pearls, in the bosom of the sea ;
Now help thee, virgin mother ! with a blessing as we go,
Upon the laughing waters, that are wandering below !

Alicia Anne Spottiswood of that ilk
LADY JOHN SCOTT   1810–1900

Durrisdeer

We'll meet nae mair at sunset, when the weary day is dune,
Nor wander hame thegither, by the lee licht o' the mune !
I'll hear your step nae longer amang the dewy corn,
For we'll meet nae mair, my bonniest, either at eve or morn.

The yellow broom is waving, abune the sunny brae,
And the rowan berries dancing, where the sparkling waters play.
Tho' a' is bright and bonnie, it's an eerie place to me,
For we'll meet nae mair, my dearest, either by burn or tree.

Far up into the wild hills, there's a kirkyard auld and still,
Where the frosts lie ilka morning, and the mists hang low and
    chill,
And there ye sleep in silence, while I wander here my lane,
Till we meet ance mair in Heaven, never to part again.

WILLIAM EDMONDSTOUNE AYTOUN

1813–65

The Massacre of the Macpherson

Fhairshon swore a feud
    Against the clan M'Tavish ;
Marched into their land
    To murder and to rafish ;
For he did resolve
    To extirpate the vipers,
With four-and-twenty men
    And five-and-thirty pipers.

But when he had gone
    Half-way down Strath Canaan,
Of his fighting tail
    Just three were remainin'.
They were all he had,
    To back him in ta battle ;
All the rest had gone
    Off, to drive ta cattle.

'Fery coot!' cried Fhairshon.
  'So my clan disgraced is;
Lads, we'll need to fight,
  Before we touch the peasties.
Here's Mhic-Mac-Methusaleh
  Coming wi' his fassals,
Gillies seventy-three,
  And sixty Dhuinéwassails!'

'Coot tay to you, sir;
  Are you not ta Fhairshon?
Was you coming here
  To fisit any person?
You are a plackguard, sir!
  It is now six hundred
Coot long years, and more,
  Since my glen was plundered.'

'Fat is tat you say?
  Dare you cock your peaver?
I will teach you, sir,
  Fat is coot pehafiour!
You shall not exist
  For another day more;
I will shoot you, sir,
  Or stap you with my claymore!'

'I am fery glad,
  To learn what you mention,
Since I can prevent
  Any such intention.'
So Mhic-Mac-Methusaleh
  Gave some warlike howls,
Trew his skian-dhu,
  An' stuck it in his powels.

In this fery way
    Tied ta failiant Fhairshon,
Who was always thought
    A most superior person.
Fhairshon had a son,
    Who married Noah's daughter ;
And nearly spoiled ta Flood,
    By trinking up ta water :

Which he would have done,
    I at least pelieve it,
Had ta mixture peen
    Only half Glenlivet.
This is all my tale :
    Sirs, I hope 'tis new t' ye !
Here's your fery good healths,
    And tamn ta whusky duty !

JAMES HEDDERWICK   born 1814

from *The Villa by the Sea*

Mine is that delightful villa,
    Sweetly nesting by the sea ;
Yet I sigh for a scintilla
    Of the bliss it promised me.

Though a pleasant cottage *orné*,
    Rich in trellis-work and flowers,
Here to sit and end my journey,
    How could I beguile the hours ?

Love of Nature is a duty,
    And I fain would love it more.
But I weary of the beauty
    I have seen for weeks before.

Lofty are the hills and regal,
    Still they are the hills of old ;
And like any other sea-gull
    Is the sea-gull I behold.

Tiresome 'tis to be a dreamer.
    When will it be time to dine ?
Oh, that almost stand-still steamer,
    How it crawls across the brine !

JOHN MITCHELL   born 1815

from *The St Rollox Lum's Address to his Brethren*

In the great cause of Art I rose,
And Art in me a wonder shows,
Such as is never seen in those
        They steeples ca',
Things gude for naething, I suppose,
        But mak streets braw.

They tell us that in days o yore
Ane Cheops Egypt's sceptre bore,
Wha built a pyramid, a score
        O feet, and mair,
Aboon where I the skies explore,
        Sae bland and fair.

But after a', wha wad compare
A pyramid to them that share,
Like me, the toils that mankind bear
    Frae morn till een,
Save sumphs, wha think that naething's rare
    That's daily seen ?

Beneath my shade Industry plies
Her eager hands to reach the prize,
That, gained, adds lustre to the eyes
    Of old and young,
And bids Hope's cheering accents rise
    Frae every tongue.

O ! when will that blest time arrive,
When men some method will contrive
To banish from Industry's hive
    The lazy drones,
Who long by fraud have learned to thrive
    On Labour's groans ?

Then future Tennants will arise,
Like those who raised me to the skies,
Some giant measure to devise,
    That even steam,
With all its powers, will in men's eyes
    A trifle seem.

Yes ! science shall the clouds dispel,
Beneath whose gloom sly birkies dwell,
Wha to their dupes some queer cracks tell
    About a chiel
Wha lang on earth has borne the bell—
    Ev'n Nick the deil.

Causey Courtship

(A Dialogue between a Besom Cadger and a Fishwoman)

SCENE—The Auld Brig, Alloa

—Lassie wi the creel, can ye loe a cadger,
licht o hert and heel, fain to be your lodger ?
Wooers like yoursel ye may hae in dizzens ;
nane my wealth may tell—*Wha'll buy besoms ?*

—Gruesome, auld and lame, dinna fleitch and flatter,
siller I hae nane in your gaet to scatter.
Up and doun I gang 'mang the gentle bodies,
roarin loud and lang—*Wha'll buy haddies ?*

—Let me pree your mou ; dinna fidge and swither,
time eneuch to rue when we gang thegither ;
come, ye dorty thing, let us weet our wizens,
owre our drappie sing—*Wha'll buy besoms ?*

—Touch me for your life ; dinna pu' my apron ;
aa the fules in Fife cudna match your caperin.
Gang ye to the bent, cuddle wi your cuddies,
there you're better kent—*Wha'll buy haddies ?*

Glacket thing, ye'll rue, sairly ye'll repent it ;
if the tether's fu' ne'er afore I kent it.
Less micht mak ye fain, drouth the timmer seasons,
I'll caa back again—*Wha'll buy besoms ?*

We'll no hae maut and meal frae Crail to Tullibody,
when I gae to the Deil on a cadger's cuddy.
Sae airt yoursel awa wi aa your tattered duddies.
A fummart ye wad staw—*Buy caller haddies.*

33

My Ain Hearthstane

'Tis sweet, when smiling Summer flings
  Her mantle owre the lea,
When scented fleurs unfold their bloom,
  And birds are a' in glee,
To wander wi the wimplin burn,
  Or 'mang the wuids alane ;
But sweeter, dearer to the heart,
  Our ain hearthstane.

When gloamin spreads out-owre the scene
  Her dewy wings o gray,
And brings the pleughman frae the furr,
  The shepherd frae the brae—
Hoo sweet the winsome wifie's smile,
  The prattlin o the wean,
That welcome wearied Labour
  To his ain hearthstane.

My hame is but a lowly bield,
  A wee bit butt and ben,
A kame intil a croodit byke
  That grandeur disna ken ;
Yet Pride within her loft wa's,
  Amid her menial train,
Micht envy me the treasures
  O my ain hearthstane.

Of gowd or gear I maunna speak ;
  Fause Fortune's aye my fae ;
She's grudged me e'en the timmer spuin,
  The breeks o hodden gray ;

34

Our kail she aye sends throu the reek,
    And clean we pyke the bane ;
Yet love maks licht o poortith
    On my ain hearthstane.

Owre weel I loe, wi genial friends,
    A social nicht o glee,
When sang and crack around the bowl
    Gar a' life's shadows flee ;
But bicker-joys are fleetin a',
    And sune the hert is fain
To toddle hame repentant
    To its ain hearthstane.

There's jags on ilka path o life,
    In ilka cup there's ga',
But poortith bydes the sairest dunts
    On mortal pows that fa' ;
For eident Toil meets cankert words,
    And luiks o sour disdain,
And Worth maun snoul to screen frae want
    Her ain hearthstane.

We've a' our ain bit weird to dree,
    Our ain bit wark to dae,
And some maun hurkle doun the howe
    While ithers speel the brae ;
But in the dub or on the dyke,
    Ye'll find it's a' in vain
To luik for lastin pleasure
    Aff your ain hearthstane.

The Auld Kirk o' Scotland

The gude auld Kirk o' Scotland,
  The wild winds round her blaw,
And when her foemen hear her sough,
  They prophecy her fa' ;
But what although her fate has been
  Amang the floods to sit—
The gude auld Kirk o' Scotland,
  She's nae in ruins yet !

There may be wrath within her wa's,
  What reck ! her wa's are wide ;
It's but the beating of a heart,
  The rushing of a tide,
Whose motion keeps its waters pure ;
  Then let them foam or fret,
The gude auld Kirk o' Scotland
  She's nae in ruins yet !

She was a lithe, she was a licht,
  When a' thing else was mirk,
An' mony a trembling heart has found
  It's bield behind the Kirk ;
She bore the brunt, and did her due,
  When Scotland's sword was wet,
The gude auld Kirk o' Scotland,
  She's nae in ruins yet !

The clouds that overcast her sky
  Maun shortly flit awa',
A bonnie, blue and peaceful heaven
  Smiles sweetly through them a' !

Her country's life-blood's in her veins,
    The wide warld's in her debt !
The gude auld Kirk o' Scotland,
    She's nae in ruins yet !

SIR JOSEPH NOEL PATON   1821–1901

Timor mortis conturbat me

Could I have sung one song that should survive
    The singer's voice, and in my country's heart
    Find loving echo—evermore a part
Of all her sweetest memories ; could I give
One great Thought to the People, that should prove
    The spring of noble action in their hour
    Of darkness, or control their headlong power
With the firm reins of Justice and of Love ;
Could I have traced one Form that should express
    The sacred mystery that underlies
    All Beauty, and through man's enraptured eyes
Teach him how beautiful is Holiness,—
    I had not feared thee.   But to yield my breath,
    Life's Purpose unfulfilled !—This is thy sting, O Death !

DOROTHEA MARIA OGILVY of Clova   1823–95

The Weary Spinnin O't

Sittin spinnin, sittin spinnin
    A' the lea-lang day,
Hearin the bit burnie rinnin,
    And the bairns at play.

37

I'm sweir to get my leg let loose,
To do a turn about the hoose ;
Oh, amna I a waefu wife
To spin awa my threid o life ?
Spinnin, spinnin, ever spinnin,
Never endin, aye beginnin ;
Hard at wark wi hand and fuit,
Oh, the weary spinnin o't !

Sittin spinnin, sittin spinnin,
   Vow but I am thrang,
My wee pickle siller winnin,
   Croonin some auld sang.
Leese me o my spinnin-wheel,
Gie's us a' oor milk and meal ;
Weet or dry, or het or cauld,
I maun spin till I grow auld.
Spinnin, spinnin, ever spinnin,
Never endin, aye beginnin,
Hard at wark wi hand and fuit
At the weary spinnin o't.

Sittin spinnin, sittin spinnin,
   Sic a wear and tear,
Taps o tow for wabs o linen,
   Till my heid is sair.
Mony a wiselike wab I've spun,
Spreid and sortit i the sun ;
Puirtith cauld is ill to bear ;
Mony bairns bring mickle care.
Spinnin, spinnin, ever spinnin,
Never endin, aye beginnin,
Hard at wark wi hand and fuit,
Oh ! the weary spinnin o't !

GEORGE MACDONALD 1824-1905

The Lord is my Shepherd

I'm a puir man, I grant,
But I am weel neepured ;
And nane sall me daunt,
Though a puir man, I grant ;
For I sall nocht want—
The Lord is my Sheepherd.
I'm a puir man, I grant,
But I am weel neepured.

That Holy Thing

They all were looking for a king
  To slay their foes and lift them high :
Thou camst, a little baby thing
  That made a woman cry.

O Son of Man, to right my lot
  Naught but Thy presence can avail ;
Yet on the road Thy wheels are not,
  Nor on the sea Thy sail.

My how or when Thou wilt not heed,
  But come down Thine own secret stair,
That Thou mayst answer every need—
  Yea, every bygone prayer.

A Sang o Zion

Ane by ane they gang awa :
The Getherer gethers grit and smaa :
Ane by ane maks ane and aa.

39

Aye whan ane sets doun the cup
Ane ahint maun tak it up :
Aa thegither they will sup.

Gowden-heidit, ripe, and strang,
Shorn will be the hairst or lang :
Syne begins a better sang.

WALTER CHALMERS SMITH

1824–1908

Miss Penelope Leith

Last heiress she of many a rood,
    Where Ugie winds through Buchan braes—
A treeless land, where beeves are good,
    And men have quaint old-fashioned ways,
And every burn has ballad-lore,
    And every hamlet has its song,
And on its surf-beat rocky shore
    The eerie legend lingers long.
Old customs live there, unaware
    That they are garments cast away,
And what of light is shining there
    Is lingering light of yesterday.

Never to her the new day came,
    Or if it came she would not see ;
This world of change was still the same
    To our old-world Penelope :
New fashions rose, old fashions went,
    But still she wore the same brocade,
With lace of Valenciennes or Ghent
    More dainty by her darning made,

A little patch upon her face,
   A tinge of colour on her cheek,
A frost of powder, just to grace
   The locks that time began to streak.

A stately lady ; to the poor
   Her manner was without reproach ;
But from the Causeway she was sure
   To snub the Provost in his coach :
In pride of birth she did not seek
   Her scorn of upstarts to conceal,
But of a Bailie's wife would speak
   As if she bore the fisher's creel.
She said it kept them in their place,
   Their fathers were of low degree ;
She said the only saving grace
   Of upstarts was humility.

The quaint old Doric still she used,
   And it came kindly from her tongue ;
And oft the ' mim-folk ' she abused,
   Who mincing English said or sung :
She took her claret, nothing loth,
   Her snuff that one small nostril curled ;
She might rap out a good round oath,
   But would not mince it for the world :
And yet the wild word sounded less
   In that Scotch tongue of other days ;
'Twas just like her old-fashioned dress,
   And part of her old-fashioned ways.

At every fair her face was known,
   Well-skilled in kyloes and in queys ;
And well she led the fiddler on
   To ' wale ' the best of his strathspeys ;

Lightly she held the man who rose
    While the toast-hammer still could rap,
And brought her gossip to a close,
    Or spoilt her after-dinner nap ;
Tea was for women, wine for men,
    And if they quarrelled o'er their cups,
They might go to the peat-moss then,
    And fight it out like stags or tups.

She loved a bishop or a dean,
    A surplice or a rochet well,
At all the Church's feasts was seen,
    And called the Kirk Conventicle ;
Was civil to the minister,
    But stiff and frigid to his wife,
And looked askance, and sniffed at her,
    As if she lived a dubious life.
But yet his sick her cellars knew,
    Well stored from Portugal or France,
And many a savoury soup and stew
    Her game-bags furnished to the Manse.

But if there was a choicer boon
    Above all else she would have missed,
It was on Sunday afternoon
    To have her quiet game of whist
Close to the window, when the Whigs
    Were gravely passing from the Kirk,
And some on foot, and some in gigs,
    Would stare at her unhallowed work :
She gloried in her ' devil's books '
    That cut their sour hearts to the quick ;
Rather than miss their wrathful looks
    She would have almost lost the trick.

Her politics were of the age
  Of Claverhouse or Bolingbroke ;
Still at the Dutchman she would rage,
  And still of gallant Graham she spoke.
She swore 'twas right that Whigs should die
  Psalm-snivelling in the wind and rain,
Though she would ne'er have harmed a fly
  For buzzing on the window-pane.
And she had many a plaintive rhyme
  Of noble Charlie and his men :
For her there was no later time,
  All history had ended then.

The dear old sinner ! yet she had
  A kindly human heart, I wot,
And many a sorrow she made glad,
  And many a tender mercy wrought :
And though her way was somewhat odd,
  Yet in her way she feared the Lord,
And thought she best could worship God
  By holding Pharisees abhorred,
By being honest, fearless, true,
  And thorough both in word and deed,
And by despising what is new,
  And clinging to her old-world creed.

ALEXANDER NICOLSON   1827-93

Skye

My heart is yearning to thee, O Skye !
  Dearest of islands !
There first the sunshine gladdened my eye,
  On the sea sparkling ;

43

There doth the dust of my dear ones lie,
    In the old graveyard.

Bright are the golden green fields to me,
    Here in the Lowlands ;
Sweet sings the mavis in the thorn tree,
    Snowy with fragrance :
But, oh ! for a breath of the great North Sea,
    Girdling the mountains !

Good is the smell of the brine that laves
    Black rock and skerry,
Where the great palm-leaved tangle waves
    Down in the green depths,
And round the craggy bluff, pierced with caves,
    Seagulls are screaming.

When the sun sinks beyond Hunish Head,
    Swimming in glory,
As he goes down to his ocean bed
    Studded with islands,
Flushing the Coolin with royal red,
    Would I were sailing !

Many a hearth round that friendly shore
    Giveth warm welcome ;
Charms still are there, as in the days of yore
    More than of mountains ;
But hearths and faces are seen no more,
    Once of the brightest.

Many a poor black cottage is there,
    Grimy with peat smoke,
Sending up in soft evening air
    Purest blue incense,
While the low music of psalm and prayer
    Rises to Heaven.

Kind were the voices I used to hear
    Round such a fireside,
Speaking the mother-tongue old and dear,
    Making the heart beat
With endless tales of wonder and fear,
    Or plaintive singing.

Great were the marvellous stories told
    Of Ossian's heroes,
Giants and witches, and young men bold,
    Seeking adventures,
Winning king's daughters and guarded gold
    Only with valour.

Reared in those dwellings have brave ones been ;
    Brave ones are still there.
Forth from their darkness on Sundays I've seen
    Coming pure linen,
And like the linen the souls were clean
    Of them that wore it.

See that thou kindly use them, O man !
    To whom God giveth
Stewardship over them, in thy short span,
    Not for thy pleasure !
Woe be to them who choose for a clan
    Four-footed people !

Blessings be with ye, both now and aye,
    Dear human creatures !
Yours is the love that no gold can buy
    Nor time can wither.
Peace be to thee and thy children, O Skye !
    Dearest of islands !

Glasgow

Sing, Poet, 'tis a merry world ;
That cottage smoke is rolled and curled
    In sport, that every moss
Is happy, every inch of soil ;—
Before *me* runs a road of toil
    With my grave across.
Sing, trailing showers and breezy downs—
I know the tragic hearts of towns.

City ! I am true son of thine ;
Ne'er dwelt I where great mornings shine
    Around the bleating pens ;
Ne'er by the rivulets I strayed,
And ne'er upon my childhood weighed
    The silence of the glens.
Instead of shores where ocean beats,
I hear the ebb and flow of streets.

Black Labour draws his weary waves
Into their secret-moaning caves ;
    But with the morning light,
The sea again will overflow
With a long weary sound of woe,
    Again to faint in night.
Wave am I in that sea of woes,
Which, night and morning, ebbs and flows.

I dwelt within a gloomy court,
Wherein did never sunbeam sport ;
    Yet there my heart was stirr'd—

My very blood did dance and thrill,
When on my narrow window-sill,
    Spring lighted like a bird.
Poor flowers—I watched them pine for weeks,
With leaves as pale as human cheeks.

Afar one summer I was borne ;
Through golden vapours of the morn,
    I heard the hills of sheep :
I trod with a wild ecstasy
The bright fringe of the living sea :
    And on a ruined keep
I sat, and watched an endless plain
Blacken beneath the gloom of rain.

O fair the lightly sprinkled waste,
O'er which a laughing shower has raced !
    O fair the April shoots !
O fair the woods on summer days,
While a blue hyacinthine haze
    Is dreaming round the roots !
In thee, O city ! I discern
Another beauty, sad and stern.

Draw thy fierce streams of blinding ore,
Smite on a thousand anvils, roar
    Down to the harbour-bars ;
Smoulder in smoky sunsets, flare
On rainy nights, with street and square
    Lie empty to the stars.
From terrace proud to alley base
I know thee as my mother's face.

When sunset bathes thee in his gold
In wreaths of bronze thy sides are rolled,
    Thy smoke is dusky fire ;

And, from the glory round thee poured,
A sunbeam like an angel's sword
   Shivers upon a spire.
Thus have I watched thee, Terror ! Dream !
While the blue Night crept up the stream.

The wild Train plunges in the hills,
He shrieks across the midnight rills ;
   Streams through the shifting glare,
The roar and flap of foundry fires,
That shake with light the sleeping shires ;
   And on the moorlands bare
He sees afar a crown of light
Hang o'er thee in the hollow night.

At midnight, when thy suburbs lie
As silent as a noonday sky,
   When larks with heat are mute,
I love to linger on thy bridge,
All lonely as a mountain ridge,
   Disturbed but by my foot ;
While the black lazy stream beneath,
Steals from its far-off wilds of heath.

And through thy heart, as through a dream,
Flows on that black disdainful stream ;
   All scornfully it flows,
Between the huddled gloom of masts,
Silent as pines unvexed by blasts—
   'Tween lamps in streaming rows.
O wondrous sight ! O stream of dread !
O long dark river of the dead.

Afar, the banner of the year
Unfurls : but dimly prisoned here,
   'Tis only when I greet

A dropt rose lying in my way,
A butterfly that flutters gay
    Athwart the noisy street,
I know the happy Summer smiles
Around thy suburbs, miles on miles.

All raptures of this mortal breath,
Solemnities of life and death,
    Dwell in thy noise alone :
Of me thou hast become a part—
Some kindred with my human heart
    Lives in thy streets of stone ;
For we have been familiar more
Than galley-slave and weary oar.

The beech is dipped in wine ; the shower
Is burnished ; on the swinging flower
    The latest bee doth sit.
The low sun stares through dust of gold,
And o'er the darkening heath and wold
    The large ghost-moth doth flit.
In every orchard Autumn stands,
With apples in his golden hands.

But all these sights and sounds are strange ;
But wherefore from thee should I range ?
    Thou hast my kith and kin ;
My childhood, youth, and manhood brave :
Thou hast that unforgotten grave
    Within thy central din.
A sacredness of love and death
Dwells in thy noise and smoky breath.

Lines in Praise of Professor Blackie

Alas ! the people's hearts are now full of sorrow
For the deceased Professor Blackie, of Edinboro',
Because he was a Christian man, affable and kind,
And his equal in charitable actions would be hard to find. . . .
Professor Blackie will be greatly missed in Edinboro',
Especially those that met him daily will feel great sorrow,
When they think of his never-failing plaid and hazel rung,
For although he was an old man, he considered he was young.
He had a very striking face, and silvery locks like a seer,
And in the hearts of the Scottish people he was loved most dear ;
And many a heart will mourn for him, but all in vain,
Because he never can return to them again.
He was a very kind-hearted man, and in no way vain ;
And I'm afraid we ne'er shall look upon his life again ;
And to hear him tell Scotch stories, the time did quickly pass,
And for singing Scotch songs few could him surpass.
But I hope he is in Heaven, singing with saints above,
Around God's throne, where all is peace and love ;
There, where God's children daily doth meet
To sing praises to God, enchanting and sweet.
He had visited almost every part of Europe in his time,
And like Lord Byron he loved the Grecian clime ;
Nor did he neglect his own dear country,
And few men knew it more thoroughly than he.
On foot he tramped o'er the most of bonnie Scotland,
And in his seventies he climbed the highest hills most grand.
Few men in his day could be compared with him,
Because he wasn't hard on fallen creatures when they did sin.
Oh, dearly beloved Professor Blackie, I must conclude my muse,
And to write in praise of thee my pen does not refuse ;
Because you were a very Christian man, be it told,
Worthy of a monument, and your name written thereon in
    letters of gold.

JAMES MACFARLAN 1832-62

from *The Lords of Labour*

They come ! they come in a glorious march !
    You can hear their steam steeds neigh,
As they dash through Skill's triumphal arch,
    Or plunge mid the dancing spray.
Their bale-fires blaze in the mighty forge,
    Their life-pulse throbs in the mill,
Their lightnings shiver the gaping gorge,
    And their thunders shake the hill.
Ho ! these are the Titans of toil and trade,
    The heroes who wield no sabre ;
But mightier conquests reapeth the blade
    That is borne by the Lords of Labour.

J. B. SELKIRK (James B. Brown) 1832-1904

from *Death in Yarrow*

It's no the sax month gane
    Sin a' our cares began—
Sin she left us here alane,
    Her callant and gudeman.
It was in the spring she dee'd,
    And noo we're in the fa' ;
And sair we've struggled wi't,
    Sin his mither gaed awa.

An awfu blow was that—
    The deed that nane can dree ;
And lang and sair we grat
    For her we couldna see.

I've aye been strong and fell,
    And can stand a gey bit thraw ;
But the laddie's no hissel
    Sin his mither gaed awa.

In a' the water-gate
    Ye couldna find his marrow—
There wasna ane his mate
    In Ettrick Shaws or Yarrow.
But he hasna noo the look
    He used to hae ava ;
He's grown sae little bouk
    Sin his mither gaed awa.

I mak his pickle meat—
    And I think I mak it weel ;
And I warm his little feet,
    When I hap him i the creel ;
And he kisses me fu' couthie,
    For he downa sleep at a'
Till he hauds up his bit mouthie,
    Sin his mither gaed awa.

And then I dander oot,
    When I can do nae mair,
And walk the hills aboot,
    I dinna aye ken where ;
For my hairt's wi ane abune,
    And the ane is growin twa,
He's dwined sae sair, sae sune,
    Sin his mither gaed awa.

And noo the lang day's dune,
    And the nicht's begun to fa',
And a bonnie harvest mune
    Rises up on Bourhope Law.

It's a bonnie warlt this,
   But it's no for me at a',
For a' thing's gane amiss
   Sin his mither gaed awa.

Second-Sight

There cometh a time in the life of man
   When earth's realities strike him less,
When the facts of the senses seem nothing, and when
The matters that move him beyond his ken
   Are the only things that impress.

Some sorrow perhaps has searched him through,
   And burned away in its cleansing fires
Life's baser belongings, and kindled anew
Those higher life-lights that strike out of view
   The earth and its low desires.

When life but lives for its holier sake,
   The lamp in a temple where no voice sings
But in prayer and praise ; those wings that make
That wafting about us, which keeps us awake
   To the sense of invisible things.

A time when a man in the world's keen eyes
   Seems fallen behind on the busy road,—
Seems making a senseless sacrifice ;
And yet he knows that his heart is wise
   In the sight of the searching God.

The world's weak wisdom has taken flight ;
   Things earthly near him, and heavenly far,
Are suddenly seen in an equal light,
And divested of argument, dumb in his sight,
   Stand out for what they are.

Slink out of his way, ye vendors of lies ;
  By a light not yours he can read you through,
Oh hollow of heart ! and oh worldly wise !
The things you would carefully screen from his eyes
  Are the things that are thrust on his view.

And to you, O soul, where the vision is shown,
  It may come but once in your earthly strife ;
Mark well what it says to you, make it your own,
Beat it out into prayer, ere the angel has flown,
  And gird it about your life.

JAMES EASSON   1833-65

The Factory Girl

In a thrifty dress of an homely guise,
  All iron'd, smooth, and clean,
The factory girl, at the brief meal hour,
  Is always to be seen.
And there is ever on her face
  That look which seems to say,
Industry is the noblest plan
  By which to live you may.'

Both snow and sleet her ceaseless feet
  Can brave without regret ;
More sweet thinks she it thus should be
  Than sleep and wake in debt.
And she lightly warbles while she works
  The moments to beguile,
As quick they fly, like the rapid wheel
  That merrily whirls the while.

Around and round the mighty arm
  Of the engine sweeps its track ;
But every turn still serves to bring
  The hour of respite back,
When the mighty bell on the lofty roof
  Calls out with clamorous din,
' To your homes now go, all ye below,
  Who closely weave and spin.'

Then home she goes to that much loved hearth,
  And there sinks down to rest ;
When a well won meal rewards her toil,
  Of all rewards the best.
Then when the happy board is swept,
  Some reading forth she'll bring ;
Or haply with her brothers young
  She tunes her voice to sing.

Year after year this is the mode
  In which she spends her days ;
An endless scene of activeness
  Her history's page displays.
And though her lot may be obscure
  The less of care has she ;
So may her happiness increase
  And toils unnoticed be.

ADAM LINDSAY GORDON   1833-70

from *Gordon's Valedictory Poem*

Lay me low, my work is done,
  I am weary.   Lay me low,
Where the wild flowers woo the sun,
  Where the balmy breezes blow,

Where the butterfly takes wing,
  Where the aspens, drooping, grow,
Where the young birds chirp and sing—
  I am weary, let me go.

I have striven hard and long
  In the world's unequal fight,
Always to resist the wrong,
  Always to maintain the right.
Always with a stubborn heart,
  Taking, giving blow for blow ;
Brother, I have played my part,
  And am weary, let me go.

Stern the world and bitter cold,
  Irksome, painful to endure ;
Everywhere a love of gold,
  Nowhere pity for the poor,
Everywhere mistrust, disguise,
  Pride, hypocrisy, and show,
Draw the curtain, close mine eyes,
  I am weary, let me go.

JAMES THOMSON   1 8 3 4 – 8 2

from *The City of Dreadful Night*

PROEM

Lo, thus, as prostrate, ' In the dust I write
  My heart's deep languor and my soul's sad tears.'
Yet why evoke the spectres of black night
  To blot the sunshine of exultant years ?

Why disinter dead faith from mouldering hidden?
Why break the seals of mute despair unbidden,
    And wail life's discords into careless ears?

Because a cold rage seizes one at whiles
    To show the bitter, old and wrinkled truth
Stripped naked of all vesture that beguiles,
    False dreams, false hopes, false masks and modes of youth;
Because it gives some sense of power and passion
In helpless impotence to try to fashion
    Our woe in living words howe'er uncouth.

Surely I write not for the hopeful young,
    Or those who deem their happiness of worth,
Or such as pasture and grow fat among
    The shows of life and feel not doubt nor dearth,
Or pious spirits with a God above them
To sanctify and glorify and love them,
    Or sages who foresee a heaven on earth.

For none of these I write, and none of these
    Could read the writing if they deigned to try:
So may they flourish, in their due degrees,
    On our sweet earth and in their unplaced sky.
If any cares for the weak words here written,
It must be some one desolate, Fate-smitten,
    Whose faith and hope are dead, and who would die.

Yes, here and there some weary wanderer
    In that same city of tremendous night,
Will understand the speech, and feel a stir
    Of fellowship in all-disastrous fight;
'I suffer mute and lonely, yet another
Uplifts his voice to let me know a brother
    Travels the same wild paths though out of sight.'

O sad Fraternity, do I unfold
    Your dolorous mysteries shrouded from of yore ?
Nay, be assured ; no secret can be told
    To any who divined it not before :
None uninitiate by many a presage
Will comprehend the language of the message,
    Although proclaimed aloud for evermore.

Part VIII

While I still lingered on that river-walk,
    And watched the tide as black as our black doom,
I heard another couple join in talk,
    And saw them to the left hand in the gloom
Seated against an elm bole on the ground,
Their eyes intent upon the stream profound.

' I never knew another man on earth
    But had some joy or solace in his life,
    Some chance of triumph in the dreadful strife :
My doom has been unmitigated dearth.

' We gaze upon the river, and we note
The various vessels, large and small, that float,
Ignoring every wrecked and sunken boat.

' And yet I asked no splendid dower, no spoil
    Of sway or fame or rank or even wealth ;
    But homely love with common food and health,
And nightly sleep to balance daily toil.

' This all-too-humble soul would arrogate
    Unto itself some signalising hate
    From the supreme indifference of Fate !

' Who is most wretched in this dolorous place ?
   I think myself ; yet I would rather be
   My miserable self than He, than He
Who formed such creatures to His own disgrace.
The vilest thing must be less vile than Thou
   From whom it had its being, God and Lord !
   Creator of all woe and sin, abhorred,
Malignant and implacable !   I vow
That not for all Thy power furled and unfurled,
   For all the temples to Thy glory built,
   Would I assume the ignominious guilt
Of having made such men in such a world.

' As if a Being, God or Fiend, could reign,
At once so wicked, foolish, and insane,
As to produce men when He might refrain !
The world rolls round for ever like a mill ;
It grinds out death and life and good and ill ;
It has no purpose, heart or mind or will.
While air of Space and Time's full river flow
The mill must blindly whirl unresting so :
It may be wearing out, but who can know ?
Man might know one thing were his sight less dim ;
That it whirls not to suit his petty whim,
That it is quite indifferent to him.
Nay, does it treat him harshly, as he saith ?
It grinds him some slow years of bitter breath,
Then grinds him back into eternal death.'

PART XVI

Our shadowy congregation rested still,
   As musing on that message we had heard

And brooding on that ' End it when you will ' ;
    Perchance awaiting yet some other word ;
When keen as lightning through a muffled sky
Sprang forth a shrill and lamentable cry :—

' The man speaks sooth, alas ! the man speaks sooth :
    We have no personal life beyond the grave ;
There is no God ; Fate knows nor wrath nor ruth :
    Can I find here the comfort which I crave ?

' In all eternity I had one chance,
    One few years' term of gracious human life :
The splendours of the intellect's advance,
    The sweetness of the home with babes and wife ;

' The social pleasures with their genial wit ;
    The fascination of the worlds of art,
The glories of the worlds of nature, lit
    By large imagination's glowing heart ;

' The rapture of mere being, full of health ;
    The careless childhood and the ardent youth,
The strenuous manhood winning various wealth,
    The reverend age serene with life's long truth :

' All the sublime prerogatives of Man ;
    The storied memories of the times of old,
The patient tracking of the world's great plan
    Through sequences and changes myriadfold.

' This chance was never offered me before ;
    For me the infinite Past is blank and dumb :
This chance recurreth never, nevermore ;
    Blank, blank for me the infinite To-come.

' And this sole chance was frustrate from my birth,
      A mockery, a delusion ; and my breath
Of noble human life upon this earth
      So racks me that I sigh for senseless death.

' My wine of life is poison mixed with gall,
      My noonday passes in a nightmare dream,
I worse than lose the years which are my all :
      What can console me for the loss supreme ?

' Speak not of comfort where no comfort is,
      Speak not at all : can words make foul things fair ?
Our life's a cheat, our death a black abyss :
      Hush and be mute, envisaging despair.'

This vehement voice came from the northern aisle,
      Rapid and shrill to its abrupt harsh close ;
And none gave answer for a certain while,
      For words must shrink from these most wordless woes ;
At last the pulpit speaker simply said,
With humid eyes and thoughtful drooping head :—

' My Brother, my poor Brothers, it is thus ;
This life itself holds nothing good for us,
      But it ends soon and nevermore can be ;
And we knew nothing of it ere our birth,
And shall know nothing when consigned to earth :
      I ponder these thoughts and they comfort me.'

'MOSES PEERIE, D.D.'   born about 1835
(Principal R. H. Story, D.D.)

from *The Goodly Ironmaster*

(A Ballad of the Iron Age)

There was an ironmaster,
   A Lord of several pits,
No man made money faster,
   None scored such lucky hits.
For him the markets waited,
   Stocks rattled up and down ;
His were the biggest money-bags
   In all St. Mammon's town.

The Levites of Philistia
   Were, mostly, rather poor ;
The decent men were scant of bread,
   Their water wasn't sure.
The man of iron's coffers
   They often eyed askance ;
'Would God,' they say, ' that of his coin
   We only had a chance !
How many a priestly household
   We'd gladden with its gleam—
How many altars dedicate—
   How many souls redeem ! '
And round the ironmaster
   They pressed in anxious throng,
Nor heeded that his mien was rough,
   His language sometimes strong ;
They praised his ' noble industry '—
   ' An honour to his race ' ;
They raised him to the Elders' seat,
   They blessed him to his face.

Where'er he went their incense
  Was burned before his nose ;
While daily upward swelling
  His hoarded treasure rose.

' God's blessing is upon him,'
  The good M'Stotty cries.
' His great increase is of the Lord,'
  M'Tattle testifies.
' Who said he was a man of wrath ? '
  Exclaims the bold M'Phun ;
' He, certes, is a man of God,
  Who's worth a million pund.'
  The gentle Humming wiped his eye—
  ' It doth a vessel good
To see the promise thus fulfilled
  About the righteous' food.'
' Yea,' quoth the gracious Chitterling,
  ' And surely if we work
The oracle aright, a share
  Should fall to Holy Kirk.'

Cries Baldykin of Greendykes
  ' My mates, leave that to me ;
The way to bleed this Mulciber
  You presently shall see.
Within his iron noddle
  Ideas there are twain,
Through dexterous play on these I trust
  The money-bags to gain.
On what he calls the Carritch
  His simple faith is pinned ;
All other theologic lore
  To him is idle wind.

Then, to his mind, the Minister
   Dealing with human souls
Is but the mate of him who digs
   At hematite or coals.
The work of each he reckons
   By what is brought to bank ;
And if the hutch be empty
   The pay is also blank.
Now let us drill the Levites
   Carritch alone to preach,
And to the hue of Carritch
   Their every thought to bleach.
A band of statisticians
   We also needs must rear,
Skilled to make smallest data
   Of vastest size appear—
By deftest tabulation
   Establishing the claim
Of earnest workmen whom their work
   Will never put to shame.
I'll pledge my floweriest sermon,
   If thus we go to work,
The ironmaster's coffers
   Will open to the Kirk.
He'll pay for nought but Carritch,
   And work reported done :
But that for this he will disburse
   Is sure as any gun.
And, hark ye, gentle comrades,
   Perchance you and me,
As deacons of the tribe, our friend
   May fling a special fee.'

ELLEN JOHNSTON

c. 1835-73

The Last Sark

Gude guide me, are ye hame again, and hae ye got nae wark ?
We've naething noo tae pit awa, unless your auld blue sark.
My heid is rinnin roond aboot, far lichter nor a flee :
What care some gentry if they're weel though a' the puir wad
  dee ?

Our merchants and mill-masters they wad never want a meal
Though a' the banks in Scotland wad for a twalmonth fail ;
For some o them hae far mair gowd than ony ane can see.
What care some gentry if they're weel though a' the puir wad
  dee ?

Oor hoose aince bien and cosy, John, oor beds aince snug and
  warm,
Feels unco cauld and dismal noo, and empty as a barn ;
The weans sit greetin in our face, and we hae nocht tae gie.
What care some gentry if they're weel though a' the puir wad
  dee ?

It is the puir man's hard-won cash that fills the rich man's purse ;
I'm sure his gowden coffers they are het wi mony a curse.
Were it no for the workin man what wad the rich man be ?
What care some gentry if they're weel though a' the puir wad
  dee ?

DAVID GRAY

1838-61

Sonnet

If it must be ; if it must be, O God !
  That I die young, and make no further moans ;

That, underneath the unrespective sod,
    In unescutcheoned privacy, my bones
Shall crumble soon,—then give me strength to bear
    The last convulsive throe of too sweet breath !
I tremble from the edge of life, to dare
    The dark and fatal leap, having no faith,
No glorious yearning for the Apocalypse ;
    But, like a child that in the night-time cries
For light, I cry ; forgetting the eclipse
    Of knowledge and our human destinies.
O peevish and uncertain soul ! obey
The law of life in patience till the Day.

THOMAS DAVIDSON   1838-70

And there will I be buried

Tell me not the good and wise
    Care not where their dust reposes—
That to him in death who lies
    Rocky beds are even as roses.

I've been happy above ground ;
    I can never be happy under
Out of gentle Teviot's sound—
    Part us not, then, far asunder.

Lay me here where I may see
    Teviot round his meadows flowing,
And around and over me
    Winds and clouds for ever going.

ROBERT BUCHANAN   1841-1901

from *The Wedding of Shon Maclean*

(A Bagpipe Melody)

To the wedding of Shon Maclean,
   Twenty Pipers together
Came in the wind and the rain
   Playing across the heather ;
Backward their ribbons flew,
Blast upon blast they blew,
Each clad in tartan new,
   Bonnet, and blackcock feather :
And every Piper was fou,
   Twenty Pipers together !—

ANDREW LANG   1844-1912

To Robert Louis Stevenson

(With Kirk's *Secret Commonwealth*)

O Louis ! you that like them maist,
Ye're far frae kelpie, wraith, and ghaist,
And fairy dames, no unco chaste,
   And haunted cell.
Amang a heathen clan ye're placed,
   That kens na hell !

Ye hae nae heather, peat, nor birks,
Nae trout in a' yer burnies lurks,
There are nae bonny U.P. kirks,
   An awfu place !
Nane kens the Covenant o Works
   Frae that o Grace !

67

But whiles, maybe, to them ye'll read
Blads o the Covenanting creed,
And whiles their pagan wames ye'll feed
    On halesome parritch ;
And syne ye'll gar them learn a screed
    O the Shorter Carritch.

Yet thae uncovenanted shavers
Hae rowth, ye sae, o clash and clavers
O gods and etins,—auld wives' havers,
    But their delight ;
The voice o him that tells them quavers
    Just wi fair fright.

And ye might tell, ayont the faem,
Thae Hieland clashes o our hame.
To speak the truth, I tak na shame
    To half believe them ;
And, stamped wi *Tusitala's* name,
    They'll a' receive them.

And folk to come ayont the sea
May hear the yowl o the Banshie,
And frae the water-kelpie flee,
    Ere a' things cease,
And island bairns may stolen be
    By the folk o peace.

from *Clevedon Church*

Westward I watch the low green hills of Wales,
    The low sky silver grey,
The turbid Channel with the wandering sails
    Moans through the winter day.
There is no colour but one ashen light
    On tower and lonely tree,

The little church upon the windy height
　　Is grey as sky or sea.

　　　.　　　.　　　.　　　.　　　.　　　.

Grey sky, brown waters, as a bird that flies,
　　My heart flies forth from these
Back to the winter rose of northern skies,
　　Back to the northern seas.
And lo, the long waves of the ocean beat
　　Below the minster grey,
Caverns and chapels worn of saintly feet,
　　And knees of them that pray.

And I remember me how twain were one
　　Beside that ocean dim,
I count the years passed over since the sun
　　That lights me looked on him,
And dreaming of the voice that, safe in sleep,
　　Shall greet me not again,
Far, far below I hear the Channel sweep
　　And all his waves complain.

In Ithaca

(' And now am I greatly repenting that ever I left my life
with thee, and the immortality thou didst promise me.'—*Letter
of Odysseus to Calypso*, Luciani *Vera Historia*)

'Tis thought Odysseus, when the strife was o'er
　　With all the waves and wars, a weary while,
　　Grew restless on his disenchanted isle,
And still would watch the sunset, from the shore,
Go down the ways of gold ; and evermore
　　His sad heart followed after, mile on mile,
　　Back to the goddess of the magic wile,
Calypso, and the love that was of yore.

69

Thou too, thy haven gained, must turn thee yet
To look across the sad and stormy space,
Years of a youth as bitter as the sea,
Ah, with a heavy heart and eyelids wet ;
Because, within a fair forsaken place,
The life that might have been is lost to thee.

Matrimony

(Matrimony—Advertiser would like to hear from well-
educated Protestant lady, under thirty, fair, with view to
above, who would have no objection to work Remington
type-writer, at home. Enclose photo. T. 99. This office.—
Cork newspaper)

T. 99 would gladly hear
From one whose years are few—
A maid whose doctrines are severe,
Of Presbyterian blue ;
Also—with view to the above—
Her photo he would see,
And trusts that she may live and love
His Protestant to be !
But ere the sacred rites are done
(And by no priest of Rome)
He'd ask, if she a Remington
Type-writer works—at home ?
If she have no objections to
This task, and if her hair—
In keeping with her eyes of blue—
Be delicately fair ;
Ah, *then*, let her a photo send
Of all her charms divine,
To him who rests her faithful friend,
Her own T. 99.

ALEXANDER ANDERSON 1845-1909
(Surfaceman)

from *The Spirit of the Times*

Where shall he come from, the poet, whose fire
   Shall place on his wild, rough page
The spirit that lurks and forever works
   In the breast of this mighty age ?
Is he yet in the cycles that loom before,
   Preparing his melody ?
Let him come, and roll through my heart and soul
   His music before I die.

But now, while we wait for the roll of his words,
   Let us work in our growing strength ;
For the earth, in her cradle since Adam died,
   Is up from her slumber at length.
Ay, up ! in the cities that roar and fret
   With the toil and the tread of men ;
And the sun shall be hurled from his course ere she sinks
   To her second childhood again.

Then, hurrah ! for our higher fellows that work
   With this thought and its Titan powers,
And cut through the jungle of creeds and fools
   A path for this planet of ours.
And hurrah for this nineteenth century time—
   What the future may grow and be !
Ah, God ! to burst up from the slumber of death
   For one wild moment to see !

JOHN YOUNG GRAY 1846–1934

My Loonie

I've a wee little loon, O ! ye ne'er saw his like,
He's as duddie and towsie as ony tint tyke ;
He trauchles his mither the weary day lang,
Yet she never ance thinks fat he daes can be wrang.

He'll climb on the back o his faither's big chair ;
Get twa stools for horses and drive to the fair,
Till coup gangs his coach and he's owre on the flure
Wi a reeshle that gars the cat flee to the door.

He'll be neist on the dresser to see and fin' oot
Fat gars the tnock chap fan the hands feeze aboot ;
Syne he'll speir fu' my watch hasna gotten a bell,
And if it will chap whan it's auld like himsel.

He'll sit doon in his chair juist like ony auld man,
And owre his bricht een gangs his wee chubby han',
For nae drap o parritch daur cross his bit mou'
Till he's socht to be made ' truly thankfu,' I trow.

I whiles think he cracks wi the birds and the bees
Whan they bum roond his heid 'mang the fleurs and the trees,
And they tell him queer stories o pairts we ne'er saw,
Till I'm maist feared the fairies will moyne him awa.

Whiles his een looks in mine wi the starnies' clear leme,
And he'll crack aboot things that I daurna weel name ;
Whar his wee sister gaed when she dwined i the fa',
And fan her and the angels will tak him awa.

72

Fan e'er he speaks that wye my hert it grows sair,
Lest they sud come tak him and lea my life bare ;
Sae I pray the gude Shepherd to spare him to me,
Till my life's darg is dune and I'm ready to dee.

HUGH HALIBURTON   1846–1922
(J. Logie Robertson)

On the Decadence of the Scots Language, Manners and Customs

They're wearin' by, the guid auld lives
O' leal an' thrifty men an' wives ;
They're wearin' oot, the guid auld creeds
That met a simple people's needs ;

The auld Scots character an' laws
That made oor kintra what it was—
Esteemed at hame, envied abroad,
Honoured o' man an' loved o' God ;
Oor nationality, oor name,
Oor patriotic love for hame—
I 'maist could greet ; I can but sigh—
They're wearin' oot, they're a' gaun by !

The gude auld honest mither tongue !
They kent nae ither, auld or young ;
The cottar spak' it in his yaird,
An' on his rigs the gawcie laird.
Weel could it a' oor wants express,
Weel could it ban, weel could it bless ;
Wi' a' oor feelin's 'twas acquent,
 Had words for pleasour an' complent.

As wide could range the auld Scots tongue ;
'Twas meet alike for auld an' young,
For jest an' earnest, joy an' wae,
For cursin' an' caressin' tae.
'Twas gentler at a hushaba
Than a wuid-muffled waterfa',
Or cushats wi' their downie croon
Heard through a gowden afternoon,
Or streams that rin wi' liquid lapse,
Or wun's among the pine-tree taps.
'Twas sweet at a' times i' the mooth
O' woman moved wi' meltin' ruth ;
But oh ! when first love was her care,
'Twas bonnie far beyond compare.
'Twas mair sonorous than the Latin,
Cam' heavier on the hide o' Satan,
When frae his Ebal o' a poopit
The minister grew hearse an' roopit,
Bannin' wi' energetic jaw
The author o' the primal fa'.
But if the poopit's sacred clangour
Was something aw'some in its anger,
Gude keep my Southlan' freen's fra' hearin'
A rouch red-headed Scotsman swearin' !
But wha would hae audacity
To question its capacity ?
The mither croon'd by cradle side,
Young Jockie woo'd his blushin' bride,
The bargain at the fair was driven,
The solemn prayer was wing'd to heaven,
The deein' faither made his will,
In gude braid Scots :—a language still !

It lives in Freedom-Barbour's lines,
In bauld Dunbar it brichtly shines,

On Lyndsay's page in licht it streams,
In Border scraps it fitful gleams,
An' like the shimmerin' spunkie strays
By Ettrick banks an' Yarrow braes.
It lives for aye in Allan's play,
In Coila's sangs, the Shepherd's lay,
The bird-like lilts fra' Paisley side,
The Wizart's tales that flew sae wide,
Forbye the vast an' various lore
O' later ballants by the score :
The gude auld Scots !—a language still,
Let fortune vary as she will.
Though banish'd from oor College ha's,
It frames the siccar auld Scots laws ;
Though from the lips, of speech the portal,
It lives in Literature immortal.

ROBERT   LOUIS   STEVENSON   1850–94

Singing

Of speckled eggs the birdie sings
    And nests among the trees ;
The sailor sings of ropes and things
    In ships upon the seas.

The children sing in far Japan,
    The children sing in Spain ;
The organ with the organ man
    Is singing in the rain.

It is not yours, O Mother

It is not yours, O mother, to complain,
   Not, mother, yours to weep,
Though nevermore your son again
   Shall to your bosom creep,
   Though nevermore again you watch your baby sleep.

Though in the greener paths of earth,
   Mother and child, no more
We wander ; and no more the birth
   Of me whom once you bore
   Seems still the brave reward that once it seemed of yore ;

Though as all passes, day and night,
   The seasons and the years,
From you, O mother, this delight,
   This also disappears— .
   Some profit yet survives of all your pangs and tears.

The child, the seed, the grain of corn,
   The acorn on the hill,
Each for some separate end is born
   In season fit, and still
   Each must in strength arise to work the almighty will.

So from the hearth the children flee,
   By that almighty hand
Austerely led ; so one by sea
   Goes forth, and one by land ;
   Nor aught of all man's sons escapes from that command.

So from the sally each obeys
   The unseen almighty nod ;
So till the ending all their ways
   Blindfolded loth have trod :
   Nor knew their task at all, but were the tools of God.

And as the fervent smith of yore
  Beat out the glowing blade,
Nor wielded in the front of war
  The weapons that he made,
    But in the tower at home still plied his ringing trade ;

So like a sword the son shall roam
  On nobler missions sent ;
And as the smith remained at home
  In peaceful turret pent,
    So sits the while at home the mother well content.

A Portrait

I am a kind of farthing dip,
  Unfriendly to the nose and eyes ;
A blue-behinded ape, I skip
  Upon the trees of Paradise.

At mankind's feast, I take my place
  In solemn, sanctimonious state,
And have the air of saying grace
  While I defile the dinner-plate.

I am ' the smiler with the knife,'
  The battener upon garbage, I—
Dear Heaven, with such a rancid life
  Were it not better far to die ?

Yet still, about the human pale,
  I love to scamper, love to race,
To swing by my irreverent tail
  All over the most holy place ;

And when at length, some golden day,
 The unfailing sportsman, aiming at,
Shall bag, me—all the world shall say :
 Thank God, and there's an end of that !

The Maker to Posterity

Far 'yont amang the years to be,
When a' we think, an' a' we see,
An' a' we luve, 's been dung ajee
 By time's rouch shouther,
An' what was richt and wrang for me
 Lies mangled throu'ther,

It's possible—it's hardly mair—
That some ane, ripin' after lear—
Some auld professor or young heir,
 If still there's either—
May find an' read me, an' be sair
 Perplexed, puir brither !

' *What tongue does your auld bookie speak ?* '
He'll spier ; an' I, his mou' to steik :
' *No' bein' fit to write in Greek,*
 I wrote in Lallan,
Dear to my heart as the peat-reek,
 Auld as Tantallon.

' *Few spak it then, an' noo there's nane.*
My puir auld sangs lie a' their lane,
Their sense, that aince was braw an' plain,
 Tint a' thegither:
Like runes upon a standin' stane
 Amang the heather.

78

' But think not you the brae to speel ;
  You, tae, maun chow the bitter peel ;
  For a' your lear, for a' your skeel,
        Ye're nane sae lucky ;
  An' things are mebbe waur than weel
        For you, my buckie.

' The hale concern (baith hens an' eggs,
  Baith books an' writers, stars and clegs)
  Noo stachers upon lowsent legs,
        An wears awa' ;
  The tack o' mankind, near the dregs,
        Rins unco law.

' Your book, that in some braw new tongue
  Ye wrote or prentit, preached or sung,
  Will still be just a bairn, an' young
        In fame an' years,
  Whan the hale planet's guts are dung
        About your ears ;

' An' you, sair gruppin' to a spar
  Or whammled wi' some bleezin' star,
  Cryin' to ken whaur deil ye are,
        Hame, France, or Flanders—
  Whang sindry like a railway car
        An' flie in danders.'

My Conscience

Of a' the ills that flesh can fear,
The loss o' frien's, the lack o' gear,
A yowlin' tyke, a glandered mear,
      A lassie's nonsense—
There's just ae thing I canna bear,
      An' that's my conscience.

When day (an' a' excüse) has gane,
An' wark is düne, and duty's plain,
An' to my chalmer a' my lane
    I creep apairt,
My conscience ! hoo the yammerin' pain
    Stends to my heart !

A' day wi' various ends in view
The hairsts o' time I had to pu'
An' made a hash wad staw a soo,
    Let be a man !—
My conscience ! whan my han's were **fu'**,
    Whaur were ye than ?

An' there were a' the lures o' life,
There pleesure skirlin' on the fife,
There anger, wi' the hotchin' knife
    Ground shairp in Hell—
My conscience !—you that's like a wife !—
    Whaur was yoursel' ?

I ken it fine : just waitin' here,
To gar the evil waur appear,
To clart the guid, confüse the clear,
    Misca' the great,
My conscience ! an' to raise a steer
    When a's ower late.

Sic-like, some tyke grawn auld and blind,
Whan thieves brok' through the gear to poind,
Has lain his dozened length an' grinned
    At the disaster ;
An' the morn's mornin', wud's the wind,
    Yokes on his master.

Youth and Love

I

Once only by the garden gate
   Our lips we joined and parted.
I must fulfil an empty fate
   And travel the uncharted.

Hail and farewell !   I must arise,
   Leave here the fatted cattle,
And paint on foreign lands and skies
   My Odyssey of battle.

The untented Kosmos my abode,
   I pass, a wilful stranger :
My mistress still the open road
   And the bright eyes of danger.

Come ill or well, the cross, the crown,
   The rainbow or the thunder,
I fling my soul and body down
   For God to plough them under.

In the Highlands

In the highlands, in the country places,
Where the old plain men have rosy faces,
And the young fair maidens
     Quiet eyes ;
Where essential silence cheers and blesses,
And for ever in the hill-recesses
Her more lovely music
     Broods and dies.

O to mount again where erst I haunted ;
Where the old red hills are bird-enchanted,
And the low green meadows
        Bright with sward ;
And when even dies, the million-tinted,
And the night has come, and planets glinted,
Lo, the valley hollow,
        Lamp-bestarred !

O to dream, O to awake and wander
There, and with delight to take and render,
Through the trance of silence,
        Quiet breath ;
Lo ! for there, among the flowers and grasses,
Only the mightier movement sounds and passes ;
Only winds and rivers,
        Life and death.

To S. R. Crockett

(In reply to a Dedication)

Blows the wind to-day, and the sun and the rain are flying,
    Blows the wind on the moors to-day and now,
Where about the graves of the martyrs the whaups are crying,
    My heart remembers how !

Grey recumbent tombs of the dead in desert places,
    Standing-stones on the vacant wine-red moor,
Hills of sheep, and the homes of the silent vanquished races,
    And winds, austere and pure :

Be it granted me to behold you again in dying,
    Hills of home ! and to hear again the call ;
Hear about the graves of the martyrs the peewees crying,
    And hear no more at all.

from *Glendale & Co.*

(After Walt Whitman)

The Firm of Glendale & Co.—
A Firm of undoubted respectability,
Its name honoured on the Exchange,
Its bills eagerly sought after, readily discounted,
Its ramifications extensive, its agencies scattered throughout the
    world.

Once on a time the Firm small and unimportant,
It has grown great from small beginnings ;
Now its factories cover acres of ground,
They have streets running through them ;
They are a city in themselves.
The buildings palatial and mammoth,
No way showy, built for endurance ;
Its chimneys tall like Egyptian obelisks ;
The clock towers aspiring also—
Lit up at night, the discs flare like angry eyes in watchful
    supervision, impressing on the minds of the workers the
    necessity of improving the hours and minutes purchased by
    Glendale & Co.

The Firm dominates the Town, it is in a sense ubiquitous ; it
    pervades it.
The workers are thousands strong :
Every morning a city-full of men, women, and children march
    through its portals ;
Every meal-hour they are disgorged,
The Town always in excitement, stir, hubbub, commotion ;
The call-boys clatter at early five ;
The bells clang, the whistles shriek at regular intervals—
The workers, slaves of the ring, hurrying to and fro in obedience
    to summons—

83

The patter of their feet like the tread of an army ;
There is a constant jostling and rumbling of lorries,
A tremendous throbbing of beams and pistons,
An incessant rattle of looms.
The atmosphere permeated with dust,
The faces of the people engrained with dirt and grime,
Their voices husky with the fluff settled on the throat and
    lungs.
It is questionable indeed if the townspeople have any real
    personal identity at all ;
If they are not really themselves part and parcel a product of
    Glendale & Co. ;
Questionable if its fluff is not also on their souls, if the interests
    of the great Firm have not dimmed their mental vision, and
    clouded their moral perceptions.
At night the Firm still predominant, still supreme,
The flame of its foundry blasts reflected on the heavens, casting
    a ruddy radiance as far as the confusion of stars in the Milky
    Way.
Great the output of the Firm ;
The machinery daily swallowing tons of the raw material,
Daily spueing forth tons of the finished webs.
It spins fine material, it spins coarse and rough material ;
The blushing bride presses with her snowy limbs the soft white
    products of its looms,
The Eastern odalisque in the harem treads on the carpets of its
    manufacture—
The Royal Squadron spreads the canvas of the Firm proudly in
    the favouring wind.
The Firm equal to any demand—
Should the globe at any time take the chills, or grow old or
    rheumatic, the Firm could supply it on the shortest of notice
    with a hap-warm, to put on its eternal spinning through
    space.
A great Firm !   A wonderful Firm !

Glendale, of Glendale & Co., is a methodical man,
A man of undoubted honesty, of unquestionable morality.
Proud of his merchant ancestry, as any lord of his pedigree :
The Firm to him is a trust—
His ambition, to make it grow greater, to hand over his charge
    to the next in succession in increased splendour ;
Political matters he has no time to attend to ;
For the solution of social problems he has no relish ;
Publicity he hates—
Nothing diverts him from the trust ;
He prides himself on being practical, on not being a dreamer, a
    sentimentalist.
Assiduous himself in attending to the interests of the Firm, he
    expects from his workers an equal assiduity—
Their individuality must be lost, swallowed up in the Firm.

Glendale is methodical—
The works an enlargement of the man ;
There nothing imperfect ; no repairing, no patching—
The imperfect machine cast into the furnace ;
Every machine with its duplicate prepared, ready to be put in
    its place.
Imperfect men and women cannot be re-cast—cannot be
    rejuvenated—
They could not endure the fiery furnace ;
They must be discharged—
To do otherwise would be to break down the system :
The works are for workers ;
The workhouses and benevolent institutions are for the old and
    infirm.
Why regret the harshness of the system ?
It is inevitable :
Glendale himself is only a part of it.

An army, the workers of Glendale & Co. ;
No army better drilled or more efficient.
Every week Glendale assembles his officers together,
They sit in solemn conclave,
They deliberate long and anxiously—
Every one answerable for his own department.
With ordinary workers Glendale comes not into contact,
His orders percolate down through various strata of officials ;
His fiat absolute as that of the Czar of all the Russias ;
He is, as an impersonal force, the lever that sets everything into
    motion, that stills everything into no motion.
He says, and it is done—
So much work on hand, so many workers taken on ;
So little work on hand, so many workers discharged :
The system, as perfect as the automatic machine that works with
    the penny shot in the slot.
Glendale is a moral man—
The works have also a tone of morality—
The morality is that of the decalogue ;
It extends as far as ' Thou shalt not ' ;
It prohibits unchastity, it disallows debt, it protests against the
    establishment of public-houses in the neighbourhood.

Yet listen a moment, Glendale, of Glendale & Co.,
I have been brooding over these things,
I have been thinking over your perfect automatical penny-in-
    the-slot system ; over your home in the suburbs ; over
    these dens in the slums—
The conclusion ? That you are not such a practical man as you
    deem yourself to be, or as others deem you to be ;
That in spite of the Scriptures we can only think of you as *raca*
    —a fool.
Do you deem that such a state of matters can continue ?
Glendale, you are the man that has built his house upon the
    sand :

Assuredly the flood will come, if not in your day, at least in the
  day of your successors.
Glendale ! there is a spiritual law of supply and demand which
  is higher than the law of the economists :
The demand of that law is that your relationship with your
  workers should be human and sympathetic.
You cannot get rid of your obligation by appealing to the
  necessity of securing cheap labour, to compete with the
  foreigner.
You use men and women as machines at the peril of yourself ;
  to the danger of society :
The demand of that law will not be evaded ;
It will be paid in some fashion or other—
God's books always balance ;
For the neglect of your workers you have the slum and its
  consequent miseries ;
Your attention to your workers would be as certainly repaid
  with blessings.

THOMAS GIVEN   1850–1917

A Song for February

Day in and day oot in his auld farrant loom,
  Time lengthens the wab o the past ;
Dame Nature steps in like a lamp tae the room,
Hir ee tae the simmer o life geein bloom.
So winter slips by, wi its mirth and its gloom,
  As spring is appearin at last.

The robin gets up and he lauchs in his glee,
  In view o the prospect so braw ;
Sets his heid tae the side, wi its feathers agee,
As he spies a bit snaw at fit o the tree,

87

And says tae himsel ' A'll hae denties tae pree
  By and by when the splash is awa.'

The blackbird keeks oot frae the fog at the broo,
  Gees his neb a bit dicht on a stane ;
His ee caught the primrose appearin in view,
And the tiny wee violet o Nature's ain blue ;
He sung them a sang o the auld and the new—
  A sang we may a' let alane.

The thrush cufft the leaves neath the skep o the bee,
  And he tirrlt them aside wae a zest ;
I maun hurry awa tae rehearsal, quo he,
This work fits the sparrow far better than me ;
His sang pleased the ear frae the tap o the tree
  As he fell intae tune wae the rest.

Thus Nature provides for hir hoose and hir wanes,
  And we may rejoice in the plan ;
The wren tae the bluebonnet sings his refrain
On causey o cottier or lordly domain ;
The wagtail looks on without shade o disdain.
  May we aye say the same o the man.

ROGER QUIN   born 1850

*To a Skylark singing above Barnhill Poorhouse,
                    Glasgow*

What blast of Fate, melodious mocker ! say,
Has blown thee here ; in airy spendthrift glee,
Wasting thy wealth of liquid ecstasy
On hearts too cold to kindle at thy lay ?
Thou sing'st of Hope above Hope's grave. . . .
        Away !

Flee this dark ' Hall of Eblis,' through whose aisles
Frail phantoms totter, or, with senile smiles,
Rake the spent ashes of dead yesterday !

Flung from Life's boiling tumult—bruised and sore ;
Sick with the shame of what I have become,
My wistful gaze follows thy flight afar—
As some late reveller when the rout is o'er
Pauses in his uncertain steps for home,
With bleared eyes blinking at the Morning Star.

ADAM WILSON   born 1850

from *The Brotherhood of Man*

Arise ! ye sons of labour, artisans of every grade,
Be up and lay aside awhile your implements of trade ;
While ' Unity is strength ' our right will be to guide the van,
For the universal fellowship and brotherhood of man.

With meagre wage and hours too long, we'll strive now to
          curtail
The working day, and have our pay set to some equal scale ;
For Labour's share in Capital's our principle and plan,
For universal fellowship and brotherhood of man.

Why should a few have all the wealth, and teeming millions be
The slaves of those in whose employ they toil for petty fee ?
Let master unto servant act the Christian, if he can,
For the universal fellowship and brotherhood of man.

Our path through life is rough and hard, but we will clear away
Whate'er impedes our progress as we plod on day by day ;
For a vast co-operation in the future dim I scan,
Bringing universal fellowship and brotherhood of man.

We do not wish to take from what already is your own ;
But let some law of equity to nations all be known ;
Let one be to the other just as when the world began,
In universal fellowship and brotherhood of man.

SIR DONALD MACALISTER 1854–1934

The Twa Traivlers

Twa traivlers gaed ance to the Hielans awa,
I' the hairst—oh ! it's then that the Heilans are braw !
The tane he gaed—to be like the lave ;
The tither his ane heart's yearning drave.

And when they baith were cam hame again,
Their friens and neighbours were unco fain,
And deaved them wi' spierin, ane and a'—
' Weel, what hae ye seen i' thae Hielans awa ? '

The tane he gantit and scartit his pow—
' Oh ! naething by-ordinar that I mind o' :
Jist hill and heather, and loch and linn,
And the blue o' the lift, and the glint o' the suin.'

The tither leuch laigh, and the like spak he,
But wi' blithesome face, and wi' glisterin' e'e—
' Ay ! hill and heather ! and loch and linn !
And the blue o' the lift ! and the glint o' the suin ! '

ROB WANLOCK

Gloaming

The hinmost whaup has quat his eerie skirl,
the flichterin gorcock tae his cover flown ;
din dwines athort the muir ; the wind sae lown
can scrimply gar the stey peat-reek play swirl
abune the herd's auld bield, or halflins droon
the laich seep-sabbin o the burn doonby,
that deaves the corrie wi its wilyart croon.
I wadna niffer sic a glisk—not I—
here wi ma fit on ane o Scotland's hills,
heather attour, and the mirk lift owre aa,
for foreign ferly or for unco sicht
e'er bragged in sang ; mair couthie joy distils
frae this than glowerin on the tropic daw,
or bleezin splendours o the norland nicht.

RONALD CAMPBELL MACFIE

A Moral

A million stars decide the place
Of any single star in space,
And though they draw it divers ways
The star in steady orbit stays :
And tho' contrariwise they draw
They all are followers of one law,—
In fact they find in mutual strife
The equilibrium of life.
They find an unanimity,
Agreeing all to disagree ;

And when they wish to peg their tether
They pull in every way together.
Moral : The remedy for schism
Is universal egotism.

Man in Evolution

Spawn he was in the steamy mire,
Fins he was in the primal sea,
Wings he was in the feathered choir,
Or ever he came a man to be.
Of dead the mountain peaks are built,
Of dead the soil, of dead the silt—
The dead that led the way to him
Through shell and claw to brain and limb.
In every thought, in every part,
Made is he of a million slain,
Blood of the dead is in his heart,
Dreams of the dead are in his brain.

W. A. MACKENZIE

Shon Campbell

Shon Campbell went to College,
Because he wanted to ;
He left the croft in Gairloch
To dive in Bain and Drew :
Shon Campbell died at College
When the spring skies were blue.

Shon Campbell went to College,
The pulpit was his aim :

By day and night he ' ground,' for he
Was Heilan', dour, and game ;
The session was a hard one,
Shon flickered like a flame.

Shon Campbell went to College,
And gave the ghost up there,
Attempting six men's ' cramming,'
On poor and scanty fare ;
Three days the Tertians mourned him,
'Twas all that they could spare.

Shon Campbell sleeps in Gairloch,
Unhooded and ungowned,
The green quadrangle of the hills
Watching his sleep profound,
And the *gaudeamus* of the burns
Making a homely sound.

But when the last great Roll is called,
And *adsums* thunder loud,
And when the quad is cumbered
With an eager, jostling crowd,
The Principal Who rules us all
Will say, ' Shon Campbell, come,
Your *Alma Mater* hails you
Magister Artium.'

JAMES KEIR HARDIE   1856-1915

Evening Prayer

When the shadows o' the e'enin' mingle wi' the summer
    gloamin',
And the bairnies tired and wearied frae their play come hirplin'
    hame ;

Auld grannie, ere she haps them in their cuddle ba' sae cosy,
Kind and couthie draws them near her as she tells them still the
 same
Auld story o' the land o' bliss, heaven's happy hame abune,
Where the bairnies dwall wi' Jesus freed frae ilka taint o' sin ;
Syne roon her lap a' kneelin' doon, wi' voice and posture meek,
They commit their souls to Jesus ere their wearied een they
 steek—

> This night I lay me down to sleep,
> I pray the Lord my soul to keep,
> If I should die before I wake,
> I pray the Lord my soul to take
> To heaven,
> For Jesus' sake,
> AMEN.

When the shadows o' death's comin' mingle wi' life's wanin'
 gloamin',
An' the weary feet o' eldhood, tired an' sair, come totterin' in,
May the simple faith o' childhood, happy confidence inspirin',
Be ours to guide us safely to the happy hame abune ;
May the loving arms o' Jesus draw us near Him as He whispers
A hope o' life for ever free frae warldly care and strife ;
May we fa' asleep committin' our souls into His keepin',
Till we wauken i' the mornin', born to everlasting life.

J. PITTENDRIGH MACGILLIVRAY   1856–1938

Glances

O weel I mind the bonnie morn,
 Richt early in the day,
When he cam' in by oor toun end
 To buy a sou o' hay.

For O he was a handsome lad,
 An' weel did cock his beaver !—

He gar't my heart play pit-a-pat :
　　Yet—speired but for my faither !

I turned aboot and gied a cast
　　That plainly said—' Ye deevil !—
Altho' ye be a braw young lad
　　Ye needna be unceevil ! '

He glower't at me like ane gaen wud
　　Wi' his daurin' rovin' een ;
At that I leuch and wi' a fling
　　Flew roun' the bourtree screen.

Abasshyd

I toke hyr heid atween my hondes
　　And kyste hyr dusky hair ;
I lyghtly touchte hyr luvely cheek, .
　　Syn kyste hyr mouth so rare.

A lityll flame cam up hyr neck
　　To tell hyr herte had fyre ;
But, sum aschamte, wyth eyen cast down,
　　Hyr mynde restrainte desyre.

A swete, pure mayde of gentyl kynd—
　　A flowr ryght fayre to see :
Yet wyth ane potent gyfte of sowle
　　Fro yll to keep hyr free.

Abasshte before hyr luvelyness
　　I knelt and kyste hyr honde ;
In token that I humbled me,
　　And stayed at hyr commaunde.

from *A Ballad in Blank Verse of the Making of a Poet*

His father's house looked out across a firth
broad-bosomed like a mere, beside a town
far in the North, where Time could take his ease,
and Change hold holiday ; where Old and New
weltered upon the border of the world.

' Oh, now,' he thought—a youth whose sultry eyes,
bold brow and wanton mouth were not all lust,
but haunted from within and from without
by memories, visions, hopes, divine desires—
' Now may my life beat out upon this shore
a prouder music than the winds and waves
can compass in their haughtiest moods. I need
no world more spacious than the region here :
the foam-embroidered firth, a purple path
for argosies that still on pinions speed,
or fiery-hearted cleave with iron limbs
and bows precipitous the pliant sea ;
the sloping shores that fringe the velvet tides
with heavy bullion and with golden lace
of restless pebble woven and fine spun sand ;
the villages that sleep the winter through,
and, wakening with the spring, keep festival
all summer and all autumn : this grey town
that pipes the morning up before the lark
with shrieking steam, and from a hundred stalks
lacquers the sooty sky ; where hammers clang
on iron hulls, and cranes in harbours creak,
rattle and swing, whole cargoes on their necks ;

where men sweat gold that others hoard or spend,
and lurk like vermin in their narrow streets :
this old grey town, this firth, the further strand
spangled with hamlets, and the wooded steeps,
whose rocky tops behind each other press,
fantastically carved like antique helms
high-hung in heaven's cloudy armoury,
is world enough for me.   Here daily dawn
burns through the smoky east ; with fire-shod feet
the sun treads heaven, and steps from hill to hill
downward before the night that still pursues
his crimson wake ; here winter plies his craft,
soldering the years with ice ; here spring appears,
caught in a leafless brake, her garland torn,
breathless with wonder, and the tears half-dried
upon her rosy cheek ; here summer comes
and wastes his passion like a prodigal
right royally ; and here her golden gains
free-handed as a harlot autumn spends ;
and here are men to know, women to love.'

His father, woman-hearted, great of soul,
wilful and proud, save for one little shrine
that held a pinch-beck cross, had closed and barred
the many mansions of his intellect.

' My son,' he said—to him, fresh from his firth
and dreams at evening ; while his mother sat,
she also with her dingy crucifix
and feeble rushlight, praying for her boy—
' My son, have you decided for the Lord ?
Your mother's heart and mine are exercised
for your salvation.   Will you turn to Christ ?
Now, young and strong, you hanker for the world ;
but think : the longest life must end at last,

and then come Death and Judgment.   Are you fit
to meet your God before the great white throne ?
If on the instant Death should summon you,
what doom would the Eternal Judge pronounce—
" Depart from me " or " Sit on my right hand " ?
In life it is your privilege to choose,
but after death you have no choice at all.
Die unbelieving, and in endless woe
you must believe throughout eternity.
My son, reject not Christ ; he pleads through me ;
the Holy Spirit uses my poor words.
How it would fill your mother's heart and mine,
and God's great heart, with joy unspeakable,
were you, a helpless sinner, now to cry,
" Lord, I believe : help Thou mine unbelief." '

He clenched his teeth ; his blood, fulfilled of brine,
of sunset, and his dreams, boomed in his ears.
A vision rose before him ; and the sound,
husky and plaintive, of his father's voice
seemed unintelligible and afar.
He saw Apollo on the Dardan beach :
the waves lay still ; the winds hung motionless,
and held their breath to hear the rebel god,
conquered and doomed, with stormy sobbing song,
and crashing discords of his golden lyre,
reluctantly compel the walls of Troy,
unquarried and unhewn, in supple lines
and massive strength to rise about the town.

A quavering voice shattered his fantasy :
his father's pleading done, his mother cried,
with twitching forehead, scalding tears, that broke
the seal of wrinkled eyelids, mortised hands

where knuckles jutted white : ' Almighty God !—
Almighty God !—Oh, save my foolish boy.'

He glanced about the dreary parlour, clenched
his teeth, and once again his blood, fulfilled
of brine, of sunset, and his dreams, exhaled
a vision.   While his parents clutched their hearts,
expecting his conversion instantly,
and listened if perchance they might o'erhear
the silent heavens burst into applause
over one lost repentant, he beheld
the Cyprian Aphrodite, all one blush
and glance of passion, from the violet sea
step inland, fastening as she went her zone.
She reached a gulf that opened in the ground
deep in a leafless wood, and waited there,
battling the darkness with her wistful eyes.
Then suddenly she blanched and blushed again,
and her divinely pulsing body bowed
with outstretched arms over the yawning earth.
Straightway Adonis, wonderstruck and pale,
stole from the sepulchre, a moonbeam wraith,
but Aphrodite, with a golden cry
that echoed round the world and shook the stars,
caught him, and thawed him in her warm embrace,
and murmuring kisses bore him to her bower.
Then all the trees were lit with budding flames
of emerald, and all the meads and leas,
coverts and shady places, glades and dells,
odoured and dimly stained with opening flowers,
and loud with love-songs of impassioned birds,
became the shrine and hostel of the spring.

His wanton face grew sweet and wonderful,
beholding Aphrodite.   But they thought—

his father and his mother, sick with hope—
it was the Holy Ghost's effectual call.
Entranced he rose and glided from the room ;
they, undeceived, like little children sobbed.

Slowly he broke his mother's tender heart,
until she died in anguish for his sins.
His father then besought him on his knees,
with tears and broken speech and pleading hands :
' My son,' he said, ' you open all the wounds
daily and nightly of the Lord of Heaven :
you killed your mother, you are killing me :
is it not sin enough, poor foolish boy ? '

For this was in the North, where Time stands still
and Change holds holiday, where Old and New
welter upon the border of the world,
and savage faith works woe.
                                        ' Oh, let me be ! '
the dreamer cried, and rushing from the house
he sought the outcast Aphrodite, dull,
tawdry, unbeautiful, but still divine
even in the dark streets of a noisome port.

            .   .   .   .   .

At times he wrote his dreams, rebellious still
that he should be constrained to please himself
as one is eased by roaring on the rack.
Desperate he grew, and wandering by his firth
exclaimed against the literature he loved.
' Lies, lies ! ' he muttered.   ' And the noblest, lies !
Why should we lie ? what penalty is this—
to write, and sing, and think, and speculate,
hag-ridden by ideas, or 'twixt the shafts

like broken horses, blinded, bitted, reined,
and whipped about the world by steel-tagged creeds ! '

.   .   .   .   .

                              ' I'll have no creed,'
he said.   ' Though I be weakest of my kind,
I'll have no creed.   Lo ! there is but one creed,
the vulture-phoenix that for ever tears
the soul of man in chains of flesh and blood
riveted to the earth ; the clime, the time,
change but its plumage.   Gluttonous bird of prey,
more fatal than all famines, plagues and wars,
I wrench you off, although my soul go too !
With bloody claws and dripping beak unfleshed,
spread out your crackling vans that darken heaven ;
rabid and curst, fly yelping where you list !
Henceforth I shall be God ; for consciousness
is God : I suffer ; I am God : this Self,
that all the universe combines to quell,
is greater than the universe ; and *I*
am that I am.   To think and not be God ?—
It cannot be ! Lo ! I shall spread this news,
and gather to myself a band of Gods—
an army, and go forth against the world,
conquering and to conquer.   Snowy steppes
of Muscovy, frost-bound Siberian plains,
and scalding sands of Ethiopia,
where groans oppress the bosom of the wind,
and men in gangs are driven to icy graves,
or lashed to brutish slavery under suns
whose sheer beams scorch and flay like burning blades,
shall ring, enfranchised, with divine delight.
At home, where millions mope, in labyrinths
of hideous streets, astray without a clue,

unfed, unsexed, unsouled, unhelped, I bring
life, with the gospel, " Up, quit you like Gods ! '

.   .   .   .   .

'. . . Subtle lie
that tempts our weakness always ; magical,
and magically changed to suit the time !
" Lo, ye shall be as Gods ! "—the serpent's cry—
rose up again, " Ye shall be sons of God " ;
and now the glozing word is in the air,
" Thou shalt be God by simply taking thought."
And if one could, believing this, convert
a million to be upright, chaste and strong,
gentle and tolerant, it were but to found
a new religion, bringing new offence,
setting the child against the father still.
Some thought imprisons us ; we set about
to bring the world within the woven spell :
our ruthless creeds that bathe the earth in blood
are moods by alchemy made dogmas of—
the petrifaction of a metaphor.
No creed for me !   I am a man apart :
a mouthpiece for the creeds of all the world ;
a soulless life that angels may possess
or demons haunt, wherein the foulest things
may loll at ease beside the loveliest ;
a martyr for all mundane moods to tear ;
the slave of every passion ; and the slave
of heat and cold, of darkness and of light ;
a trembling lyre for every wind to sound.
I am a man set by to overhear
the inner harmony, the very tune
of Nature's heart ; to be a thoroughfare
for all the pageantry of Time ; to catch
the mutterings of the Spirit of the Hour

and make them known ; and of the lowliest
to be the minister, and therefore reign
prince of the powers of the air, lord of the world,
and master of the sea.   Within my heart
I'll gather all the universe, and sing
as sweetly as the spheres ; and I shall be
the first of men to understand himself. . . .
And lo ! to give me courage comes the dawn,
crimsoning the smoky east ; and still the sun
with fire-shod feet shall step from hill to hill
downward before the night ; winter shall ply
his ancient craft, soldering the years with ice ;
and spring appear, caught in a leafless brake,
breathless with wonder and the tears half-dried
upon her rosy cheek ; summer shall come
and waste his passion like a prodigal
right royally ; and autumn spend her gold
free-handed as a harlot ; men to know,
women to love, are waiting everywhere.'

Thirty Bob a Week

I couldn't touch a stop and turn a screw,
   and set the blooming world a-work for me,
like such as cut their teeth—I hope, like you—
   on the handle of a skeleton gold key ;
I cut mine on a leek, which I eat it every week :
   I'm a clerk at thirty bob as you can see.

But I don't allow it's luck and all a toss ;
   there's no such thing as being starred and crossed ;
it's just the power of some to be a boss,
   and the bally power of others to be bossed :
I face the music, sir ; you bet I ain't a cur ;
   strike me lucky if I don't believe I'm lost !

For like a mole I journey in the dark,
    a-travelling along the underground
from my Pillared Halls and broad Suburbean Park,
    to come the daily dull official round ;
and home again at night, with my pipe all alight,
    a-scheming how to count ten bob a pound.

And it's often very cold and very wet,
    and my missis stitches towels for a hunks ;
and the Pillared Halls is half of it to let—
    three rooms about the size of travelling trunks.
And we cough, my wife and I, to dislocate a sigh,
    when the noisy little kids are in their bunks.

But you never hear her do a growl or whine,
    for she's made of flint and roses, very odd ;
and I've got to cut my meaning rather fine,
    or I'd blubber, for I'm made of greens and sod :
so perhaps we are in Hell, for all that I can tell,
    and lost and damned and served up hot to God.

I ain't blaspheming, Mr Silver-Tongue ;
    I'm saying things a bit beyond your art :
of all the rummy starts you ever sprung,
    thirty bob a week's the rummiest start !
With your science and your books and your theories
      about spooks,
    did you ever hear of looking in your heart ?

I didn't mean your pocket, Mr, no :
    I mean that having children and a wife,
with thirty bob on which to come and go,
    isn't dancing to the tabor and the fife :
when it doesn't make you drink, by Heaven ! it makes
      you think,
    and notice curious items about life.

I step into my heart and there I meet
  a god-almighty devil singing small,
who would like to shout and whistle in the street,
  and squelch the passers flat against the wall ;
if the whole world was a cake he had the power to take,
  he would take it, ask for more, and eat them all.

And I meet a sort of simpleton beside,
  the kind that life is always giving beans ;
with thirty bob a week to keep a bride
  he fell in love and married in his teens :
at thirty bob he stuck ; but he knows it isn't luck :
  he knows the seas are deeper than tureens.

And the god-almighty devil and the fool
  that meet me in the High Street on the strike,
when I walk about my heart a-gathering wool,
  are my good and evil angels if you like.
And both of them together in every kind of weather
  ride me like a double-seated bike.

That's rough a bit and needs its meaning curled.
  But I've a high old hot un in my mind—
a most engrugious notion of the world,
  that leaves your lightning 'rithmetic behind :
I give it at a glance when I say, ' There ain't no chance,
  nor nothing of the lucky-lottery kind.'

And it's this way that I make it out to be :
  no fathers, mothers, countries, climates—none ;
not Adam was responsible for me,
  nor society, nor systems, nary one :
a little sleeping seed, I woke—I did, indeed—
  a million years before the blooming sun.

I woke because I thought the time had come ;
    beyond my will there was no other cause ;
and everywhere I found myself at home,
    because I chose to be the thing I was ;
and in whatever shape, of mollusc or of ape,
    I always went according to the laws.

I was the love that chose my mother out ;
    I joined two lives and from the union burst ;
my weakness and my strength without a doubt
    are mine alone for ever from the first :
it's just the very same, with a difference in the name,
    as ' Thy will be done.'   You say it if you durst !

They say it daily up and down the land
    as easy as you take a drink, it's true ;
but the difficultest go to understand,
    and the difficultest job a man can do,
is to come it brave and meek with thirty bob a week,
    and feel that that's the proper thing for you.

It's a naked child against a hungry wolf ;
    it's playing bowls upon a splitting wreck ;
it's walking on a string across a gulf
    with millstones fore-and-aft about your neck ;
but the thing is daily done by many and many a one ;
    and we fall, face forward, fighting, on the deck.

Decadents

(Prologue to *Earl Lavender*)

Though our eyes turn ever waveward,
    where our sun is well-nigh set ;
though our Century totters graveward,
    we may laugh a little yet.

Oh ! our age-end style perplexes
    all our elders Time has tamed ;
on our sleeves we wear our sexes,
    our diseases, unashamed.

Have we lost the mood romantic
    that was once our right by birth ?
Lo ! the greenest girl is frantic
    with the woe of all the earth !

But we know a British rumour,
    and we think it whispers well :
' We would ventilate our humour
    in the very jaws of Hell.'

Though our thoughts turn ever Doomwards,
    though our sun is well-nigh set,
though our Century totters tombwards,
    we may laugh a little yet.

WALLACE MARTIN LINDSAY   1858–1937

A Song of Putting

O' a' the strokes that's in the game
Which is your choice ?   Gie it a name.
The drive, say you ; the loft, say you ;
The brassy-shot, the cleek-shot—but
        Gie me the putt.
The wee bit pat, nae mair nor that,
The canny touch, scarcely sae much.
The stroke that sends the ballie in,
O that's the stroke to gar you win !

107

Your ' far and sure ' 's a splendid motto.
When I was young, 'twas a' I tho't o',
To swipe my fill, to hae my will,
To lace intil't wi fury—but
    Gie me the putt.
The wee bit pat, nae mair nor that,
The canny touch, scarcely sae much.
The drive's but silver, solid gold
The stroke that sees the ballie holed.

I've watched them stand wi feet wide planted
And swing their club like men demented ;
Then crack ! and whew ! awa she flew,
The soarin, sounin rocket—but
    Gie me the putt,
The wee bit pat, nae mair nor that,
The canny touch, scarcely sae much.
Yon drive, the talk o half the toun,
It didna send the ballie doon.

On life's last green ane wish I'll utter :
' Leave to my han' my faithful putter,
My steps to stay on my lang way.
I fain wad tak nane ither but
    The club to putt,
To gie the pat, nae mair nor that,
The canny touch, scarcely sae much.
St Peter willna think it sin
To let my wee bit putter in.'

DUGALD SUTHERLAND MacCOLL   1859-1948

What are We Fighting for—Scotland

LOWLANDERS

To thriftless England we have lent
The frugal life, the fervent mind,
And where the wanderers of us went
A mighty realm of human kind
Keeps guard upon the Seven Seas,
And orders the Antipodes.

Us too the fog has sore beset,
The din of wheels, the reek, the mud,
But not commuted in us yet
The thrillings of the battle-blood ;
From close and wynd, from cot and manse,
Old wayfarers, we turn to France.

HIGHLANDERS

To fight for loyalty outworn,
For leaders fallen, for cause betrayed,
The battle lost, the hope forlorn,
This from of old was all our trade,
And scanty is the remnant here
Among the pastures of the deer.

Yet from the corrie and the glen
Where lingers any fighting clan,
Sutherland, Gordon, Seaforth men,
Black Watch, we muster to a man.
Charge Cluny, Murray, with the steel !
On Fraser, Appin, and Lochiel !

A Cry from the Poor

O is there a God in the Heavens ?
   Or has He been drowned in the sea ?
Or feedeth He only the ravens
   Who feast on the feeble with glee ?
No ; He hath appointed Him stewards
   To deal out the gifts of His hand ;
But faithless are all but a few hearts,
   And fettered with foibles the land.

The earth is the Lord's and its fulness,
   The land, as the wave and its wealth ;
Deem ye, silly dolts, in your dulness,
   That stealing from God is not stealth.
Your calves feed and fatten on riches,
   While hunger is gnawing God's poor ;
Your statues have canopied niches,
   While human heads houseless endure.

Come down from your temples of splendour
   To Misery's squalid ravines—
More cursed the bright guilt of your grandeur
   Than all the dark guilt of these scenes.
Stretch the hand to your brethren who languish
   In slums for the sake of a crust,
And own in the hell of high anguish
   How sadly you've failed in your trust.

But a muffled cheer breaks from the masses,
   Like the breath of a Samson unbound,
As, thro' clenched teeth, the hissed whisper passes
   ' Too long in the prison we've ground.'

Then remember, ye brothers of Abel,
  As ye bring of the fruit of the ground,
God's altar is Poverty's table—
  Take care it be worthily crowned.

Fragment to His Mother

(In Shetland Norn)

O' a' da sangs I'm ever sung
  I'm never sung o' dee,
To' a' da sang du ever sang
  Wis ' Hushie ba' ' to me.

Du's hed de mony a weary oor
  Sin' first du cradled me,
But du's taen a' dy care ta Christ,
  An' I'm taen mine ta dee.

Sae let me tak de roond da neck
  An' look deep i' dy ee :—
Na ! Na ! I widna gie dee yet
  For ony lass I see.

DAVID RORIE

The Pawky Duke

There aince was a very pawky duke,
  Far kent for his joukery-pawkery,
Wha owned a hoose wi' a grand outlook,
  A gairden and a rockery.
Hech mon ! The pawky duke !
  Hoot ay ! An' a rockery !
For a bonnet-laird wi' a sma' kailyard
  Is naethin' but a mockery !

He lived far up a Heelant glen,
    Where the foamin' flood an' the crag is,
An' he dined each day on the usquebae
    An' he washed it doon wi' haggis.
Hech mon !   The pawky duke !
    Hoot ay !   An' a haggis !
For that's the way the Heelanters dae,
    Where the foamin' flood and the crag is !

He wore a sporran and a dirk
    An' a beard like besom bristles,
He was an elder o' the kirk
    An' he hated kists o' whistles.
Hech mon !   The pawky duke !
    An' doon on kists o' whistles !
They're a' reid-heidit fowk up North
    Wi' beards like besom bristles !

Then ilka four hoors through the day
    He took a muckle jorum,
An' when the gloamin' gathered gray
    Got fou' wi' great decorum.
Hech mon !   The pawky duke !
    Blin' fou' wi' great decorum !
There ne'er were males amang the Gaels
    But loo'ed a muckle jorum !

His hair was reid as ony rose,
    His legs were lang an' bony,
He keepit a hoast an' a rubbin'-post
    An' a buskit cockernony.
Hech mon !   The pawky duke !
    Wi' a buskit cockernony !
Ye ne'er will ken true Heelant men
    Who'll own they hadna ony !

An' if he met a Sassenach loon
  Attour in Caledonia,
He gar'd him lilt in a cotton kilt
  Till he had an acute pneumonia.
Hech mon !   The pawky duke !
  An' a Sassenach wi' pneumonia !
He lat him feel that the land o' the leal
  Is gey near Caledonia.

He never went awa' doon Sooth
  To mell wi' legislation,
For weel he kent sic things to be
  Unfitted for his station.
Hech mon !   The pawky duke !
  An' weel he kent his station,
For dustmen noo we a' alloo
  Are best at legislation !

Then aye afore he socht his bed,
  He danced the Ghillie-Callum,
An' wi's Kilmarnock owre his neb
  What evil could befall 'im ?
Hech mon !   The pawky duke !
  What evil could befall 'im,
When he cast his buits and soupled his cuits
  With a gude-gaun Ghillie-Callum ?

But they brocht ae day a muckle joke
  For his ducal eedification,
An' they needit to trephine his heid,
  An' he dee'd o' the operation !
Hech mon !   The pawky duke !
  Wae's me for the operation !
For weel I wot this typical Scot
  Was a michty loss to the nation !

J. J. HALDANE BURGESS 1863-1927

from *Dokkins*

Dir üsliss deevils here an dere,
   Ipo Güd's frütfil laand,
At for da pür hae deil-a-care,
   Dey muv no fit or haand.
Bit Laabir, feth ! will conquer yit
   In spite o aa, I view.
Dir aristocracies is bit
   Da dokkin on da scroo.

ROBERT FULLER MURRAY 1863-93

Αἰὲν Ἀριστεύειν

Ever to be the best.   To lead
   In whatsoever things are true ;
   Not stand among the halting crew,
The faint of heart, the feeble-kneed,
Who tarry for a certain sign
   To make them follow with the rest—
Oh, let not their reproach be thine !
   But ever be the best.

For want of this aspiring soul,
   Great deeds on earth remain undone,
   But, sharpened by the sight of one,
Many shall press toward the goal.
Thou running foremost of the throng,
   The fire of striving in thy breast,
Shalt win, although the race be long,
   And ever be the best.

And wilt thou question of the prize ?
  'Tis not of silver or of gold,
  Nor in applauses manifold,
But hidden in the heart it lies :
To know that but for thee not one
  Had run the race or sought the quest,
To know that thou hast ever done
  And ever been the best.

MARY SYMON   1863–1938

The Glen's Muster-Roll : The Dominie Loquitur

Hing it up aside the chumley-cheek, the aul' glen's Muster-Roll,
A' names we ken fae hut an' ha', fae Penang to the Pole,
An' speir na gin I'm prood o't—Losh ! coont them line by line,
Near haun' a hunner fechtin' men, an' they a' were Loons o'
    Mine.

A' mine.   It's jest like yesterday they sat there raw on raw,
Some tchyauvin' wi' the ' Rule o' Three,' some widin' throu'
    ' Mensa ' ;
The map o' Asia's shoggly yet faur Dysie's sheemach head
Gaed cleeter-clatter a' the time the carritches was said.
' A limb,' his greetin' grannie swore, ' the aul' deil's very limb '—
But Dysie's deid an' drooned lang syne ; the *Cressy* coffined him.
' Man guns upon the fore barbette ! ' . . . What's that to me
    an' you ?
Here's moss an' burn, the skailin kirk, aul' Kissack beddin's soo.
It's Peace, it's Hame,—but ower the Ben the coastal searchlights
    shine,
And we ken that Britain's bastions mean—that sailor Loon o'
    Mine.

The muirland's lang, the muirland's wide, an' fa says 'ships' or
    'sea'?
But the tang o' saut that's in wir bleed has puzzled mair than me.
There's Sandy wi' the birstled shins, faur think ye's he the day?
Oot where the hawser's tuggin' taut in the surf o' Suvla Bay;
An' ower the spurs o' Chanak Bahr gaed twa lang stilpert chiels,
I think o' flappin' butteries yet or weyvin' powets' creels—
Exiles on far Australian plains—But the Lord's ain boomerang
'S the Highland heart that's aye for hame hooever far it gang.
An' the winds that wail ower Anzac an' requiem Lone Pine
Are nae jest a' for stranger kin, for some were Loons o' Mine.

They're comin' hame in twas an' threes: there's Tam frae
    Singapore—
Yon's his, the string o' buckie-beads abeen the aumry door—
An' Dick Macleod, his sanshach sel' (Guid sake, a bombardier!)
I see them yet ae summer day come hodgin' but the fleer:
'Please, sir' (a habber an' a hoast), 'Please, sir' (a gasp, a gulp,
Syne wi' a rush), 'Please, sir-can-we-win-oot-to-droon-a-fulp?'
. . . Hi, Rover, here, lad!—ay, that's him, the fulp they didna
    droon,
But Tam—puir Tam lies cauld an' stiff on some grey Belgian
    dune,
An' the Via Dolorosa's there, faur a wee bit cutty queyn
Stan's lookin' doon a teem hill-road for a sojer Loon o' Mine.

Fa's neist? The Gaup—a Gordon wi' the 'Bydand' on his
    broo,
Nae murlacks dreetlin' fae his pooch or roon the weeks o's mou',
Nae word o' groff-write trackies on the 'Four best ways to
    fooge'—
He steed his grun' an' something mair, they tell me, oot at Hooge.
But ower the dyke I'm hearin' yet: 'Lads, fa's on for a swap?—
A lang sook o' a pandrop for the sense o' "verbum sap."
116

Fack's death I tried to min' on't—here's my gairten wi' the knot—
But—bizz ! a dhubrack loupit as I passed the muckle pot.'
Ay, ye didna ken the classics, never heard o' a co-sine,
But here's my aul' lum aff to ye, dear gowkit Loon o' Mine.

They're handin' oot the haloes, an' three's come to the glen—
There's Jeemack taen his Sam Browne to his mother's but an'
    ben.
Ay, they ca' me ' Blawin' Beelie,' but I never crawed sae crouse
As the day they ga' the V.C. to my *filius nullius*.
But he winna sit ' Receptions ' nor keep on his aureole,
A' he says is ' Guide the gabbin', and rax ower the Bogie Roll.'
An' the Duke an's dother shook his han' an' speirt aboot his kin.
' Old family, yes : here sin' the flood,' I smairtly chippit in.
(Fiech ! Noah's ? Na—We'd ane wirsels, ye ken, in '29.)
I'm nae the man to stan' an' hear them lichtlie Loon o' Mine.

Wir Lairdie. That's his mither in her doo's-neck silk gaun by,
The puddock, so she tells me, 's haudin' up the H.L.I.
An' he's stan'in ower his middle in the Flanders clort an' dub,
Him that ee'st to scent his hanky an' speak o's mornin' ' tub.'
The Manse loon's dellin' divots on the weary road to Lille,
An' he canna flype his stockin's, 'cause they hinna tae nor heel.
Sennelager's gotten Davie—a' mou' fae lug to lug—
An' the Kaiser's kyaak, he's writin', 'll neither ryve nor rug.
' But mind ye ' (so he post-cairds), ' I'm already ower the Rhine.'
Ay, there's nae a wanworth o' them, though they werena Loons
    o' Mine.

. . . You—Robbie. Memory pictures : Front bench. A curly
    pow,
A chappit hannie grippin' ticht a Homer men't wi' tow—
The lave a' scrammelin' near him, like bummies roon a byke,
' Fat's this ? ' ' Fat's that ? ' He'd tell them a'—ay speir they
    fat they like.

My hill-foot lad ! A' sowl an' brain fae's bonnet to his beets,
A ' Fullarton ' *in posse*, nae the first fun' fowin' peats.
An' I see a blythe young Bajan gang whistlin' doon the brae,
An' I hear a wistful Paladin his patriot *credo* say.
An' noo, an' noo I'm waitin' till a puir thing hirples hame—
Ay, 't's the Valley o' the Shadow, nae the mountain heichts o'
    Fame.
An' where's the nimble nostrum, the dogma fair and fine,
To still the ruggin' heart I hae for you, oh, Loon o' Mine.

My Loons, my Loons ! Yon winnock gets the settin' sun the
    same,
Here's sklates and skailies, ilka dask a' futtled wi' a name.
An' as I sit a vision comes : Ye're troopin' in aince mair,
Ye're back fae Aisne an' Marne an' Meuse, Ypres an' Festubert ;
Ye're back on weary bleedin' feet—you, you that danced an'
    ran—
For every lauchin' loon I kent I see a hell-scarred man.
Not mine but yours to question now ! You lift unhappy eyes—
  Ah, Maister, tell's fat a' this means.' And I, ye thocht sae wise,
Maun answer wi' the bairn words ye said to me langsyne :
' I dinna ken, I dinna ken.' Fa does, oh, Loons o' Mine ?

VIOLET JACOB   1 8 6 3 – 1 9 4 6

Jock to the First Army

O Rab an' Dave an' rantin' Jim,
    The geans were turnin' reid
When Scotland saw yer line grow dim,
    Wi' the pipers at its heid ;
Noo, i' yon warld we dinna ken,
    Like strangers ye maun gang—
' *We've sic a wale o' Angus men*
    That we canna weary lang.'

And little Wat—my brither Wat,
   Man, are ye aye the same ?
Or is yon sma' white hoose forgot
   Doon by the strath at hame ?
An' div ye mind foo aft we trod
   The Isla's banks before ?—
  ' *My place is wi' the Hosts o' God*
    But I mind me o' Strathmore.'

It's deith comes skirlin' through the sky,
   Below there's nocht but pain,
We canna see whaur deid men lie
   For the drivin' o' the rain ;
Ye a' hae passed frae fear an' doot,
   Ye're far frae airthly ill—
  ' *We're near, we're here, my wee recruit,*
    And we fecht for Scotland still.'

The Field by the Lirk o' the Hill

   Daytime and nicht,
   Sun, wind an' rain,
   The lang cauld licht
   O' the spring months again ;
   The braird's a' weed
   And the fairm's a' still—
   Wha'll sow the seed
   I' the field by the lirk o' the hill ?

   Prood maun ye lie,
   Prood did ye gang,
   Auld, auld am I
   And oh ! life's lang !

Ghaists i' the air,
Whaups' voices shrill,
And you nae mair
I' the field by the lirk o' the hill—
Ay, bairn, nae mair, nae mair,
I' the field by the lirk o' the hill.

Tam i' the Kirk

O Jean, my Jean, when the bell ca's the congregation
O'er valley and hill wi' the ding frae its iron mou',
When a'body's thochts is set on their ain salvation,
                    Mine's set on you.

There's a reid rose lies on the Buik o' the Word afore ye
That was growin' braw on its bush at the keek o' day,
But the lad that pu'd yon flower i' the mornin's glory
                    He canna pray.

He canna pray, but there's nane i' the kirk will heed him
Whaur he sits sae still his lane at the side o' the wa',
For nane but the reid rose kens what my lassie gied him—
                    It and us twa.

He canna sing for the sang that his ain he'rt raises,
He canna see for the mist that's afore his een,
And a voice droons the hale o' the psalms and the paraphrases
                    Crying 'Jean! Jean! Jean!'

Baltic Street

My dainty lass, lay you the blame
    Upon the richtfu' heid;

'Twas daft ill-luck that bigg'd yer hame
  The wrang side o' the Tweed.
Ye hae yer tocher a' complete,
  Ye're bonnie as the rose,
But I was born in Baltic Street,
  In Baltic Street, Montrose !

Lang syne on mony a waefu' nicht,
  Hie owre the sea's distress,
I've seen the great airms o' the licht
  Swing oot frae Scurdyness ;
An' prood, in sunny simmer blinks,
  When land-winds rase an' fell,
I'd flee my draigon on the links
  Wi' callants like mysel'.

Oh, Baltic Street is cauld an' bare
  An' mebbe no sae grand,
But ye'll feel the smell i' the caller air
  O' kippers on the land.
'Twixt kirk an' street the deid fowk bide,
  Their feet towards the sea,
Ill neebours for a new-made bride,
  Gin ye come hame wi' me.

The steeple shades the kirkyaird grass,
  The seamen's hidden banes,
A dour-like kirk to an English lass
  Wha kens but English lanes ;
And when the haar, the winter through,
  Creeps blind on close and wa',
My hame micht get a curse frae you,
  Mysel' get mebbe twa.

I'll up an' aff the morn's morn
     To seek some reid-haired queyn,
Bauld-he'rted, strang-nieved, bred an' born
     In this auld toon o' mine.
And oh ! for mair I winna greet,
     Gin we hae meal an' brose
And a but an' ben in Baltic Street,
     In Baltic Street, Montrose !

Pride

Did iver ye see the like o' that ?
The warld's fair fashioned to winder at !
Heuch—dinna tell me !   Yon's Fishie Pete
That cried the haddies in Ferry Street
Set up wi' his coats an' his grand cigars
In ane o' thae stinkin' motor cars !

I mind the time (an' it's no far past)
When he wasna for fleein' alang sae fast,
An' doon i' the causey his cairt wad stand
As he roared oot ' Haddies ! ' below his hand ;
Ye'd up wi' yer windy an' doon he'd loup
Frae the shaft o' the cairt by the sheltie's doup.

Aye, muckle cheenges an' little sense,
A bawbee's wit an' a poond's pretence !
For there's him noo wi' his neb to the sky
I' yon deil's machinery swiggit by,
An' me, that whiles gied him a piece to eat,
Tramps aye to the kirk on my ain twa feet.

An neebours, mind ye, the warld's agley
Or we couldna see what we've seen the day ;

Guid fortune's blate whaur she's weel desairv't,
The sinner fu' an' the godly stairv't,
An' fowk like me an' my auld guidman
Jist wearied daein' the best we can !

I've kept my lips an' my tongue frae guile
An' kept mysel' to mysel' the while ;
Agin a' wastrels I've aye been set
And I'm no for seekin' to thole them yet ;
A grand example I've been through life,
A righteous liver, a thrifty wife.

But oh ! the he'rt o' a body bleeds
For favours sclarried on sinfu' heids.
Wait you a whilie !   Ye needna think
They'll no gang frae him wi' cairds an' drink !
They'll bring nae blessin', they winna bide,
For the warst sin, neebours, is pride, aye, pride !

NEIL MUNRO   1864-1930

from *Bannocks o Barley*

Just gie us a griddle, a guid Culross griddle,
    A nievefu o salt and the side o a burn,
We'll feed like our fathers that never kent famine,
    Wi meal and a griddle nae Scottie 'll mourn !
It's no the day's provand that maks ye the sodger,
    It's milk o your mither that fills ye wi steel ;
And sae we'll be couthy, and sae we'll be canty,
    As lang's we hae bannocks o barley meal.

Lament for Macleod of Raasay

Allan Ian Og Macleod of Raasay,
   Treasure of mine, lies yonder dead in Loos,
His body unadorned by Highland raiment,
   Trammelled, for glorious hours, in Saxon trews.
Never man before of all his kindred
   Went so apparelled to the burial knowe,
But with the pleated tartan for his shrouding,
   The bonnet on his brow.

My grief ! that Allan should depart so sadly,
   When no wild mountain pipe his bosom wrung,
With no one of his race beside his shoulder
   Who knew his history and spoke his tongue.
Ah, lonely death and drear for darling Allan !
   Before his ghost had taken wings and gone,
Loud would he cry in Gaelic to his gallants,
 ' Children of storm, press on ! '

Beside him, when he fell there in his beauty,
   Macleods of all the islands should have died ;
Brave hearts his English !—but they could not fathom
   To what old deeps the voice of Allan cried ;
When in that strange French country-side war-battered,
   Far from the creeks of home and hills of heath,
A boy, he kept the old tryst of his people
   With the dark girl Death.

Oh Allan Ian Og ! Oh Allan *aluinn* !
   Sore is my heart remembering the past,
And you of Raasay's ancient gentle children
   The farthest-wandered, kindliest and last !
It should have been the brave dead of the islands
   That heard ring o'er their tombs your battle cry,

To shake them from their sleep again, and quicken
  Peaks of Torridon and Skye.

Gone in the mist the brave Macleods of Raasay,
  Far furth from fortune, sundered from their lands,
And now the last grey stone of Castle Raasay,
  Lies desolate and levelled with the sands.
But pluck the old isle from its roots deep-planted
  Where tides cry coronach round the Hebrides,
And it will bleed of the Macleods lamented,
  Their loves and memories !

CHARLES MURRAY   1864-1941

The Hint o' Hairst

O for a day at the Hint o' Hairst,
  With the craps weel in an' stackit,
When the farmer steps thro' the corn-yard,
  An' counts a' the rucks he's thackit :

When the smith stirs up his fire again,
  To sharpen the ploughman's coulter ;
When the miller sets a new picked stane,
  An' dreams o' a muckle moulter :

When cottars' kail get a touch o' frost,
  That mak's them but taste the better ;
An' thro' the neeps strides the leggined laird,
  Wi' 's gun an' a draggled setter :

When the forester wi' axe an' keel
  Is markin' the wind-blawn timmer,
An' there's truffs aneuch at the barn gale
  To reist a' the fires till simmer.

Syne O for a nicht, ae lang forenicht,
  Owre the dambrod spent or cairtin',
Or keepin' tryst wi' a neebour's lass—
  An' a mou' held up at pairtin'.

Gin I was God

Gin I was God, sittin' up there abeen,
Weariet nae doot noo a' my darg was deen,
Deaved wi' the harps an' hymns oonendin' ringin',
Tired o' the flockin' angels hairse wi' singin',
To some clood-edge I'd daunder furth an', feth,
Look ower an' watch hoo things were gyaun aneth.
Syne, gin I saw hoo men I'd made mysel'
Had startit in to pooshan, sheet an' fell,
To reive an' rape, an' fairly mak' a hell
O' my braw birlin' Earth,—a hale week's wark—
I'd cast my coat again, rowe up my sark,
An', or they'd time to lench a second ark,
Tak' back my word an' sen' anither spate,
Droon oot the hale hypothec, dicht the sklate,
Own my mistak', an', aince I'd cleared the brod,
Start a'thing owre again, gin I was God.

DR JOHN FERGUS

Blin'

Blin' ! an I'll hae to fin' for the face o my wife an wean.
Blin' an I'll never see the sun on the braes again ;
an the ling 'll licht to a lowe, an the trees i the spring turn green,
an the lift 'll be blue owreheid, but no for my sichtless een.

An the stooks 'll stand like gowd i the licht o the autumn sun,
an the river be lippin' fu' wi saumon an troot on the run,
an the loch 'll be white wi faem when the win' frae the Nor'lan'
    blaws,
an the hills, when the hairst is owre, 'll be poothert wi early
    snaws ;
an aa will be as it was i the lichtsome days sinsyne,
the cosy white-washed cot, the sheep, an the couthy kine,
an the dowg wi his wistfu face, aye ready to tak the hill,
an the bairns comin up the glen, het-fuit frae the wee bit schuil ;
an the guidwife, braw as a lass, eident aa roun' the place,
wi the glint o gowd in her hair, an the kindly luik in her face ;
an me ! sic a sichtless loon, wi naethin' to dae but fin',
an fin' whaurever I gang, for I'm blin' frae the war, I'm blin'.

WALTER WINGATE   1865-1918

Conscience

'Twas a bonnie day—and a day o' dule
The day I plunkit the Sawbath schule !

I wan'ert awa' ayont the knowes,
Where the bluebell blaws and the arnut grows ;
The bee on the thistle, the bird on the tree—
A'thing I saw was blithe—but me.

Weary and wae at last I sank
'Mang the gowan beds on the railway bank—
But never a train cam' whistlin' by—
And oh ! but a lanely bairn was I.

And I joukit hame frae tree to tree—
For I kent that I was whaur I sudna be,

When I saw the bad men—the men that play
At cartes and quoits on the Sawbath Day.

But—cunnin' wee cowart—I waitit till
It was time to skail frae the Sawbath schule ;
Naebody kent—but I kent mysel'—
And I gaed to my bed in the fear o' hell.

Conscience, thou Justice cauld and stern,
Aften thy sairest word I earn :
But this is a thing I'll ne'er forgie—
It wisna fair wi' a bairn like me.

After

We foucht the Prussian Guairds :
    It took us a' oor wecht.
I wish them sic anither day,
The folk that sit at hame and say
    The Germans canna fecht.

It took us a' we kent :
    We bate them in the en' ;
And comin' hame we saw them lie,
Wi' blin' een starin' at the sky,
    And a' bonnie men !

Fu' fain wad mony a lass
    A man like yon hae won :
And mony a mither's hert's been prood
When to his gallant heicht he stood,
    Her muckle sojer son.

They were as braw's oorsell's ;
  But a'e side maun be bate ;
And something seemed my hert to draw,
And peety wadna bide awa'
  To see them lie say quate.

RUDYARD KIPLING   1865-1936

from *McAndrew's Hymn* (1893)

Lord, Thou hast made this world below the shadow of a dream,
An', taught by time, I tak' it so—exceptin' always Steam.
From coupler-flange to spindle-guide I see Thy Hand, O God—
Predestination in the stride o yon connectin-rod.
John Calvin might ha' forged the same—enorrmous, certain,
    slow—
Ay, wrought it in the furnace-flame—*my* ' Institutio.'
I cannot get my sleep to-night ; old bones are hard to please ;
I'll stand the middle watch up here—alone wi God and these
My engines, after ninety days o race and rack and strain
Through all the seas of all Thy world, slam-bangin home again.
Slam-bang too much—they knock a wee—the crosshead-gibs
    are loose,
But thirty thousand mile o sea has gied them fair excuse. . . .
Fine, clear and dark—a full-draught breeze, wi Ushant out o
    sight,
And Ferguson relievin Hay.   Old girl, ye'll walk to-night !
His wife's at Plymouth. . . .   Seventy- One- Two- Three since
    he began—
Three turns for Mistress Ferguson . . . and who's to blame the
    man ?
There's none at any port for me, by drivin fast or slow,
Since Elsie Campbell went to Thee, Lord, thirty years ago

(The year the *Sarah Sands* was burned.   Oh, roads we used to
 tread,

Fra Maryhill to Pollokshaws—fra Govan to Parkhead !)

Not but they're ceevil on the Board.   Ye'll hear Sir Kenneth
 say :

' Good morrn, McAndrew !   Back again ?   And how's your
 bilge to-day ? '

Miscallin technicalities but handin me my chair

To drink Madeira wi three Earls—the auld Fleet Engineer

That started as a boiler-whelp—when steam and he were low.

I mind the time we used to serve a broken pipe wi tow !

Ten pound was all the pressure then—Eh ! Eh !—a man wad
 drive ;

And here, our workin gauges give one hunder sixty-five !

We're creepin on wi each new rig—less weight and larger
 power ;

There 'll be a loco-boiler next and thirty mile an hour !

Thirty and more.   What I ha' seen since ocean-steam began

Leaves me na doot for the machine : but what about the man ?

The man that counts, wi all his runs, one million mile o sea :

Four times the span from earth to moon. . . . How far, O Lord,
 from Thee

That wast beside him night and day ?   Ye mind my first
 typhoon ?

It scoughed the skipper on his way to jock wi the saloon.

Three feet were on the stokehold-floor—just slappin to and fro—

And cast me on a furnace-door.   I have the marks to show.

Marks !   I ha' marks o more than burns—deep in my soul and
 black,

And times like this, when things go smooth, my wickedness
 comes back.

The sins o four and forty years, all up and down the seas,

Clack and repeat like valves half-fed. . . .   Forgie's our tres-
 passes !

Nights when I'd come on deck to mark, wi envy in my gaze,
The couples kittlin in the dark between the funnel-stays ;
Years when I raked the Ports wi pride to fill my cup o wrong—
Judge not, O Lord, my steps aside at Gay Street in Hong-Kong !
Blot out the wastrel hours of mine in sin when I abode—
Jane Harrigan's and Number Nine, The Reddick and Grant
　　Road !
And waur than all—my crownin sin—rank blasphemy and wild.
I was not four and twenty then—Ye wadna judge a child ?
I'd seen the Tropics first that run—new fruit, new smells, new
　　air—
How could I tell—blind-fou wi sun—the Deil was lurkin there ?
By day like playhouse-scenes the shore slid past our sleepy eyes ;
By night those soft, lasceevious stars leered from those velvet
　　skies ;
In port (we used no cargo-steam) I'd daunder down the streets—
An ijjit grinnin in a dream—for shells and parrakeets,
And walkin-sticks o carved bamboo and blowfish stuffed and
　　dried—
Fillin my bunk wi rubbishry the Chief put overside.
Till, off Sambawa Head, Ye mind, I heard a land-breeze ca',
Milk-warm wi breath o spice and bloom : ' McAndrew, come
　　awa ! '
Firm, clear and low—no haste, no hate—the ghostly whisper went,
Just statin eevidential facts beyon' all argument :
' Your mither's God's a graspin deil, the shadow o yoursel,
Got out o books by meenisters clean daft on Heaven and Hell.
They mak him in the Broomielaw, o Glasgie cold and dirt,
A jealous, pridefu fetich, lad, that's only strong to hurt.
Ye'll not go back to Him again and kiss His red-hot rod,
But come wi Us ' (Now, who were *They* ?) ' and know the
　　Leevin God,
That does not kipper souls for sport or break a life in jest,
But swells the ripenin cocoanuts and ripes the woman's breast.'

131

And there it stopped—cut off—no more—that quiet, certain
  voice—
For me, six months o twenty-four, to leave or take at choice.
'Twas on me like a thunderclap—it racked me through and
  through—
Temptation past the show o speech, unnameable and new—
The Sin against the Holy Ghost ? . . . And under all, our
  screw.

That storm blew by but left behind her anchor-shiftin swell.
Thou knowest all my heart and mind, Thou knowest, Lord, I
  fell—
Third on the *Mary Gloster* then, and first that night in Hell !
Yet was Thy Hand beneath my head, about my feet Thy Care—
Fra Deli clear to Torres Strait, the trial o despair,
But when we touched the Barrier Reef Thy answer to my
  prayer ! . . .
We dared na run that sea by night but lay and held our fire,
And I was drowsin on the hatch—sick—sick wi doubt and tire :
' *Better the sight of eyes that see than wanderin o desire !* '
Ye mind that word ? Clear as our gongs—again, and once
  again,
When rippin down through coral-trash ran out our moorin-
  chain :
And, by Thy Grace, I had the Light to see my duty plain.
Light on the engine-room—no more—bright as our carbons
  burn.
I've lost it since a thousand times, but never past return !

Memory (for S.G.)

See the leaves are falling faster,
   Wet with rain from autumn trees,
All in brown and gold disaster—
   Is your memory dead with these?

No, never dead, for every season
   (We were lovers all a year)
Has for me a mystic reason,
   Breathes her subtle atmosphere.

So in change of form and features
   Seen in strangers leagues apart,
In the gambols of earth's creatures,
   Strikes her memory to my heart.

When the world to ruin crashes,
   Lying where all manhood must,
Dust myself, from other ashes
   I shall know her delicate dust.

Serenade (from the Sanskrit)

Lady of the lovely thighs
   Curving like banana fruit,
Hither glance with those dear eyes,
   Idly then will Kama shoot
All his arrows—better he
   Lay aside his bow, while you
Playful raise your brow for me—
   Speak with sweetness throbbing through

133

Utterance just above the mute,
    Such as to the ear may come
Like the music of the lute
    Mingling with the muffled drum.

Father JOHN GRAY   1866–1934

Ad Matrem

Lord, if thou art not present, where shall I
Seek thee the absent ?   If thou art everywhere,
How is it that I do not see thee nigh ?

Thou dwellest in a light remote and fair.
How can I reach that light, Lord ?   I beseech
Thee, teach my seeking, and thyself declare

Thyself the sought to me.   Unless thou teach
Me, Lord, I cannot seek ; nor can I find
Thee, if thou wilt not come within my reach.

Lord, let me seek, with sturdy heart and mind,
In passion of desire and longingly.
Let me desire thee, seeking thee ; and find. . . .

Loving thee, find thee ; love thee, finding thee.

A Prelate

The rest of us enjoy the earth
and drink the light and taste the feast ;
while I lie quietly deceased ;
ordained to be so from my birth.

Ettrickdale

Overburdened, out you clear ;
be dried and toasted in the air,
along the unfrequented road ;
and in the evening walk with God.

The waters of the winding dale,
whatever may, will never fail ;
from hidden sources, springs afar,
these million ages purr and roar.

No lips of men have shaped the word
to name what all have often heard ;
so willingly believe the noise
is like the uncreated voice.

The fiftieth time the lisping rush
has died upon a silver hush ;
and, faithful to the downward hue,
another element is blue.

White pathway in the darkening hills,
soft salve for nearly all your ills,
on bruise and scar a healing drip,
the wanderers' companionship.

A planet, rose on tender green,
tugs at its radius unseen,
and draws its complicated arc ;
until it blaze against the dark.

On earth no sight or sound at all ;
unless an owl's alternate call ;
or Tushielaw, if there you sup,
a furlong off is lighted up.

The Wild Lass

Hameward ye're travellin' in the saft hill rain,
The day lang by, that ye wearied o' the glen,
Nae ring upon your hand, nae kiss upon your mou',
        Quaiet noo !

There's fiddlers and dancin' and steps gaun by the doors,
But nane o' them sall fret ye in the lang nicht hours,
Oh, Peace come on the wind, Peace fa' with the dew,
        Quaiet noo !

Cauld was the lift abune ye, the road baith rauch and steep,
Nae farrer sall ye wander nor greet yersel' to sleep,
My ain wild Lass, my bonnie, hurtit, doo,
        Quaiet, quaiet noo !

Alas ! Poor Queen

She was skilled in music and the dance
And the old arts of love
At the court of the poisoned rose
And the perfumed glove,
And gave her beautiful hand
To the pale Dauphin
A triple crown to win—
And she loved little dogs
       And parrots
         And red-legged partridges
And the golden fishes of the Duc de Guise
And a pigeon with a blue ruff
She had from Monsieur d'Elbœuf.

Master John Knox was no friend to her ;
She spoke him soft and kind,
Her honeyed words were Satan's lure
The unwary soul to bind
' Good sir, doth a lissome shape
And a comely face
Offend your God His Grace
Whose Wisdom maketh these
Golden fishes of the Duc de Guise ? '

She rode through Liddesdale with a song ;
' Ye streams sae wondrous strang,
Oh, mak' me a wrack as I come back
But spare me as I gang,'
While a hill-bird cried and cried
Like a spirit lost
By the grey storm-wind tost.

Consider the way she had to go.
Think of the hungry snare,
The net she herself had woven,
Aware or unaware,
Of the dancing feet grown still,
The blinded eyes—
Queens should be cold and wise,
And she loved little things,
        Parrots
    And red-legged partridges
And the golden fishes of the Duc de Guise
And the pigeon with the blue ruff
She had from Monsieur d'Elbœuf.

from *Autumn in Denmark* (1892)

O leaf that blowest westward, where the sighing
   Of fir-trees answers to the wind's loud boasts,
Bear thou my greeting onward where the flying
   White-crested billows beat on far-off coasts.

And when thou there hast found a willing hearer,
   Use but the words that many a poet has sung,
And say, ' Three things by distance still grow dearer—
   Our loves, our native land, our mother-tongue.'

GEORGE DOUGLAS BROWN   1869–1902

Covenanter's Deathbed

I canna dee, tho' I fain wud dee,
   For I'm tired o' the world wide,
An' nae grave will ever be rest to me
   But a grave on the green hill-side.

Bury me deep on the Bennan Hill,
   Whaur I may face the sea,
An' sleep a lang an' blessèd sleep
   Till Christ shall wauken me.

Oh ! to be quat o' life's stoury faucht
   An' this dull hot bed o' pain,
Tae lie a' nicht in the windy waucht
   O' the clear caul' mornin' rain :—

And the whaup may skirl in the lanely sky,
  An' the sun shine miles aroon' ;
And quately the stately ships gae by,
  But I'll be sleepin' soun'.

ROBERT MURRAY   1869–1950

The Bairn

I saw the Bairn in a city car,
  And thin and pale was he ;
His wee white heid in an auld grey rag
  As he sat on his mither's knee.

And she was as wan as the Wean himsel,
  Sae shrunk wi cauld and want ;
The marks o hunger across her cheek,
  And her briests for the Bairn were scant.

Tainted and torn the auld dune duds
  That wrapt her body numb,
And they held a smell, like the reek o hell,
  The smell o a Calton slum.

The Bairn was fractious and couldna rest,
  Nor wad his sorrow cease ;
And nocht his puir wee mither micht dae
  Could win his hert to peace.

And aye he wheeng'd and aye he grat,
  While aa the folk looked on ;
And twa bonnie bairns, weel fed and cled,
  Thocht ' Whit kind o laddie's yon ? '

Troubled and shy, like a frichtit bird,
    She cuddled him close and ran ;
And oot on the black, rain-blattered street,
    Bewildert I saw her stand.

O God forgie a coward like me,
    That moved nor fuit, nor hand ;
Nor kindly word, nor a broon bawbee,
    For her or the puir wee man.

But my hert went wi them, step by step,
    Their dark Golgotha way ;
To the loathsome hole the Bairn maun thole
    For the sins of a soulless day.

M. C. SMITH   1869-

The Boy in the Train

Whit wey does the engine say *Toot-toot* ?
    Is it feart to gang in the tunnel ?
Whit wey is the furnace no pit oot
    When the rain gangs doon the funnel ?
What'll I hae for my tea the nicht ?
    A herrin', or maybe a haddie ?
Has Gran'ma gotten electric licht ?
    Is the next stop Kirkcaddy ?

There's a hoodie-craw on yon turnip-raw !
    An' sea-gulls !—sax or seeven.
I'll no fa' oot o' the windae, Maw,
    It's sneckit, as sure as I'm leevin'.

We're into the tunnel ! we're a' in the dark !
    But dinna be frichtit, Daddy,
We'll sune be comin' to Beveridge Park,
    And the next stop's Kirkcaddy !

Is yon the mune I see in the sky ?
    It's awfu' wee an' curly.
See ! there's a coo and a cauf ootbye,
    An' a lassie pu'in a hurly !
He's chackit the tickets and gien them back,
    Sae gie me my ain yin, Daddy.
Lift doon the bag frae the luggage rack,
    For the next stop's Kirkcaddy !

There's a gey wheen boats at the harbour mou',
    And eh ! dae ye see the cruisers ?
The cinnamon drop I was sookin' the noo
    Has tummelt an' stuck tae ma troosers. . . .
I'll sune be ringin' ma Gran'ma's bell,
    She'll cry, ' Come ben, my laddie,'
For I ken mysel' by the queer-like smell
    That the next stop's Kirkcaddy !

G. K. MENZIES   1869 –

Poaching in Excelsis

(' Two men were fined £120 apiece for poaching a white
rhinoceros.'—South African Press)

I've poached a pickle paitricks when the leaves were turnin' sere,
I've poached a twa-three hares an' grouse, an' mebbe whiles a
    deer,
But ou, it seems an unco thing, an' jist a wee mysterious,
Hoo any mortal could contrive tae poach a rhinocerious.

I've crackit wi' the keeper, pockets packed wi' pheasants' eggs,
An' a ten-pun' saumon hangin' doun in baith my trouser legs,
But eh, I doot effects wud be a wee thing deleterious
Gin ye shuld stow intil yer breeks a brace o' rhinocerious.

I mind hoo me an' Wullie shot a Royal in Braemar,
An' brocht him doun tae Athol by the licht o' mune an' star.
An' eh Sirs ! but the canny beast contrived tae fash an' weary
    us—
Yet staigs maun be but bairn's play beside a rhinocerious.

I thocht I kent o' poachin' jist as muckle's ither men,
But there is still a twa-three things I doot I dinna ken ;
An' noo I cannot rest, my brain is growin' that deleerious
Tae win awa' tae Africa an' poach a rhinocerious.

WILL H. OGILVIE   1869–

The Blades of Harden

Ho ! for the blades of Harden !
    Ho ! for the driven kye !
The broken gate and the lances' hate,
    And a banner red on the sky !
The rough road runs by the Carter ;
    The white foam creams on the rein ;
Ho ! for the blades of Harden !
    ' There will be moonlight again.'

The dark has heard them gather,
    The dawn has bowed them by,
To the guard on the roof comes the drum of a hoof
    And the drone of a hoof's reply.

There are more than birds on the hill tonight,
   And more than winds on the plain !
The threat of the Scotts has filled the moss,
  ' There will be moonlight again.'

Ho ! for the blades of Harden !
   Ho ! for the ring of steel !
The stolen steers of a hundred years
   Come home for a Kirkhope meal !
The ride must risk its fortune,
   The raid must count its slain,
The March must feed her ravens,
  ' There will be moonlight again ! '

Ho ! for the blades of Harden !
   Ho ! for the pikes that cross !
Ho ! for the king of lance and ling
   —A Scott on the Ettrick moss !
The rough road runs by the Carter,
   The white foam creams on the rein ;
And aye for the blades of Harden
  ' There will be moonlight again ! '

LORD ALFRED DOUGLAS 1870–1945

from *The City of the Soul*

What shall we do, my soul, to please the King ?
Seeing he hath no pleasure in the dance,
And hath condemned the honeyed utterance
Of silver flutes and mouths made round to sing.
Along the wall red roses climb and cling,
And oh ! my prince, lift up thy countenance,
For there be thoughts like roses that entrance
More than the languors of soft lute-playing.

Think how the hidden things that poets see
In amber eves or mornings crystalline,
Hide in the soul their constant quenchless light,
Till, called by some celestial alchemy,
Out of forgotten depths, they rise and shine
Like buried treasure on Midsummer night.

Lighten our Darkness
(England, 1918)

In the high places lo ! there is no light,
The ugly dawn beats up forlorn and grey.
Dear Lord, but once before I pass away
Out of this Hell into the starry night
Where still my hopes are set in Death's despite,
Let one great man be good, let one pure ray
Shine through the gloom of this my earthly day
From one tall candle set upon a height.
Judges and prelates, chancellors and kings,
All have I known and suffered and endured,
(And some are quick and some are in their graves).
I looked behind their masks and posturings
And saw their souls too rotten to be cured,
And knew them all for liars, rogues and knaves.

JOHN FERGUSON

Sonnet No. III from Thyrea

He caught a chill in Leicester, he came here ;—
    He came here with his little store of gold,
    To this grim dwelling, bare, and clean, and cold,
Where life joins hands with death, and hope with fear :

He told us how in Leicester's city drear,
  On coughing slightly, down his garments rolled
  The warm and scarlet flood ; and oft he told
How softly he would tread from year to year.

His wife came for him, and he left to-day
  Because his little store of gold was done ;
  My God ! I knew not gold and life were one
Till he shook hands with us and went away :
  His limbs all fever-thinned, and hope all gone—
O Christ in Heaven, how he longed to stay !

Ad majorem Dei gloriam

They call Him the Good Shepherd and the Lamb,
  The Rose, the Prince of Peace, Emmanuel ;
  And yet, half-vaunting, of His vengeance tell
On all who traffic in deceit and sham ;
They boast much knowledge of the dread I AM,
  And babble of a Book whose pages swell
  With record of men's faults since Adam fell—
Nay, He inscribeth every muttered ' Damn.'

They have not seen the Lord who tell such things,
  They have not touched His garment in the throng,
    The foolish folk who know not what they say. . . .
No book of doom is hid beneath His wings,
  And when men stumble in blind paths of wrong
    How often doth He look the other way !

HAMISH HENDRY

Saunders MacSiccar

Ae müneless nicht in a blear October
   Auld Saunders MacSiccar gaed dodderin' hame ;
He wasna near fou, nor he wasna richt sober,
   Though I sair misdoot if he kent his name ;
When there at the cross-roads, staked and tethered,
   Glowered a black goat !   Or was it a deevil ?
' Preserve us,' quo Saunders, ' since noo we've forgethered,
   A sinfu' auld man had better be ceevil ! '
        ' You're richt,' quo the Goat.

Guid guide us ! thocht Saunders, sure this is no' canny,
   It's as true as I'm sober I heard the baste speak ;
A clever wee deil could change hides wi' a nanny,
   And still mak' its hame in the Brunstane Reek ;
But natheless it's tied wi' a gey stout tether,
   Sae I'll speak it fair, for this cowes the cuddy ;—
' Braw nicht,' quo Saunders, ' and no' bad weather
   For deils, or goats, or a daunderin' buddy ! '
        ' Braw nicht,' quo the Goat.

Weel, that's fair and friendly, thocht Saunders MacSiccar,
   And it's plain as his beardie I've naething to fear ;—
Though I'm no' gaun to argy, and it's ower dark to bicker,
   There's twa-three bit questions I'd like fine to speer !
I'm a Scotsman mysel, I was born oot at Fintry,
   And this deil has the Scots twang, whaever has bred 'um :—
' Do you no' think,' quo Saunders, ' oor grand auld kintry
   Has drapped a gey hantle o' its dour smeddum ? '
        ' You're richt,' quo the Goat.

146

' I kent I was richt, man ; and this is the way o't—
  The flyte and the fecht are noo clean oot o' fashion ;
Ye daurna noo thraw for the yea or the nay o't,
  But pouch your opinions row'd up like a rashion ;
It's no' your ain tüne, but what ither folk whistle
  That noo ye maun dance till, or else ye'll repent it !
Am I no' richt in saying the prood Scottish thistle
  Is no' just as jaggie as what we hae kent it ? '
          ' You're richt,' quo the Goat.

' The kirks noo,' quo Saunders, ' hae tint a' their flyting,
  Since I was a laddie and crooned ower the Carritch ;
Oh ! the brisk collyshangie !   Oh, the barking and biting,—
  Lord ! yon was the spurtle steered saut in oor parritch !
But noo things are wersh,—ilka poopit's bow-wowless,
  While the Carritch, Guid help us, grows shorter and shorter ;
It's a dowie auld Scotland, forjeskit and thowless,
  Noo the kirks are mixed throwther and brayed in a morter ! '
          ' You're richt,' quo the Goat.

' And whare is the freedom that made Scotland prooder
  Than ony prood kintry frae here to the Indies,—
The freedom oor faithers won, shooder to shooder,
  When Scotland was Scotland, and shindies were shindies ?
Sma' drams for the drouthy, nae honest free drinking ;
  Laws here and rules there, wi' teetotalers to hinder ;
But between oor twa sels, am I no' richt in thinking
  We're no' jist the folk to gang dry as a cinder ? '
          ' You're richt,' quo the Goat.

' Fine I kent I was richt ; I've a wonderfu' noddle ;
  I can see through a whinstane as far as anither ;
And if ye're the deil, Gosh ! I carena a boddle
  For we've 'greed on a' hands, as brither wi' brither.

But I maun get hame, sae I bid ye guid nicht noo ;
   This road is gey dark, yet I ken a' the links o't ;
It's just like the world ; and am I no richt noo,—
    The deil and a Scotsman, they ken a' the kinks o't ! '
        ' You're richt,' quo the Goat.

LEWIS SPENCE   1874 -

The Prows o' Reekie

O wad this braw hie-heapit toun
Sail aff like an enchanted ship,
Drift owre the warld's seas up and doun
And kiss wi' Venice lip to lip,
Or anchor into Naples Bay
A misty island far astray,
Or set her rock to Athens' wa',
Pillar to pillar, stane to stane,
The cruikit spell o' her backbane,
Yon shadow-mile o' spire and vane,
Wad ding them a' !   Wad ding them a' !
Cadiz wad tine the admiralty
O' yonder emerod fair sea,
Gibraltar frown fro frown exchange
Wi' Nigel's Crags at elbuck-range,
The rose-red banks o' Lisbon make
Mair room in Tagus for her sake.

A hoose is but a puppet-box
To keep life's images frae knocks,
But mannikins scrieve oot their sauls
Upon its craw-steps and its walls :
Whaur hae they writ them mair sublime
Than on yon gable-ends o' time ?

The Queen's Bath-House, Holyrood

Time that has dinged doun castels and hie toures,
And cast great crouns like tinsel in the fire,
That halds his hand for palace nor for byre,
Stands sweir at this, the oe of Venus' boures.
Not Time himself can dwall withouten floures,
Though aiks maun fa' the rose sall bide entire ;
So sall this diamant of a queen's desire
Outflourish all the stanes that Time devours.
Mony a strength his turret-heid sall tine
Ere this sall fa' whare a queen lay in wine,
Whose lamp was her ain lily flesh and star.
The walls of luve the mair triumphant are
Gif luve were waesome habiting that place ;
Luve has maist years that has a murning face.

Portrait of Mary Stuart, Holyrood

Wauken be nicht, and bydand on some boon,
　　Glamour of saul, or spirituall grace,
　　I haf seen sancts and angells in the face,
And like a fere of seraphy the moon ;
But in nae mirk nor sun-apparelled noon
　　Nor pleasance of the planets in their place
　　Of luve devine haf seen sae pure a trace
As in yon shadow of the Scottis croun.

Die not, O rose, dispitefull of hir mouth,
Not be ye lillies waeful at hir snaw ;
This dim devyce is but hir painted sake,
The mirour of ane star of vivand youth,
That not hir velvets nor hir balas braw
Can oueradorn, or luve mair luvely make.

The Pavone

(In the quhilk the makar, in the auld Scottis, compares Juno's
bird with Houp)

Now in the none the prowde pavone, his ryall rone,
  Apollo of the fowlis with plumis clere,
With princelie pretts his fedderis frets, thir amulets
  Quhilk maydens luve but luvaris hald in fear.
    Like Tytan owre the gowand swaird he gangs,
    Ane gramest galleoun tynsellit of sprangs.
Als the sones ee he may nocht be
  Seen bot with peryll of unvisored sicht.
Emerant is he als is the sea,
  Ane Bezant bird, birnand the air with licht.
Swa haf I seen in dell or dene some houp amene
For-dele my daie and blind my seelie sicht,
Lyke the pavone at hicht of none, with set of sone
  Vanish awaie als all of borrowit licht.
    Sic angell is for man bot maltalent,
    Fata Morgana of the feynds intent.
Nor yow I rede list to that leid ;
  Bot seik for that quhilk is of farrer gloir,
That lowe that scheid frae wonderheid
  Nocht of this yirth but of yon evirmoir.

The Carse

It is a thousand sunsets since I lay
In many-birded Gowrie, and did know
Its shadow for my soul, that passionate Tay
Out of my heart did flow.

The immortal hour the hate of time defies.
Men of my loins a million years away

Shall have the gloom of Gowrie in their eyes,
And in their blood the Tay.

JOHN BUCHAN (1st Lord Tweedsmuir)   1875–1940

Home Thoughts from Abroad (1917)

Aifter the war, says the papers, they'll no be content at hame,
    The lads that hae feucht wi' death twae 'ear i' the mud and the
        rain and the snaw ;
For aifter a sodger's life the shop will be unco tame ;
    They'll ettle at fortune and freedom in the new lands far awa'.

No me !
By God !   No me !
Aince we hae lickit oor faes
And aince I get oot o' this hell,
For the rest o' my leevin' days
I'll mak a pet o' mysel'.
I'll haste me back wi' an eident fit
And settle again in the same auld bit.
And oh ! the comfort to snowk again
The reek o' my mither's but-and-ben,
The wee box-bed and the ingle neuk
And the kail-pat hung frae the chimley-heuk !
I'll gang back to the shop like a laddie to play,
Tak doun the shutters at skreigh o' day,
And weigh oot floor wi' a carefu' pride,
And hear the clash o' the countraside.
I'll wear for ordinar' a roond hard hat,
A collar and dicky and black cravat.
If the weather's wat I'll no stir ootbye
Wi' oot an umbrella to keep me dry.

I think I'd better no tak a wife—
I've had a' the adventure I want in life.—
But at nicht, when the doors are steeked, I'll sit,
While the bleeze loups high frae the aiken ruit,
And smoke my pipe aside the crook,
And read in some douce auld-farrant book ;
Or crack wi' Davie and mix a rummer,
While the auld wife's pow nid-nods in slum'er ;
And hark to the winds gaun tearin' bye
And thank the Lord I'm sae warm and dry.

When simmer brings the lang bricht e'en,
I'll daunder doun to the bowling-green,
Or delve my yaird and my roses tend
For the big floo'er-show in the next back-end.
Whiles, when the sun blinks aifter rain,
I'll tak my rod and gang up the glen ;
Me and Davie, we ken the püles
Whaur the troot grow great in the howes o' the hills ;
And, wanderin' back when the gloamin' fa's
And the midges dance in the hazel shaws,
We'll stop at the yett ayont the hicht
And drink great wauchts o' the scented nicht,
While the hoose lamps kin'le raw by raw
And a yellow star hings ower the law.
Davie will lauch like a wean at a fair
And nip my airm to make certain shüre
That we're back frae yon place o' dule and dreid,
To oor ain kind warld—
                              But Davie's deid !
Nae mair gude nor ill can betide him.
We happit him doun by Beaumont toun,
And the half o' my hert's in the mools aside him.

A Prayer

(With acknowledgments to W. H. Auden)

God, give us the grace to hate
our unemancipated state,
and to wipe from Scotland's face
her intellectual disgrace.

The eye that peers forth cannily,
how can it reach the stars on high ?
The ear that waits on market price
obeys the voice of cowardice.

The mouth that babbles out ' Ay, ay '
how shall it utter prophecy ?
Who on self-interest spends his days
forgets the noble art of praise.

Free us from fear of other folk,
our minds from weight of foreign yoke ;
teach us to take our true delight
in things that are our own by right.

The soil that nourished flesh and bones,
the chemistry of Scotland's stones,
in our bodily substance shout
what we ought to be about.

Unmistakeable the note
the Northern Wind sings in its throat ;
the Highland rivers' sudden rush
raises the authentic blush.

Our mountains that above us tower
alone can judge our ' finest hour ' ;
to clear our word-beclouded minds
we need the Bible of the Winds.

The things for which we ought to die
are plainly written on the sky ;
God, now to us the vision give
to know for what we ought to live.

RACHEL ANNAND TAYLOR   1876-

The Princess of Scotland

' Who are you that so strangely woke,
    And raised a fine hand ? '
Poverty wears a scarlet cloke
    In my land.

' Duchies of dreamland, emerald, rose
    Lie at your command ? '
Poverty like a princess goes
    In my land.

' Wherefore the mask of silken lace
    Tied with a golden band ? '
Poverty walks with wanton grace
    In my land.

' Why do you softly, richly speak
    Rhythm so sweetly scanned ? '
Poverty hath the Gaelic and Greek
    In my land.

154

' There's a far-off scent about you seems
      Born in Samarkand.'
Poverty hath luxurious dreams
          In my land.

' You have wounds that like passion-flowers you hide :
      I cannot understand.'
Poverty hath one name with Pride
          In my land.

' Oh !   Will you draw your last sad breath
      'Mid bitter bent and sand ? '
Poverty begs from none but Death
          In my land.

The Doubles

When straight and still the body lies
      Upon the cool white bed,
When from the mouth and ears and eyes
      Their proper bliss has fled ;
When hands are crossed above the heart
      To bar the door to Sin ;—
The Spiritual Counterpart
      Floats upward from her Twin.

Strange love-talk in the land of Sleep,
      Fantastic, obsolete !
Strange murder in the land of Sleep
      And snaring of swift feet !
Oh !   When the urns of Dawn are spilt,
      The Waking hardly know
What rangers in the Woods of Guilt
      Nightlong their spirits go.

Proud faces in the land of Sleep
    Long sunken in the clay !
And kisses in the land of Sleep
    Where lowes red hate by day !
And struggles to the very death
    Until the dreamer wake
With wounded soul and failing breath
    Upon a white daybreak.

The Doubt

I am pure, because of great illuminations
    Of dreamy doctrine caught from poets of old,
Because of delicate imaginations,
    Because I am proud, or subtle, or merely cold.
Natheless my soul's bright passions interchange
    As the red flames in opal drowse and speak :
In beautiful twilight paths the elusive strange
    Phantoms of personality I seek.
If better than the last embraces I
    Love the lit riddles of the eyes, the faint
Appeal of merely courteous fingers,—why,
    Though 'tis a quest of souls, and I acquaint
My heart with spiritual vanities,—
    Is there indeed no bridge twixt me and these ?

ROBERT CRAWFORD   1877–1931

Darkness Visible

I speak of ebon tracts, whose sullen gloom
    Is heavy as Fate's scowl—a murky pit
    So dark the sun might be encased in it,
A yellow, round and ineffectual bloom

That could its own circumference scarce illume.
  For I have seen, from sockets globed with awe,
  Hope wandering blindly to that fearful maw
Where tiger rocks suspended wait like doom.

  And oh ! the pathos of the feeble lamp !
  The sad impertinence of flesh and bone
Loosening the tonnage that with angry stamp
  Blots a kind brother out—with not a groan !
Trade of compassionless shudder, scornèd mud,
Romanceless danger, sober selling of blood !

A. W. MAIR

The Prayer of the Lover

A little while, O Love, and thou and I
  Dwell in the darksome chambers of the dead,
  Heeding nor hearing aught, while overhead
The careless footsteps of the world go by :
Yet, O my Love, I would not choose to lie
  Idle for ever, afar from life's grey sea,
  Where no salt wind should ever visit me,
Culling the bloom of pleasure till I die :
Mine rather be it amid the moil of men
  To war all day beneath the weary sun,
    Under the blinding dust and parching heat,
Drawing hard breath until the even : and then,
  The good fight finished and the long day done,
    To lay the wreath of victory at thy feet.

Epitaph

Here I, Jock Scott, frae Peterheid
At saxty year lie dour and deid,
A bachelor,—for wed I wadna :
And och ! I wish my father hadna !

JOSEPH LEE   1878-1949

The Bullet

Every bullet has its billet ;
    Many bullets more than one.
God !   Perhaps I killed a mother
    When I killed a mother's son.

German Prisoners

When first I saw you in the curious street,
Like some platoon of soldier ghosts in grey,
My mad impulse was all to smite and slay,
To spit upon you, tread you 'neath my feet.
But when I saw how each sad soul did greet
My gaze with no sign of defiant frown,
How from tired eyes looked spirits broken down,
How each face showed the pale flag of defeat,
And doubt, despair, and disillusionment,
And how were grievous wounds on many a head,
And on your garb red-faced was other red ;
And how you stooped as men whose strength was spent,
I knew that we had suffered each as other,
And could have grasped your hand and cried, ' My brother.'

Sair Wark's Nae Easy

Doon at Nether Dallachy there's neither watch nor knock,
but denner time and supper time, and aye yoke, yoke.
It's hingin in, aye hingin in, aa day fae sax tae sax,
the deil a meenit div ye get tae gie yoursel a rax.
In winter time it's plooin ley, or anse it's caain muck,
or neeps tae ser' the byllie's nowt, or thrashin a bit ruck.
The stem-mill at a neep'rin toon is shortsome, but it's sair—
a fraucht o barley's nae that licht tae shouther up a stair.
But files there'll be a bonny ploy, fan lassies tramp the soo,
and filies tee an anterin dram for sweelin doon the stew.
Syne roon again comes shaavin time, wi grubber, roller,
    harra—
tae haud fowk oot o langer, dod, the hairst's its only marra.
Ye're skilpin on throw steens and stour until ye've firet your
    feet,
and aye the grieve is girnin, ' Jock, hing in, ye dozy breet.'
Syne birze and scraap and birze again, fan neeps come tae the
    hyow ;
yon foreman chiel, he's sic a deil for hashin, hashin throw.
Your back may crack, it doesna mak, ye be tae caa awa—
sae fa's wyte is't ye canna wale the big anes fae the smaa ?
And neist ye're ootbye at the moss tae cast the winter's peat :
a fusome, clorty business, gin the lair be saft and weet.
Ye've syne the hey tae tak about, and gin the wither's shouery
it's nesty, scutterin kind o wark ; and fan it's dry it's stoury.
The hairst ! My certies, thon's the job tae gar ye pech and
    swyte,
and gin ye faa ahint the lave the grieve gangs fairly gyte.
It's fine, nae doubt, tae hurl about for him that caas the reaper,
but nae sae fine tae bin' and stook aside a forcey neeper.

Fae morn tae nicht there's nae devaal fae trauchlin aye and
     tyaavin,
ye've hardly time tae claw yoursel fan yoky wi a yaavin.
It's boo and lift and boo again until ye're like tae drap,
and maybe files ye'll hae tae scythe a laid and tousled crap.
A weel, at lang length clyak comes, ye've stookt the hinmaist
     rigg ;
the warst o't's by, but still and on it's aa tae fork and bigg.
There's eident days, and forenichts tee, aneth a muckle meen,
afore ye've gotten winter and anither hairst is deen.
Dod, man, it's grand tae see the rucks straucht standin and weel-
     shapeit :
ye've deen your darg, and there it is, aa thackit braw and raipit.
But hear the grieve : ' Ye glaikit gype, there's nae time tae be
     lost ;
awa and get the tatties up and happit fae the frost.'
Or lang ye're at the ploo again, sae roond the sizzens rin,
and aye by tearin out the life ye try tae haud it in.
Doon at Nether Dallachy there's neither watch nor knock,
but denner time and supper time, and aye yoke, yoke.

HAROLD MONRO   1879–1932

Week-end

The train !   The twelve o'clock for Paradise.
     Hurry, or it will try to creep away.
Out in the country everyone is wise :
     We can be wise only on Saturday.
There you are waiting, little friendly house :
     Those are your chimney stacks, with you between,
Surrounded by old trees and strolling cows,
     Staring through all your windows at the green.

Your homely floor is creaking for our tread :
   The smiling teapot with contented spout
Thinks of the boiling water, and the bread
   Longs for the butter.   All their hands are out
To greet us, and the gentle blankets seem
Purring and crooning :—' Lie in us, and dream.'

JOHN MACDOUGALL HAY 1881-1919

Celtic Melancholy

It is not in the sorrow of the deep,
For sunset's magic turns to pearls her tears ;
Nor in old forests stiff with frost that sleep
Bowed with the legend of her ghostly years ;
Nor in the sombre grandeur of the hills,
Whose snows have cold communion with the skies ;
Not in the mourning of the moor with rain,
         Or solemn mist that spills
Its weariness of silence : or the cries
Of great winds wandering through the glens in pain.

Thou hadst no knowledge of the market-place
And cities white and glad with statuary ;
The hiving ports of a far-travelled race,
Idols in gold and jewelled sacristy ;
Men hot with story from the ends o' earth,
Plaudits in theatres ; an eager fleet
Taking the tide, bound for the goodly wars.
         Such stuff of song and mirth
Was never thine amidst the sleet
And noise of black whales spouting to the stars.

Thine is the heritage of wandering men
Whose deeds are fragments passing like the stream ;
They build the tower ; they forge the shield ; and then
Their labours vanish like a fragrant dream.
Wistful and dim with sad magnificence
Ye are the men destined to doom and death.
A purpose ye could never realise ;
    And stable recompense
Of victory was fleeting as a breath.
Only the face of death is kind and wise.

Ye are the men of perished hopes, of things
Most dear that now are ever lost—home, name,
And country—song of triumph never brings
Like requiem the meaning that's in fame.
Slogan ne'er stirred the heart to dare and die
As coronach loud wailing in the glen.
Ah ! aye for you the best's beneath the sod ;
    Over the sea to Skye ;
All's over ; falls the night on broken men,
Culloden's sword with blood writes *Ichabod.*

WILLIAM MOIR CALDER   1881-

Moray Sang

The win' blaws oot o' Orkney
A winter month or twa,
An' rievin' ower the Moray Firth
It lifts the gangrel snaw,
An' sets it doon on Badenoch
A hunder mile awa.

The April win' fae Athol
Blaws up wi' breath o' balm,
An' melts the snaw's caul hairt tae ruth
For yeanin' ewe an' lam' ;
An' Spey maun post it doon the strath
The hunder mile it cam'.

An Epitaph

(Hic sita est Amymone Marci optima et pulcherrima lanifica pia pudica frugi casta domiseda)

Here lies Rob Allan's bonny Bell,
A tenty dame,
That span her 'oo an' said her prayers,
An' bade at hame.

W. D. COCKER   1882–

The Deluge

The Lord took a staw at mankind,
A righteous an' natural scunner ;
They were neither to haud nor to bind,
They were frichtit nae mair wi' his thun'er.

They had broken ilk edic' an' law,
They had pitten his saints to the sword,
They had worshipped fause idols o' stane ;
' I will thole it nae mair,' saith the Lord.

' I am weary wi' flytin' at folk ;
I will dicht them clean oot frae my sicht ;
But Noah, douce man, I will spare,
For he ettles, puir chiel, to dae richt.'

So he cried unto Noah ae day,
When naebody else was aboot,
Sayin' : ' Harken, my servant, to Me
An' these, my commands, cairry oot :

' A great, muckle boat ye maun build,
An ark that can float heich an' dry,
Wi' room in't for a' yer ain folk
An' a hantle o' cattle forby.

' Then tak' ye the fowls o' the air,
Even unto the big bubbly-jocks ;
An' tak' ye the beasts o' the field :
Whittrocks, an' foumarts, an' brocks.

' Wale ye twa guid anes o' each,
See that nae cratur rebels ;
Dinna ye fash aboot fish :
They can look efter theirsels.

' Herd them a' safely aboard,
An' ance the Blue Peter's unfurled,
I'll send doun a forty-day flood
And de'il tak' the rest o' the world.'

Sae Noah wrocht hard at the job,
An' searched to the earth's farthest borders,
An' gathered the beasts an' the birds,
An' tellt them to staun' by for orders.

An' his sons, Ham an' Japheth an' Shem,
Were thrang a' this time at the wark ;
They had fell'd a wheen trees in the wood
An' biggit a great, muckle ark.

This wasna dune juist on the quate,
An' neebours would whiles gether roun' ;
Then Noah would drap them a hint
Like : ' The weather is gaun to break doun.'

But the neebours wi' evil were blin'
An' little jaloused what was wrang,
Sayin' : ' That'll be guid for the neeps,'
Or : ' The weather's been drouthy ower lang.'

Then Noah wi' a' his ain folk,
An' the beasts an' the birds got aboard ;
An' they steekit the door o' the ark,
An' they lippened theirsels to the Lord.

Then doun cam' a lashin' o' rain,
Like the wattest wat day in Lochaber ;
The hailstanes like plunkers cam' stot,
An' the fields turned to glaur, an' syne glabber.

An' the burns a' cam' doun in a spate,
An' the rivers ran clean ower the haughs,
An' the brigs were a' soopit awa',
An' what had been dubs becam' lochs.

Then the folk were sair pitten aboot,
An' they cried, as the weather got waur :
' Oh ! Lord, we ken fine we ha'e sinn'd
But a joke can be cairried ower faur ! '

Then they chapp'd at the ark's muckle door,
To speer gin douce Noah had room ;
But Noah ne'er heedit their cries,
He said : ' This'll learn ye to soom.'

An' the river roar'd loudly an' deep ;
An' the miller was droon't in the mill ;
An' the watter spread ower a' the land,
An' the shepherd was droon't on the hill.

But Noah, an' a' his ain folk,
Kep' safe frae the fate o' ill men,
Till the ark, when the flood had gi'en ower,
Cam' dunt on the tap o' a ben.

An' the watters row'd back to the seas,
An' the seas settled doun and were calm.
An' Noah replenished the earth—
But they're sayin' he took a guid dram !

SIR ALEXANDER GRAY   1882–

Scotland

Here in the Uplands
The soil is ungrateful ;
The fields, red with sorrel,
Are stony and bare.
A few trees, wind-twisted—
Or are they but bushes ?—
Stand stubbornly guarding
A home here and there.

Scooped out like a saucer,
The land lies before me ;
The waters, once scattered,
Flow orderedly now

Through fields where the ghosts
Of the marsh and the moorland
Still ride the old marches,
Despising the plough.

The marsh and the moorland
Are not to be banished ;
The bracken and heather,
The glory of broom,
Usurp all the balks
And the fields' broken fringes,
And claim from the sower
Their portion of room.

This is my country,
The land that begat me.
These windy spaces
Are surely my own.
And those who here toil
In the sweat of their faces
Are flesh of my flesh,
And bone of my bone.

Hard is the day's task—
Scotland, stern Mother —
Wherewith at all times
Thy sons have been faced :
Labour by day,
And scant rest in the gloaming,
With Want an attendant,
Not lightly outpaced.

Yet do thy children
Honour and love thee.
Harsh is thy schooling,
Yet great is the gain :

True hearts and strong limbs,
The beauty of faces,
Kissed by the wind
And caressed by the rain.

Lairhillock, Kincardine

Grief

What ails you, you puir auld body ?
   What gars you greet sae sair ?
Hae you tint the man that's been kind to you
   This forty year and mair ?

O, I didna greet when I tint him,
   Not yet on the burrel-day ;
But though I saw to the hoose and the byre,
   God kens that my hert was wae.

But this mornin' I cam on his bauchles ;
   What cud I dae but greet ?
For I mindit hoo hard he had wrocht for me,
   Trauchlin' wi' sair, sair feet.

IVO MACNAUGHTON CLARK   1883–1950

Ascensioun

He cam tae mend the broken wheels o life,
   A vricht fae roadside shop in Nazareth ;
They stabbed His hert wi hate as cruel's a knife—
   The arles o His luve the stang o death.

In cauld mort-chaumer for three days He lay—
    An end, they howped, tae aa His God-gien pouers—
Syne furth He cam intil the gairden gray
    By starn illumed and censed by breath o fleurs.

He cam and gaed 'mang freens for twa score days ;
    They kentna faur at nicht He laid His heid ;
He spak, e'en supped wi them ; tae their amaze
    They saw He was alive that aince was deid.

Syne on a roch hill-tap in Galilee
    A clood cam wraith-like ower dumbfoundert men,
And swirlan round took Him up bodily
    Richt oot o sicht ayont aa mortal ken.

Upliftit were their lives tae Halysted,
    Abeen wanhap and ocht that micht befaa,
Upo His throne the King wi airms outspread
    His bairns welcomes Hame baith ane and aa.

ANDREW YOUNG   1885 -

Field-Glasses

Though buds still speak in hints
And frozen ground has set the flints
As fast as precious stones
And birds perch on the boughs, silent as cones,

Suddenly waked from sloth
Young trees put on a ten years' growth
And stones double their size,
Drawn nearer through field-glasses' greater eyes.

Why I borrow their sight
Is not to give small birds a fright
Creeping up close by inches ;
I make the trees come, bringing tits and finches.

I lift a field itself
As lightly as I might a shelf,
And the rooks do not rage
Caught for a moment in my crystal cage.

And while I stand and look,
Their private lives an open book,
I feel so privileged
My shoulders prick, as though they were half-fledged.

A. M. DAVIDSON

Auld Fowk

The auld wife sat ayont her man,
   But nae auld carle saw she ;
And, gin he keekit owre at her,
   An auld wife saw na he.

Wi tousy heid a cottar lad
   Sat in the auld man's place,
And glowered, tongue-tackit, at the stars
   That lauched in Jeanie's face.

HELEN BURNESS CRUICKSHANK   1886–

Overdue

O ragin' wind
An' cruel sea,

Ye put the fear
O' daith on me.
I canna sleep,
I canna pray,
But prowl aboot
The docks a' day,
An' pu' my plaid
Aboot me ticht.
'Nae news yet, mistress!'—
Ae mair nicht!

Comfort in Puirtith

The man that mates wi' Poverty,
　An' clasps her tae his banes,
Will faither lean an' lively thochts,
　A host o' eident weans—
But wow! they'll warstle tae the fore
　Wi' hunger-sharpit brains!

But he that lies wi' creeshy W'alth
　Will breed a pudden thrang,
Owre cosh tae ken their foziness,
　Owre bien tae mak' a sang—
A routh o' donnert feckless fules
　Wha dinna coont a dang!

The Stranger

I met a man when I was drinkin' ale,
Wha yammert like a bird at break o' day;
But tho' his tongue was licht wi' joke an' tale,
His een were wae.

171

'Ye're whistlin' in the dark, my lad, that's clear,
Tae keep your spunk up,' thinks I tae mysel';
But what his trouble was I'll never speir—
The deid ne'er tell.

Sae Lang has Sorrow

Sae lang has Sorrow tenanted
   The hoose o' Life wi' me
An' saut-like seasoned ilka meal
   Wi' sharpened ecstasie,
That gin she cam' tae say Fareweel,
   An' Joy hersel' cam' ben
I doobt I wadna welcome her,
   The bonny smilin' quean.

And at the lanely hinderend
   Gin I sud tak' the road
Tae regions yont the yett o' Daith,
   A sorrowless abode,
I doobt I wadna feel at hame
   Sans sorrow an' sans sin,
An' fleein' frae the wersh-like place
   I'd tirl *anither* pin.

The Ponnage

   . . . Sing
Some simple silly sang
O' willows or o' mimulus
A river's banks alang.
        Hugh MacDiarmid

I mind o' the Ponnage Pule,
The reid brae risin',

Morphie Lade,
An' the saumon that louped the dam,
A tree i' Martin's Den
Wi' names carved on it ;
But I ken na wha I am.

Ane o' the names was mine,
An' still I own it.
Naething it kens
O' a' that mak's up me.
Less I ken o' mysel'
Than the saumon wherefore
It rins up Esk frae the sea.

I am the deep o' the pule,
The fish, the fisher,
The river in spate,
The broon o' the far peat-moss,
The shingle bricht wi' the flooer
O' the yellow mim'lus,
The martin fleein' across.

I mind o' the Ponnage Pule
On a shinin' mornin',
The saumon fishers
Nettin' the bonny brutes—
I' the slithery dark o' the boddom
O' Charon's coble
Ae day I'll faddom my doobts.

Glenskenno Wood

Under an arch o' bramble
    Saftly she goes,
Dark broon een like velvet,
    Cheeks like the rose.

Ae lang branch o' the bramble
　　Dips ere she pass,
Tethers wi' thorns the hair
　　O' the little lass.

Ripe black fruit, an' blossom
　　White on the spray,
Leaves o' russet an' crimson,
　　What wad ye say ?

What wad ye say to the bairn
　　That ye catch her snood,
Haudin' her there i' the hush
　　O' Glenskenno Wood ?

What wad ye say ?　The autumn
　　O' life draws near.
Still she waits, an' listens,
　　But canna hear.

Ealasaid

Here are the shores you loved,
The tumbling waters
Curling and foaming on Atlantic strands,
The ocean gentian-blue beyond believing,
The clean white sands.

And here the ancient speech
You loved essaying,
Rising and falling like the wave-borne birds ;
The cadences that wind and tide are weaving
In Gaelic words.

And here the little crofts
With thatch stone-weighted
You told me of, so often ere I came.
How strange that I am here without you, grieving
Your lost, loved name.

O sleep you soundly now,
Ealasaid darling,
Beneath the sandy turf on Tiree's shore.
No more your island home you need be leaving,
Be sad no more.

Spring in the Mearns

(For Lewis Grassic Gibbon, 23 February 1935)

Clouds of smoke on the hill
where the whin is burning,
staining the clear cold sky
as the sun goes down.
Brighter the fire leaps up
as night grows darker ;
wild and lovely the light
of the flaming whin.

Blackened the stubborn bush ;
no more the golden
nut-sweet blossom shall lure
the wandering bee.
Twisted branches sink
to a sullen smoulder
where the small stonechat clinked
contentedly.

Come again when the rains
have carried the ashes
into the hungry soil
and lo ! the green !
Earth that was seared by fire
has now begotten
tender herbage for tough,
and grain for whin.

Body of man to death,
flesh to ashes,
muscle and tissue and bone
to dust are come.
Ah, but the spirit leaps
from the cindered fibre,
living, laughs at death
that is but a name.

Life goes on for ever ;
the body smoulders,
dies in the heat of the pace,
is laid in earth.
Life goes on ; the spirit
endures for ever,
wresting from death in earth
a brave new birth.

He who set the flame
of his native genius
under the cumbering whin
of the untilled field
lit a fire in the Mearns
that illumines Scotland,
clearing her sullen soil
for a richer yield.

Armistice Day

If Edward Thomas or Rupert Brooke
Or the maker of that good Marlborough book
Could have lived on if I had died
I hope I should have sunk my pride,
Though futile deemed I war, and wrong,
And been more proud to die for song.

Or if some certain friends of mine
Who fell in France and Palestine
Would have lived still instead of me,
Perchance unhesitatingly
I then had leapt when rang the drums.
I know that when November comes.

But they who knew me not, or knew,
Went out as if 'twere naught to do,
And gave their song and friendship rare
To death, as though they did not care
Worthy who were the gift they brought . . .
I have been died for—who has not ?

EDWIN MUIR   1887–

Scotland's Winter

Now the ice lays its smooth claws on the sill,
The sun looks from the hill
Helmed in his winter casket,
And sweeps his arctic sword across the sky.
The water at the mill
Sounds more hoarse and dull.

The miller's daughter walking by
With frozen fingers soldered to her basket
Seems to be knocking
Upon a hundred leagues of floor
With her light heels, and mocking
Percy and Douglas dead,
And Bruce on his burial bed,
Where he lies white as may
With wars and leprosy,
And all the kings before
This land was kingless,
And all the singers before
This land was songless,
This land that with its dead and living waits the Judgment Day.
But they, the powerless dead,
Listening can hear no more
Than a hard tapping on the sounding floor
A little overhead
Of common heels that do not know
Whence they come or where they go
And are content
With their poor frozen life and shallow banishment.

The Transmutation

That all should change to ghost and glance and gleam,
And so transmuted stand beyond all change,
And we be poised between the unmoving dream
And the sole moving moment—this is strange
Past all contrivance, word, or image, or sound,
Or silence, to express, that we who fall
Through Time's long ruin should weave this phantom ground
And in its ghostly borders gather all.

There incorruptible the child plays still,
The lover waits beside the trysting tree,
The good hour spans its heaven, and the ill,
Rapt in their silent immortality,
As in commemoration of a day
That having been can never pass away.

The Stronghold

This is our native land.
By strict inheritance
Our lives are free.   A hand
Strange to us set us here,
Ordained this liberty,
And gave us hope and fear
And the endless mines of chance.

To weave our tale sublime
Rhyme was knit to rhyme
So close, it seemed a proof
That nothing else could be
But this one tapestry,
Where gleams under the woof
A giant Fate half-grown,
Imprisoned and its own.

To our unquestioned rule
No bound is set.   We were
Made for this work alone.
This is our native air.
We could not leave these fields.
And when Time is grown
Beneath our countless hands,
They say this kingdom shall
Be stable and beautiful.

But at its centre stands
A stronghold never taken,
Stormed at hourly in vain,
Held by a force unknown,
That neither answers nor yields.
There our fate is shaken,
There the hero was slain
That bleeds upon our shields.

The Return

The veteran Greeks came home
Sleepwandering from the war.
We saw the galleys come
Blundering over the bar.
Each soldier with his scar
In rags and tatters came home.

Reading the wall of Troy
Ten years without a change
Was such intense employ
(Just out of the arrows' range),
All the world was strange
After ten years of Troy.

Their eyes knew every stone
In the huge heartbreaking wall
Year after year grown
Till there was nothing at all
But an alley steep and small,
Tramped earth and towering stone.

Now even the hills seemed low
In the boundless sea and land,
Weakened by distance so.

How could they understand
Space empty on every hand
And the hillocks squat and low ?

And when they arrived at last
They found a childish scene
Embosomed in the past,
And the war lying between—
A child's preoccupied scene
When they came home at last.

But everything trite and strange,
The peace, the parcelled ground,
The vinerows—never a change !
The past and the present bound
In one oblivious round
Past thinking trite and strange.

But for their grey-haired wives
And their sons grown shy and tall
They would have given their lives
To raise the battered wall
Again, if this was all
In spite of their sons and wives.

Penelope in her tower
Looked down upon the show
And saw within an hour
Each man to his wife go,
Hesitant, sure and slow :
She, alone in her tower.

Song

Why should your face so please me
That if one little line should stray

Bewilderment would seize me
And drag me down the tortuous way
Out of the noon into the night ?
But so, into this tranquil light
You raise me.

How could our minds so marry
That, separate, blunder to and fro,
Make for a point, miscarry,
And blind as headstrong horses go ?
Though now they in their promised land
At pleasure travel hand in hand
Or tarry.

This concord is an answer
To questions far beyond our mind
Whose image is a dancer.
All effort is to ease refined
Here, weight is light ; this is the dove
Of love and peace, not heartless love
The lancer.

And yet I still must wonder
That such an armistice can be
And life roll by in thunder
To leave this calm with you and me.
This tranquil voice of silence, yes,
This single song of two, this is
A wonder.

The Rider Victory

The rider Victory reins his horse
Midway across the empty bridge
As if head-tall he had met a wall.
Yet there was nothing there at all,

No bodiless barrier, ghostly ridge
To check the charger in his course
So suddenly, you'd think he'd fall.

Suspended, horse and rider stare,
Leaping on air and legendary.
In front the waiting kingdom lies,
The bridge and all the roads are free ;
But halted in implacable air
Rider and horse with stony eyes
Uprear their motionless statuary.

The Castle

All through that summer at ease we lay,
And daily from the turret wall
We watched the mowers in the hay
And the enemy half a mile away.
They seemed no threat to us at all.

For what, we thought, had we to fear
With our arms and provender, load on load,
Our towering battlements, tier on tier,
And friendly allies drawing near
On every leafy summer road.

Our gates were strong, our walls were thick,
So smooth and high, no man could win
A foothold there, no clever trick
Could take us, have us dead or quick.
Only a bird could have got in.

What could they offer us for bait ?
Our captain was brave and we were true. . . .
There was a little private gate,
A little wicked wicket gate.
The wizened warder let them through.

Oh then our maze of tunnelled stone
Grew thin and treacherous as air.
The cause was lost without a groan,
The famous citadel overthrown,
And all its secret galleries bare.

How can this shameful tale be told?
I will maintain until my death
We could do nothing, being sold;
Our only enemy was gold,
And we had no arms to fight it with.

The Swimmer's Death

He lay outstretched upon the sunny wave,
That turned and broke into Eternity.
The light showed nothing but a glassy grave
Among the trackless tumuli of the sea.
Then over his buried brow and eyes and lips
From every side flocked in the homing ships.

Epitaph

Into the grave, into the grave with him.
Quick, quick, with dust and stones this dead man cover
Who living was a flickering soul so dim
He was never truly loved nor truly a lover.

Since he was half and half, now let him be
Something entire at last here in this night
Which teaches us its absolute honesty
Who stray between the light and the half-light.

He scarce had room for sorrow, even his own ;
His vastest dreams were less than six feet tall ;
Free of all joys, he crept in himself alone :
To the grave with this poor image of us all.

If now is Resurrection, then let stay
Only what's ours when this is put away.

Variations on a Time Theme, VII

Ransomed from darkness and released in Time,
Caught, pinioned, blinded, sealed and cased in Time ;
Summoned, elected, armed and crowned by Time,
Tried and condemned, stripped and disowned by Time ;
Suckled and weaned, plumped and full-fed by Time,
Defrauded, starved, physicked and bled by Time ;
Buried alive and buried dead by Time :

If there's no crack or chink, no escape from Time,
No spasm, no murderous knife to rape from Time
The pure and trackless day of liberty ;
If there's no power can burst the rock of Time,
No Rescuer from the dungeon stock of Time,
Nothing in earth or heaven to set us free :
Imprisonment's for ever ; we're the mock of Time,
While lost and empty lies Eternity.

Merlin

O Merlin in your crystal cave
Deep in the diamond of the day,
Will there ever be a singer
Whose music will smooth away

The furrow drawn by Adam's finger
Across the meadow and the wave ?
Or a runner who'll outrun
Man's long shadow driving on,
Break through the gate of memory
And hang the apple on the tree ?
Will your magic ever show
The sleeping bride shut in her bower,
The day wreathed in its mound of snow
And Time locked in his tower ?

from *The Journey Back*

Through countless wanderings,
Hastenings, lingerings,
From far I come,
And pass from place to place
In a sleep-wandering pace
To seek my home.

I wear the silver scars
Of blanched and dying stars
Forgotten long,
Whose consternations spread
Terror among the dead
And touched my song.

The well-bred animal
With coat of seemly mail
Was then my guide.
I trembled in my den
With all my kindred when
The dragon died.

Through forests wide and deep
I passed and as a sleep
My wandering was.
Before the word was said
With animal bowed head
I kept the laws.

I thread the shining day ;
The mountains as in play
Dizzily turn
My wild road round and round.
No one has seen the ground
For which I burn.

Through countless wanderings,
Hastenings, lingerings,
Nearer I come,
In a sleep-wandering pace
To find the secret place
Where is my home.

ANON.   *c.* 1887

The Station-Master's Dochter

(Otherwise, *The Lament of Tammas Claiker, Bill-Sticker*)

O wae's me for the station-master's dochter !
 She doesna care a preen for me, tho I wad fain hae socht her.
She cocks a purple tammie on a stook o yalla hair :
A jersey haps her shouthers, but she keeps her thrapple bare,
in a what-d'ye-caa-'t—invitin ye tae tak a second luik—
a chemie, caad a blouse, wi a snippit gushet-neuk.
                    Snippit, rippit, snippit,
                    Rippit, snippit, rippit,
A chemie, caad a blouse, wi a snippit gushet-neuk.

Ay, see the stuck-up stockie standan there afore the wicket.
she kens she has a dainty hand for takin up your ticket.
But in the train at fowks like me she winna fling a word,
she's aye in sic a hurry nippin tickets in the third.
But I wad like to tell her—I wad tell her gin I durst—
she's an unco time in nippin wi the billies in the first !
   Nippin, clippin, nippin,
   Clippin, nippin, clippin,
she's an unco time in nippin wi the billies in the first.

Aince, at the Coperative Ball, I thocht I'd hae a dance wi her,
but—set her up, the besom !—I could never get a chance wi her,
sae I had juist tae skutch about the slippy flure and watch her
trippin here and trippin there and skippin round and round,
whiles slippin intae corners wi the gentry frae the toun.
   Trippin, skippin, slippin,
   Slippin, skippin, trippin,
slippin intae corners wi the gentry frae the toun.

O wae's me for the station-master's dochter !
She winna gie a luik at me—she's no the lass I thocht her.
An honest man's a worthy man, whatever be his trade ;
the lass that lichtlies him for that deserves tae dee a maid.
Ye getna muckle guid, but ye get the fewer ills
in pickin up a livin, rinnin round and stickin bills.
   Pickin, stickin, pickin,
   Stickin, pickin, stickin,
in pickin up a livin rinnin round and stickin bills.

JAMES BRIDIE   1888-1951

Martha's Prayer to St. Eloi

Sweet Saint Eloi, bend a convenient ear
to me, your suppliant, her pious moans ;

who finds small comfort and but little cheer
in kneeling on these cold, damp, hard, sharp stones :
for my Goodman, for all his goods and gear,
lies mournfully on his four-post bed and groans
he has been badly for this past long year.
The rheumatism racks his aching bones.
He cannot eat ; he cannot take his beer ;
and yestereve, Saint Eloi, he depones
that he heard harping and the distant, clear
voices of heavenly tenors, baritones,
sopranos, altos, coming ever more near—
strange and celestial. And the Doctor owns
his nostrums baffled, as, with gaze austere
and wagging pow, his thirsty knife he hones.
Ah ! Save, Saint Eloi, save my husband dear !
Accept these humble . . . shall I call them loans ?
For, it is said, whatever we give to thee
promptly repaid a thousand fold shall be.

The Three Tykes

' I had three tykes,' the silly old Man saith,
' called Discipline, Imagination, Faith.
They kept my soul and its bigging safe from skaith.

' Ae night in the bygoing came a fellow fell
who's tongue gaed clatter like the College bell
that secret ferlies told and garred me tell.

' As frae an ower-turned blanket sprint the bugs
sae crept his words intil my bizzing lugs
and syne the wight unchristened my three dugs.

' The bulldog he called *Refrenatio* ;
the whippet he called *Aberratio* ;
the terrier, Faith, was *Cupida Ratio.*

'The Latin words disjaskit me;
I hung the curs upon a tree,
and there they hang for a' to see.

'Doon cam the riever lads frae the Hanging Shaw
and riped my bigging to the naked wa'
wi never a tyke to bark at them ava.'

WALTER ELLIOT   1888 –

Sestette to Fish

Let us praise the humble fish,
Though not all that one could wish,
'Tis an inexpensive dish—
                              Pisces Benedicite.

Whiles when us ill fortune scuppers,
Prowl we Sauchie on our uppers,
Kind friends stand Adelphi suppers—
                              Pisces Benedicite.

Though the casual Govan herring
Warns us by a sense unerring
That the dead need but interring—
                              Pisces Benedicite.

Taken fresh and all unspotted,
Rolled in vinegar and potted,
O, it tickles the parotid—
                              Pisces Benedicite.

Gone Rectorials' great issues,
Gone the fried and midnight fishes,
Balm they brought to craving tissues—
                              Pisces Benedicite.

Fishes boiled or fishes fried,
Fishes sailing in the tide,
Or decently interred inside—

Pisces Benedicite.

ISOBEL WYLIE HUTCHISON   1889–

Advent Sunday at Umanak

The church is bright with candlelight,
  (The snow lies thick and broad) ;
Here for a space by Heaven's grace
  The folk may sup with God.
They have gone up by three and four
  And five and six and seven.
The cloth is spread, the grace is said,
  The door stands wide to Heaven.

Now every guest has donned his best ;
  With hands and faces clean,
With *anoraq* of blue or black
  Or red or white or green,
Kamiker new of scarlet hue
  And sealskin *bukser* brown,
They have gone up to sup with God,
  Out of this little town.

Now like a rose the Pastor glows
  In cope of gold and red ;
In surplice white, with chalice bright
  He blesses each bent head ;
He breaks the bread and pours the wine
  And in his office waits—
A servant found on holy ground
  And watchful at God's gates.

Oh ! little kirk amid the mirk,
　　The icebergs and the frost ;
A place of rest for every guest—
　　The glad, the tempest-tost ;
Here mid the dark that draws around
　　As sinks our earthly sun,
The Light is found that shall abound
　　When day and night are done.

BESSIE J. B. MACARTHUR　　　1889-

The Collady-Stane

O Truth's a braw collady-stane,
　　sae fu' o licht
it leams, a muckle siller stern,
　　athort the nicht.

But some wad hae it reid as bluid,
　　some gowd, or green,
and some they canna see't for mist
　　afore their een.

But aye they ettle to be richt,
　　theirsels—or nane—
gin they but get an orra glisk
　　o yon braw stane.

O green, or gowd, or cramasie,
　　or siller licht—
which will you hae to traivel wi
　　athort the nicht ?

Last Leave

O I remember you so lithe and gay,
    yet with a wistfulness you could not hide ;
clear eyes that questioned in some subtle way,
    and would not be denied.

So young you seemed in battle-dress of blue,
    almost a radiance shone about your head ;
such delicate awareness filtering through,
    I cannot dream you dead.

Vanished perchance, with spirit strong and wise,
    none left the tale of valour to unfold ;
only the echo of your brave emprise
    for memory to hold.

Vanished perchance, yet with familiar grace,
    when sudden silence falls across the room,
smiling you steal to your accustomed place
    and know yourself at home.

G. BRUCE THOMSON

McFarlane o' the Sprots o' Burnieboozie

Afore that I'd be terraneezed as I this file hae been,
I'd raither rin' frae here tae Birse wi' peez in baith ma sheen,
I'd raither dee for want o' breath than pine for want o' love,
And it's a' because McFarlane merrit Sousie.
Sousie's kankert faither wi' mine could niver gree,
And aye fan I'd gang ower that gait he'd turn his dog at me.
So I sent ma freen McFarlane doon to see fit he could dee,
McFarlane o' the Sprots o' Burnieboozie.

I dinna like McFarlane, I'm safe enough tae state.
His lug wad cast a shadow ower a sax-fit gate.
He's soft as ony goblin and sliddery as a skate,
McFarlane o' the Sprots o' Burnieboozie.

McFarlane spak nae wird for me but plenty for himsel',
He reesed the lassie's barley scones, her kebbick and her kail.
Her faither cried oot 'Sprottie, man, ye should try yer luck
    yersel','
Tae McFarlane o' the Sprots o' Burnieboozie.
Though McFarlane is the grimmest chiel for twenty miles aroon,
Though they buy his fottygraph tae fleg the rottens frae a toon,
He kittled up his spunk at this and spiered gin she'd come doon
And be mistress o' the Sprots o' Burnieboozie.

I dinna like McFarlane, I tell ye it's a fac' ;
He's a nose for splittin' hailstanes and a humphy back ;
He's legs like guttaperka, ilka step his knees gang knack—
McFarlane o' the Sprots o' Burnieboozie.

Oh, a dirl o' the teethache's nae particularly sweet,
Bit love's the only power on earth that iver gart me greet ;
It's like kittlie chilblains roon yer heart instead o' roon yer feet—
They were aggravated wi' the sicht o' Sousie.
Noo freens and kind philosophers, ye've heard what me befell ;
Niver lippen tae the middle man, bit dee yer work yersel',
Or I'll bet my hinmost sarkit ye're a day ahin the markit
As fan I sent Jock McFarlane roon tae Sousie.

I dinna like McFarlane, it's affa bit it's true ;
A pewter speen wis tint in Jock McFarlane's moo.
He couldnae weel be grimmer, sups his brose wi' the skimmer—
McFarlane o' the Sprots o' Burnieboozie.

194

GEORGE BUCHANAN-SMITH 1890–1915

Fragment

Courage, faint heart, press forward to the hill !
  The ridge looms dark ?   It only hides the day.
Wait for the dawn to come ?   O forward still,
  And meet the sun halfway !

WILLA MUIR 1890 –

Speerin'

Lyin' on a hillside
Wi' heather to my chin,
I speered at a' the wee things
Gaein' oot an' in :
Wee things, near things,
We're livin' a' thegither,
Me an' ants an' forkytails
Doon in the heather.

Syne on a grassy brae
Amang the carle doddies
I speered in the gloamin'
At the heavenly bodies :
Big things, far things,
Stars an' suns by dozens,
We're a' gaein' the same road,
We're a' cater-cousins.

WILLIAM OGILVIE   1891-1939

There's Nane o' My Ain to Care

There's nane o' my ain to care,
   There's nane to mind me noo,
There's nane o' my ain to comb my hair,
   There's nane to sponge my mou'.
There's nane o' my ain to care,
   Strange han's sall straighten me,
Strangers sall fauld about my limbs
   The claes o' my deid body.

IVOR BROWN   1891-

Never Go Back

(Lines written after revisiting a Scottish country house where I lived
as a small boy)

Oh, never revisit !   The burn that I thought was a Spey,
Full of baitable monsters, has withered and dwined away,
And the trout in the pool would go into a sardine-tin,
But once they were salmon-splendid.   And what of the linn ?

There's a bath-tap bitty where once was a torrent a-whummle :
As the Hydro-Electrics can make a canal of the Tummel,
So Time turns the Findhorn of fancy to trickle of Ouse ;
Its boulders are pebbles : you'd cross it, not wetting your shoes,

And the great hill beyond and its blackness of firs, where the roe
Would leap like a wapiti,—boy saw the wee buckie so—
Is only a five minutes' clamber, no more than a tump,
And the quivering woods have been axed to a desert of stump.
196

The heron that mocked me so long—children ever would slay—
Has gone with its great, lazy wings and its glimmer of grey ;
The rubious squirrel has fled from its larch ; there are dairies,
So couthy and trim, where once were my jungle and prairies.

Tamed by man's tidying hand is the maze of young eyes :
Time, the assassin of glory, the slayer of size,
Turns the ben of the boy to a hummock, the burn to a drain.
Oh, folly of follies—to grasp at young heaven again.

The hill may be ghosted with game—but what is a spectre ?
Spring the waters I drank—but now only whisky is nectar.
The Big House of the bairn, so enormous, majestic, what is it ?
Just decently earning its keep as a farm.   Oh, never revisit !

NEIL M. GUNN   1891-

The Serpent

Outpouring from an earth
close-bound by antique roots
of blackened heather runts
whose high green shoots
lifting frail buds of birth
shiver
as your cold coils meet
their anguished feet :

Outpouring from my mind
dark-bound by primal fears
your arrowy diamond head
in glittering spell uprears—
uprears   and sways   and dips—
feeling among the flowers
whole shivering hours.

MARGARET WINEFRIDE SIMPSON

Villanelle

O winter wind, lat grievin be,
Lat grievin be, and murn nae mair :
Simmer sall set thy sorrow free.

New hurt the heavy hert sall dree ;
Thy weariness awa sall wear :
O winter wind, lat grievin be.

Wi a' the waes the warld sall see
What wae hast thou that can compare ?
Simmer sall set thy sorrow free,

Yet what delicht sall puirtith pree
When time sall solace thy despair ?
O winter wind, lat grievin be.

What fear onkent can trouble thee,
What misery that nane can share ?
Simmer sall set thy sorrow free,

But man in dule doth live and dee ;
A birn mair brief is thine to bear :
O winter wind, lat grievin be :

Simmer sall set thy sorrow free !

FREDERICK VICTOR BRANFORD   1892–1941

Ardgay

A hundred pontiff hills entomb,
Passionlessly, my purple home.

Buried in a haunted cup
Where the flashing snakes writhe up
In coils of crested foam.

Secret Treaties, II

Is it a god that thunders like a sea
Upon the gates of Gaza ; should I play
Samson and bear the brazen strengths away,
Leaving this wooden citadel to be
The sport of every storm successively ?
Beleaguered by the embattled stars, the bay
Of marching winds, the desperate array
Of anarchs banded in the heart of me,
I cannot hear the sacred bugles blow
Nor see the white battalions of the Cross.
Each head is Janus.   Every proud crusade
Boasts on its hell-wrought banners holy braid,
While o'er the dead uncowering harpies crow
Patriot fervours and batten on our loss.

To D.C.B.

' Others had parents, you had only me,
An ugly, cross, auld buddie,' so you sighed
When many years ago my mother died
In far-off foreign London.   And then we
Fled to the hills like deer in jeopardy.
Mine infant hands you laid on power, and plied
My heart with flame, and bade me fearless ride
Away from you to meet the advancing sea.
Robed in red dreams with Ninus have I gone
To win Semiramis at Babylon,

Travelled in Faerie, bright with elfin dames
Who had instructed Phidias in despair.
Evil and good with all they held most rare
Are to your central splendour but dim frames.

The Iron Flower

Long ago in a lonely land
Where no bloom hath ever been,
Gnarled thistles only and
Wizened grasses mean—
Like a temple to the sun
On a star that hath none,
Like an altar to a god
In an atheist's abode,
A poet at his duty,
Where men hated beauty,
Made an iron flower,
And it withered in an hour.

HUGH MacDIARMID (C. M. Grieve)   1892-

Cophetua

Oh ! The King's gane gyte,
Puir auld man, puir auld man,
An an ashypet lassie
Is Queen o the lan'.
Wi a scoogie o silk
An a bucket o siller
She's showin the haill Coort
The smeddum intil her.

The Watergaw

Ae weet forenicht i the yow-trummle
I saw yon antrin thing,
A watergaw wi its chitterin licht
Ayont the on-ding ;
An I thocht o the last wild look ye gied
Afore ye deed !

There was nae reek i the laverock's hoose
That nicht—and nane i mine ;
But I hae thocht o that foolish licht
Ever sin syne ;
An I think that mebbe at last I ken
What your look meant then.

O Jesu Parvule

(' Followis ane sang of the birth of Christ, with the tune
of *Baw lu la law*.'—*Godly Ballates*)

His mither sings to the bairnie Christ
Wi the tune o *Baw lu la law*.
The bonnie wee craturie lauchs in His crib
An aa the starnies an he are sib.
 Baw, baw, my loonikie, baw, balloo.
' Fa' owre, ma hinny, fa' owre, fa' owre,
Aabody's sleepin binna oorsels.'
She's drawn Him in tae the bool o her breist,
But the byspale's nae thocht o sleep i the least.
 Balloo, wee mannie, balloo, balloo.

The Eemis-stane

I' the how-dumb-deid o the cauld hairst nicht
The warl like an eemis-stane

201

Wags i the lift ;
An my eerie memories fa'
Like a yowdendrift.

Like a yowdendrift so's I couldna read
The words cut oot i the stane
Had the fug o fame
An history's hazelraw
No' yirdit thaim.

Empty Vessel

I met ayont the cairney
A lass wi tousie hair
Singin till a bairnie
That was nae langer there.

Wunds wi warlds tae swing
Dinna sing sae sweet.
The licht that bends owre aathing
Is less taen up wi't.

At My Father's Grave

The sunlicht still on me, you row'd in clood,
We look upon ilk ither noo like hills
Athort a valley.   I'm nae mair your son.
It is my mind, nae son o yours, that looks,
And the great darkness o your death comes up
And equals it across the way.
A livin man upon a deid man thinks
And ony sma'er thocht's impossible.

Milk-wort and Bog-cotton

Cwa een like milk-wort and bog-cotton hair !
I love you, earth, in this mood best o a'
When the shy spirit like a laich wind moves
And frae the lift nae shadow can fa'
Since there's nocht left to thraw a shadow there
Owre een like milk-wort and milk-white cotton hair.

Wad that nae leaf upon anither wheeled
A shadow either and nae root need dern
In sacrifice to let sic beauty be !
But deep surroondin darkness I discern
Is aye the price o licht.   Wad licht revealed
Naething but you, and nicht nocht else concealed.

Water Music

(To William and Flora Johnstone)

Wheesht, Joyce, wheesht, and let me hear
   Nae Anna Livvy's lilt,
But Wauchope, Esk, and Ewes again,
   Each wi its ain rhythms till't.

Archin here and arrachin there,
   Allevolie or allemand,
Whiles appliable, whiles areird,
   The polysemous poem's planned.

Lively, louch, atweesh, atween,
   Auchimuty or aspate,
Threidin through the averins
   Or bightsom in the aftergait.

Or barmybrained or barritchfu,
  Or rinnin like an attercap,
Or shinin like an Atchison,
  Wi a blare or wi a blawp.

They ken a' that opens and steeks,
  Frae Fiddleton Bar to Callister Ha',
And roon aboot for twenty miles,
  They bead and bell and swaw.

Brent on or boutgate or beshacht,
  Bellwaverin or borne-heid,
They mimp and primp, or bick and birr,
  Dilly-dally or show speed.

Brade-up or sclafferin, rouchled, sleek,
  Abstraklous or austerne,
In belths below the brae-hags,
  And bebbles in the fern.

Bracken, blaeberries, and heather
  Ken their amplefeysts and toves,
Here gangs ane wi aiglets jinglin,
  Through a gowl anither goves.

Lint in the bell whiles hardly vies
  Wi ane the wind amows,
While blithely doon abradit linns
  Wi gowd begane anither jows.

Cougher, blocher, boich and croichle,
  Fraise in ane anither's witters,
Wi backthraws, births, by-rinnins,
  Beggar's-broon or blae—the critters !

Or burnet, holine, watchet, chauve,
  Or wi a' the colours dyed
O' the lift abune and plants and trees
  That grow on either side.

Or coinyelled wi the midges,
  Or swallows a' aboot,
The shadow o an eagle,
  The aiker o a troot.

Toukin ootrageous face
  The turn-gree o your mood,
I've climmed until I'm lost
  Like the sun ahint a clood.

But a tow-gun frae the boon-tree,
A whistle frae the elm,
A spout-gun frae the hemlock,
And, back in this auld realm,
Dry leafs o dishielogie
To smoke in a ' partan's tae ' !

And you've me in your creel again,
  Brim or shallow, bauch or bricht,
Singin in the mornin,
  Corrieneuchin a' the nicht.

With a Lifting of the Head

PLOTINUS

Scotland, when it is given to me
      As it will be
To sing the immortal song
The crown of all my long

Travail with thee
I know in that high hour
I'll have, and use, the power
Sublime contempt to blend
With its ecstatic end
As who, in love's embrace,
Forgetfully may frame
Above the poor slut's face
Another woman's name.

The Skeleton of the Future

(At Lenin's Tomb)

Red granite and black diorite, with the blue
Of the labradorite crystals gleaming like precious stones
In the light reflected from the snow : and behind them
The eternal lighting of Lenin's bones.

The Parrot Cry

Tell me the auld, auld story
O hoo the Union brocht
Puir Scotland into being
As a country worth a thocht.
England, frae whom a' blessings flow,
What could we dae withoot ye ?
Then dinna threip it doon oor throats
As gin we e'er could doot ye !
 My feelings lang wi' gratitude
 Ha'e been sae sairly harrowed
 That dod ! I think it's time
 The claith was owre the parrot !

Tell me o' Scottish enterprise
And canniness and thrift,
And hoo we're baith less Scots and mair
Than ever under George the Fifth,
And hoo to ' wider interests '
Oor ain we sacrifice
And yet tine naething by it
As aye the parrot cries.
    Syne gie's a chance to think it oot
    Aince we're a' weel awaur o't,
    For, losh, I think it's time
    The claith was owre the parrot !

Tell me o' love o' country
Content to see't decay,
And ony ither paradox
Ye think o' by the way.
I doot it needs a Hegel
Sic opposites to fuse ;
Oor education's failin'
And canna gie's the views
    That were peculiar to us
    Afore oor vision narrowed
    And gar'd us think it time
    The claith was owre the parrot !

A parrot's weel eneuch at times
But whiles we'd liefer hear
A blackbird or a mavis
Singin' fu' blythe and clear.
Fetch ony native Scottish bird
Frae the eagle to the wren,
And faith ! you'd hear a different sang
Frae this painted foreigner's then.

The marine that brocht it owre
Believed its every word
—But we're a' deeved to daith
Wi' his infernal bird.

It's possible that Scotland yet
May hear its ain voice speak
If only we can silence
This endless-yatterin' beak.
The blessing wi' the black
Selvedge is the clout !
It's silenced Scotland lang eneuch,
Gi'e England turn aboot,
   For the puir bird needs its rest—
   Wha else 'll be the waur o't ?
   And it's lang past the time
   The claith was owre the parrot !

And gin that disna dae, lads,
We e'en maun draw its neck
And heist its body on a stick
A' ither pests to check.
I'd raither keep't alive, and whiles
Let bairns keek in and hear
What the Balliol accent used to be
Frae the Predominant Pairtner here !
   —But save to please the bairns
   I'd absolutely bar it
   For fegs, it's aye high time
   The claith was owre the parrot !

On Reading Professor Ifor Williams's ' Canu Aneirin ' in Difficult Days

('Only barbarism, villainy and ignorance do not respect the
past, cringing before the present alone.'—PUSHKIN)

Stay me with mosses, comfort me with lichens.
Opening the Gododdin again and renewing
My conscious connection with the gwyr y gogledd
I who never fail to detect every now and again,
In the Hebridean and Shetland and Cornish waters I most
    frequent,
By subtle signs Myrddin's ship of glass
Which has floated invisibly around the seas
Ever since Arfderydd a millennium and half ago
(Since Arfderydd—a few miles from where I was born !)
I am as one who sees again in a stark winter wood
(And the forest of Celyddon subdued in death's grip to-day)

The lichens and mosses, earth's first mercies, shine forth
—The dusk of Lincoln green warming the ragged tree-bole,
Dark flaked liverwort on dank cliff,
Rich velvet mosses making a base
For the old stone dykes—all glowing
In a lustrous jewel-like beauty for the enjoyment of which
One might well endure the rigours of winter !
Contrary to common belief, the lichens and mosses
Love the winter sunlight as wise human beings do.
(Thus, of two retaining walls of a sunk lane,
The lichens and mosses are most abundant and vigorous
On the side that receives the largest volume of sunlight,
And a warm stretch of dykefoot facing the low-set
Southern winter sun is the most resplendent
In fairy velvet of any exposure known to me.)

Even so, at the feet of the great grim vertical problems
Of contemporary life I am sustained and cheered

By the perennial shining of a few
Little personal relationships.
Surely in these days of Massenmensch
A singularly blessed example
Of the transcendent function emerging
From an enantiodromic movement.

Even so in these sterile and melancholy days
The ghastly desolation of my spirit is relieved
As a winter wood by glowing moss or lichen,
And the sunk lane of my heart is vivified,
And the hidden springs of my life revealed
Still patiently potent and humbly creative
When I spy again the ancestral ties between Scotland and
Wales,
And, weary of the senseless cacophony of modern literature,
Recur to Aneirin's Gododdin, one of the oldest poems
In any European vernacular—far older indeed
Than anything ever produced on the Continent
Outside Greek and Latin ; and not only
Note how (great topical lesson for us to-day)
It is not the glory, but the pity and waste, of war
That inspires its highest passages, but realise
That the profoundest cause in these Islands to-day,
The Invisible War upon which Earth's greatest issues depend,
Is still the same war the Britons fought in at Catraeth
And Aneirin sings.   The Britons were massacred then.   Only
one
Escaped alive.   His blood flows in my veins to-day
Stronger than ever, inspires me with his unchanged purpose,
And moves me alike in Poetry and Politics.

Between two European journeys of Neville Chamberlain's
And two important speeches of Herr Hitler's
I return to the Taliesin and Llywarch Hen poems,

Full of hiraeth, of angry revolt
Against the tyranny of fact, even as Malesherbes
Spent the time lesser men would have devoted
To preparing their case against the forty-three accusations
Contained in the Acte énonciatif
Of December 11, 1792
In reading Hume's History of the House of Stuart.

So I am delivered from the microcosmic human chaos
And given the perspective of a writer who can draw
The wild disorder of a ship in a gale
Against the vaster natural order of sea and sky.
If man does not bulk too big in his rendering
He does not lose the larger half of dignity either.

Aneirin stays me with mosses
And comforts me with lichens
In the winter-bound wood of the world to-day
Where the gaunt branches rattle like gallow bones.
It is like one of the commonest and at the same time
One of the most indeterminate factors in the life of men
—An experience so intensely private
And so jealously guarded and protected
It scarcely reaches the level of articulation.
It is felt to be precious and indispensable.
It belongs to the very foundations
Of temperament and character,
Yet it seldom rises to the clear-cut stage
Of positive affirmation.
It lies somewhere between wistfulness and perception,
In the borderland between longing and knowing.
It is like music from some far-off shore
Or a light that never was on land or sea.

The Seamless Garment

When'er the mist which stands 'twixt God and thee
Defecates to a pure transparency.

COLERIDGE

You are a cousin of mine
   Here in the mill.
It's queer that born in the Langholm
   It's no' until
Juist noo I see what it means
To work in the mill like my freen's.

I was trying to say something
   In a recent poem
Aboot Lenin.   You've read a guid lot
   In the news—but ken the less o'm ?
Look, Wullie, here is his secret noo
In a way I can share it wi you.

His secret and the secret o a'
   That's worth ocht.
The shuttles fleein owre quick for my een
   Prompt the thocht.
And the coordination atween
Weaver and machine.

The haill shop's dumfounderin
   To a stranger like me,
Second nature to you ; you're perfectly able
   To think, speak and see
Apairt frae the looms, though to some
That doesna sae easily come.

Lenin was like that wi workin-class life,
   At hame wi't a'.

His fause movements couldna been fewer,
    The best weaver Earth ever saw.
A' he'd to dae moved intact,
Clean, clear, and exact.

A poet like Rilke did the same
    In a different sphere,
Made a single reality—a' ae oo—
    O' his love and pity and fear ;
A seamless garment o music and thought,
But you're owre thrang wi puirer to tak tent o't.

What's life or God or what you may ca't
    But something at ane like this ?
Can you divide yoursel frae your breath
    Or—if you say yes—
Frae your mind that as in the case
O' the loom keeps that in its place ?

Empty vessels mak the maist noise
    As weel you ken.
Still waters rin deep, owre fu' for soond.
    It's the same wi men.
Belts fleein, wheels birlin—a river in flood
Fu' flow and tension o' poo'er and blood.

Are you equal to life as to the loom ?
    Turnin oot shoddy or what ?
Claith better than man ?   D'ye live to the full,
    Your poo'er's a' deliverly taught ?
Or scamp a'thing else ?   Border claith's famous,
Shall things o mair consequence shame us ?

Lenin and Rilke baith gied still mair skill,
    Coopers o Stobo, to a greater concern

Than you devote to claith in the mill.
    Wad it be ill to learn
To keep a bit eye on their looms as weel
And no' be hailly taen up wi your ' tweel ' ?

The womenfolk ken what I mean.
    Things maun fit like a glove,
Come clean off the spoon—and syne
    There's time for life and love.
The mair we mak natural as breathin the mair
Energy for ither things we'll can spare
But as long as we bide like this
Neist to naething we hae, or miss.

Want to gang back to the handloom days ?
    Nae fear !
Or paintin oor hides ?   Hoo d'ye think we've got
    Frae there to here ?
We'd get a million times faurer still
If maist folk change profits didna leave't till
A wheen here and there to bring it aboot
—Aye, and hindered no' helped to boot.

Are you helpin ?   Machinery's improved, but folk ?
    Is't no high time
We were tryin to come into line a' roun ?
    (I canna think o a rhyme.)
Machinery in a week maks greater advances
Than Man's nature 'twixt Adam and this.

Hundreds to the inch the threids lie in,
    Like the men in a communist cell.
There's a play o licht frae the factory windas.
    Could you no' mak mair yoursel ?
Mony a loom mair alive than the weaver seems
For the sun's still nearer than Rilke's dreams.

Ailie Bally's tongue's keepin time
   To the vibration a' richt.
Clear through the maze your een signal to Jean
   What's for naebody else's sicht.
Short skirts, silk stockings—fegs, hoo the auld
Emmle-deugs o the past are curjute and devauld !

And as for me in my fricative work
   I ken fu' weel
Sic an integrity's what I maun hae,
   Indivisible, real,
Woven owre close for the point o a pin
Onywhere to win in.

The Little White Rose

The Rose of all the world is not for me.
I want for my part
Only the little white rose of Scotland
That smells sharp and sweet—and breaks the heart.

EWART ALAN MACKINTOSH   1893–1916

In Memoriam Private D. Sutherland,
*Killed in action in the German trench 16 May 1916, and
the others who died*

So you were David's father,
And he was your only son,
And the new-cut peats are rotting
And the work is left undone,
Because of an old man weeping,
Just an old man in pain,
For David, his son David,
That will not come again.

Oh, the letters he wrote you
And I can see them still,
Not a word of the fighting
But just the sheep on the hill
And how you should get the crops in
Ere the year got stormier,
And the Bosches have got his body,
And I was his officer.

You were only David's father,
But I had fifty sons
When we went up in the evening
Under the arch of the guns,
And we came back at twilight—
O God !   I heard them call
To me for help and pity
That could not help at all.

Oh, never will I forget you,
My men that trusted me,
More my sons than your fathers',
For they could only see
The little helpless babies
And the young men in their pride.
They could not see you dying,
And hold you while you died.

Happy and young and gallant,
They saw their first-born go,
But not the strong limbs broken
And the beautiful men brought low,
The piteous writhing bodies,
They screamed ' Don't leave me, sir,'
For they were only your fathers
But I was your officer.

NAN SHEPHERD   1893-

Above Loch Avon

So on we marched.   That awful loneliness
Received our souls as air receives the smoke.
Then larger breath we drew, felt years gone by,
And in a new dimension turned and spoke.

In the Cairngorms

XVIII

Cauld, cauld as the wall
That rins frae under the snaw
On Ben a'Bhuird,
And fierce, and bricht,
This water's nae for ilka mou,
But him that's had a waucht or noo
Nae wersh auld waters o the plain
Can sloke again,
But aye he clim's the weary hicht
To fin' the wall that lowps like licht,
Caulder than mou can thole, and aye
The warld cries out on him for fey.

WILLIAM JEFFREY   1894-1946

John Knox in the Galleys (1547-49)

1

A bitter meditation in the mirk it is,
The hert ootcrying till the mind's eye sees
Lomond clad in emerant and the Howe flure-lit,

The flesh the while subjected to the whup's shrill wheeze,
The galley bucking, billows foamed and snell,
The Watchman frozen to the wode cross-trees.

II

A pretty sicht had Andrews' lordis noo,
The man wha prophesied by kirk and field
Ourhailet thus and melled wi' sons o' whures !
Ane glance wad send them blinkand for a bield.
'Tis guts alane may stand this.   Yea, my God
My God ! the lift sall split or ere I yield !

III

Yet will may weakened be when, burned in pain,
The back o'erscabbit and the bellox dry,
The body crieth that the jaws o' daith
Pronounce an ending, or that the sun on high
Put ferlies in the brain till cleft waves seem
Bricht stags and kennettis on the rin ootby !

IV

At times abominations flaunt the deep's
Green tenements and causeys quick wi' hell,
And maist that lassock frae the Cyprian shore,
Wha's temple stoud on ane Ephesian fell :
Withouten sark she smites the licht o' day
And wins the feeblit flesh intil her spell.

V

Sall I, at times ourhailet, being Adam-born,
Tak tent on Origen and his remede ?
That were ane monkish way.   Unmanned, I were
Nocht but ane straw tae tackle Scotland's need.
Besides, a manchild made, a man I sall remain,
By God's grace keeper o' mine ain het seed !

Lauch then, ye selie waves and flichtering mews !
This mannie, think ye, noo sae starved and raw,
Wad be but spindrift in his kittok's bed ?
'Tis true.   A routh o' thochts that keep nae law
Torment this sinner bounden till ane oar
And slashed wi' sunlicht and the whup's reid claw.

Yet that Egyptian wha taucht in schules
Had lordship o' the mind : a clerk he was
In turnings o' the sternes, in scriptures auld.
Sic learning man micht use, that is but as,
His warldlie nature setting up in power,
Though kenning in his hert it can but pass.

Sall I appraise that guid and studious birk
Abune the Carthaginian, that cunning wicht
Wha gat the language o' the Kirk o' Rome
And held the gnosis scarcely worth a dicht ?
Wi' choice o' ane, I dae the spirit wrang :
I maun hae baith to drive this life aricht.

How think ye, burdies o' the southron touns,
That man in boreal clime may haud the road
Licht happit, scant o' flesh or scant o' brain ?
Sae beggarly, he is na worth ane toad !
A pickle win', and soop ! he's owre the knowe,
Sair shockit and forfochen, and perilous wode.

Wi' routh o' flesh and brain, the Scot maun rise
A very Samson at the gates o' Rome

And dirl them doun and ilka gowden gaud
Till they lie streikit on the bluid-reid loam.
The vision this, strang beltit like the sun,
That steels my spirit when the hert maks moan.

XI

'Tis nae presumption.   God is throned abune
The flesh, the brain, the floreal earth and heaven.
Afore Him what is man but scatterit gerss ?
Yet Grace is his.   Though meanest o' the livin'
He can, as Dauvit tells in pointed writ,
Rax till his strength encreases seven times seven.

XII

A bitter meditation, maister mew, it is !
Nae doot thou's taen the measure o' my fear :
A pechin, peekie fellow, peenged and flayed
By carnal deils !   Indeed, it is a bier
I suld clap banes in, so but Nature guides the day
And I keep sconsit in this galley here.

XIII

But there's a sang abounding in the hert
And raised at dawing when the caller air
Trips like a damakie that sees her luve.
I ken I'll see Auld Reekie's rocky stair
Upliftit as was Jacob's in a cloud o' sternes,
And I sall smell bluid scailt on Holyrood's flair.

XIV

Thy servant, Lord, he sall na dee a nameless thing,
A larach heapit wi' the galley's dung.
He'll tread on gerss agen and see the bewis green
And hear in cleansit kirk the royal psalms sung.
My God ! he'll speil in power and plunk his heel,
And wae to them that thraw him, though their wames be young !

The Song of the Ungirt Runners

We swing ungirded hips,
   And lightened are our eyes,
The rain is on our lips,
   We do not run for prize.
We know not whom we trust
   Nor whitherward we fare,
But we run because we must
   Through the great wide air.

The waters of the seas
   Are troubled as by storm.
The tempest strips the trees
   And does not leave them warm.
Does the tearing tempest pause ?
   Do the tree-tops ask it why ?
So we run without a cause
   'neath the big bare sky.

The rain is on our lips,
   We do not run for prize.
But the storm the water whips
   And the wave howls to the skies.
The winds arise and strike it
   And scatter it like sand,
And we run because we like it
   Through the broad bright land.

To Germany

You are blind like us.   Your hurt no man designed,
And no man claimed the conquest of your land.

221

But gropers both through fields of thought confined
    We stumble and we do not understand.
    You only saw your future bigly planned,
And we the tapering paths of our own mind,
    And in each other's dearest ways we stand,
And hiss and hate.   And the blind fight the blind.

When it is peace, then we may view again
    With new-won eyes each other's truer form
    And wonder.   Grown more loving-kind and warm
We'll grasp firm hands and laugh at the old pain,
    When it is peace.   But until peace, the storm,
The darkness and the thunder and the rain.

JAMES PEACOCK   1895–1933

from *Desideria* (a Sonnet Sequence)

The first cold doubts of new experience
Chilled, like a plunge into a morning sea,
My sleep-warmed thoughts.   I found it strange to be
So near that I might stretch my fingers hence
And touch thy face in very truth and sense.
Oh, art thou but one girl made dear to me,
As others might, by distant wizardry,
A new thing quite apart from my pretence ?
Or art thou she, the Eve, created whole
Out of my fragment dreams by God's avail ?
A Galatea sculptured in my soul
For whom the blood responsive will not fail ?—
I feel like one who watches morning roll
Its light along a dim and lovely vale.

ALAN FLEMING McGLASHAN

Anaesthesia

Over my nose and mouth a cold, hard cone
   of silvered steel ; eyes blanketed with wool . . .
A vapour rolls, oily and sickening-sweet,
heavily down my throat : a drowsy heat
   spreads thro' my limbs. . . . Within my throbbing skull
a great Bell tolls, hollow and deep of tone. . . .
Someone says ' *Take deep breaths.*' The tenuous sound
   seems to descend a million miles to find
my buried consciousness,—but yet I hear,
and feel I must obey, though palsied fear
   grips the small cowering fragment of my mind
that's conscious still : a mole in frozen ground.
I breathe more deeply ; and the great Bell tolls
   loudly, more loudly yet,—until its hum
seems as the beating wings of some fierce gull
trapped in the bony dungeon of my skull. . . .
   Now I sink downwards, blind and chilled and numb . . .
down through the Earth's damp bosom. . . . Pallid souls
I meet, that gaze on me from age-old graves
   as I pass dumbly down. At length the Bell
softens its tone to wave-beats. . . . And I reach
a strange-familiar, grey-green, twilight beach,
   littered with bones that yield an earthy smell,
and fringed by softly lapping, grey-green waves.

ANON.   *c.* 1895

The Dundonian at Bonn

   Here in the land of *Würste* (*id est* sausages,
     Which idle *Burschen* swallow by the score,

Adding the while, in oft-repeated tossages,
  Beer from a beaker, brown and brimming o'er,
  Then, thumping on the table, call for more),

Here where established usage runs contrarily
  In everything to what obtains at home,
The guileless *Ausländer* must walk it warily,
  Among the Romans doing as in Rome.
  (Beer is a thing I *never* drink at home.)

Here where the institutions all are model ones,
  And law and order hold supremest sway,
From aged *Burgers* down to little toddle ones
  The highest thought of all is to obey,
  And policemen are the heroes of the day.

Here where the Rhein flows rapidly and pabulous—
  (*Rein* = clean, but this is not the case),
Home of romance, and haunt of creatures fabulous—
  I mourn the inroads of the commonplace.
  (Beer, bricks, and Baedeker are commonplace.)

Here where the *Damen* clothe themselves atrociously
  And tartan frocks are matched with yellow boots,
Where children all are fattened up precociously
  And nearly split their little sailor suits—
  (Myself am spare, and hate your yellow boots).

Here in a land of merriment and jollity,
  Far from the smoky realms of jute and jam,
Here where I spend an educative holiday,
  Here—well, that's all about it, here I am !

RODERICK WATSON KERR 1895–

The Grave-digger

A digger he digs in the dark,
   In the naked remains of a wood,
For his friend that lies stiff and stark,
   On his head hard blood for a hood :
The digging is painful and slow,
   Yet the digger he sweats like a slave ;
But he did not know what I now know :
   The digger he dug his own grave.

GABRIEL RIVERS 1896–

Last Lullaby

(For a Child, Sick unto Death)

Fair angels will sing tae ye,
Sweet cherubim wing tae ye,
And the earth-born saints
In a ring round ye stand.
Mither Mary will hap ye,
Young Jesus will clap ye,
Till your ain mither comes
At the Father's command.

True Wedlock

What tho his grave hauds naething mair
Than gowden hair and banes,
God give my ain be lockt wi his,
Weel happit round wi stanes !

Sae that when dawns the dreadfu day
When earth stops birlin round,
And the clash o planets is the trump
That wauks us frae our swound :
New aeons o consummate fire
Sall bind our stour again ;
And suld our ghaists come seekin us,
Ae hoose maun dae for twain.

NAOMI MITCHISON 1897–

Lament

Green graves in the Southland.   My heart it is sair
For the braw lads and bonnie I'll never see mair ;

The lads that hae lassies, the lads that hae nane,
I the weet o the carses they lie by their lane,

On dune and in braeside, by muir and by burn,
Under aits o the hairst, under ruits o the fern,

And faur doun frae Scotland, on hearts that are sair,
Lie deid lads, lie dear lads, we'll never see mair.

Westminster

(Specially for J. P. W. Mallalieu)

The clever and angry
Confident on Benches :
The humble and crazy
Little in the Lobby
Under decent statues'
Discreet disapproval.

Men on strings,
Three line whips,
Strings on men :
Sooner, later,
Luckiest trips.
Laughter then
From Snip and Snitch,
Tadpole and Taper.
Mother of Parliaments,
That old bitch,
Gets her men.

In Westminster Hall
Various horrors have been enacted, judicial
   and otherwise.
To Big Ben's vacant face
The eager eyes of suicides gaze up.
All as it will be, was : was, as will be.

WILLIAM SOUTAR   1898–1943

The Bairn

The winter's awa : and yonder's the spring
coman owre the green braes :
and I canna but greet, while aa the birds sing,
I canna but greet ;
for it micht hae been you, wi your smaa, lauchan face,
coman in frae the weet.

The Tryst

O luely, luely, cam she in
and luely she lay doun :

227

I kent her by her caller lips
and her breists sae smaa and round.

Aa throu the nicht we spak nae word
nor sindered bane frae bane :
aa throu the nicht I heard her hert
gang soundin wi my ain.

It was about the waukruif hour
whan cocks begin to craw
that she smooled saftly throu the mirk
afore the day wad daw.

Sae luely, luely, cam she in,
sae luely was she gane ;
and wi her aa my simmer days
like they had never been.

The Lanely Müne

Saftly, saftly, throu the mirk,
the müne walks aa hersel :
ayont the brae ; abüne the kirk ;
and owre the dunnlan bell.
I wadna be the müne at nicht
for aa her gowd and aa her licht.

The Sea-shell

Listen ! for a lost warld maunners here
frae the cauld mou o a shell ;
and sae far awa the blufferts blare
and the sea-birds skreel :

and the wail o women alang yon shore
whaur the swaw comes rowin in ;
and the swurly waters whummlin owre
the cry o the sailor-men.

The Makar

Nae man wha loves the lawland tongue
but warsles wi the thocht—
there are mair sangs that bide unsung
nor aa that hae been wrocht.

Ablow the wastery o the years,
the thorter o himsel,
deep buried in his bluid he hears
a music that is leal.

And wi this lealness gangs his ain ;
and there's nae ither gait
though aa his feres were fremmit men
wha cry : *Owre late, owre late.*

Content

Wi meal in the girnel,
and milk in the bowl,
a man will haud thegither
baith body and soul.

And wi a hert that's ready
to thole the rochest days
a man will hairst contentment
frae a gey puir place.

Riddle on a Library

It's no the resurrection day
owre aa the warld's kirk-yairds ;
yet here the deid in thrangety
stand up atween their buirds.

They clype o heaven and o hell ;
they lee and dinna lee ;
but wha wad tak in what they tell
maun listen wi his ee.

The Auld House

There's a puckle lairds in the auld house
   wha haud the waas thegither :
there's no muckle graith in the auld house
   nor smeddum aither.

It was aince a braw and bauld house
   and guid for onie weather :
kings and lords thranged in the auld house
   or it gaed a'smither.

There were kings and lords in the auld house
   and birds o monie a feather :
there were sangs and swords in the auld house
   that rattled ane anither.

It was aince a braw and bauld house
   and guid for onie weather :
but it's noo a scruntit and cauld house
   whaur lairdies forgaither.

Lat's caa in the folk to the auld house,
   the puir folk aa thegither :
it's sunkit on rock is the auld house,
   and the rock's their brither.

It was aince a braw and bauld house
   and guid for onie weather :
but the folk maun funder the auld house
   and bigg up anither.

The Earth Abides

When our loud days are chronicles
of rancour and revenge
whoever walks upon these hills
shall not remember change.

He shall be moulded by their mood :
their granite and their grass
through secret ways of sense and blood
into his life will pass.

And he shall love his native land ;
and still an exile be
if in its name he lift a hand
to smite an enemy.

And he shall look upon the sun
and see his ensign there
if earth belong to all, and none ;
gifted as light and air.

The Unicorn

When from the dark the day is born
life's glory walks in white :
upon the hills the unicorn
glitters for mortal sight.

Out of their dream the hunters wake
with brightness in their eyes :
the foolish hurry forth to take,
but gently go the wise.

They only are the wise who claim
this for their foolishness :
to love the beast they cannot tame,
yet cheer the unending chase.

Reality

There are clear moments when we truly know
The realness of our lone experience ;
As if the mind saw past its screen of sense
Into the light which shapes time's shadow-show.
Nothing of earth in this unearthy glow
Is changed ; but we are changed by the intense
Revealment, and our dull intelligence
Stares upon truth but cannot prove it so.
Whate'er the source of this pervasive beam
(Which is, and is not, in a moment's space)
Only its noon quickens to doubtless sight ;
And, being gone, shall not our reason seem
A fool—with tapers—coming, in the night,
To name the truth upon a sundial's face :

Healing Moment

What mind
Is not made whole
By earthy loveliness
Which troubles its Bethesda pool
Of blood ?

For a Sundial

Hold not the hour,
loving what you have lost ;
only the gifted hour can be your guest :
gladly accept the flower and the frost :
the sun goes down and shadows are at rest.

The Permanence of the Young Men

No man outlives the grief of war
Though he outlive its wreck :
Upon the memory a scar
Through all his years will ache

Hopes will revive when horrors cease ;
And dreaming dread be stilled ;
But there shall dwell within his peace
A sadness unannulled.

Upon his world shall hang a sign
Which summer cannot hide :
The permanence of the young men
Who are not by his side.

233

Song

Whaur yon broken brig hings owre,
Whaur yon water maks nae soun',
Babylon blaws by in stour :
Gang doun wi a sang, gang doun.

Deep, owre deep, for onie drouth,
Wan eneuch an ye wud droun,
Saut, or seelfu', for the mouth :
Gang doun wi a sang, gang doun.

Babylon blaws by in stour
Whaur yon water maks nae soun' :
Darkness is your only door ;
Gang doun wi a sang, gang doun.

ROBERT RENDALL   1898–

Cragsman's Widow

' He was aye vaigan b' the shore,
    An' climman amang the craigs,
Swappan the mallimaks,
    Or taakan whitemaa aiggs.

' It's six year bye come Lammas,
    Sin' he gaed afore the face,
An' nane but an aald dune wife
    Was left tae work the place.

' Yet the sun shines doun on a' thing,
    The links are bonnie and green,
An' the sea keeps ebban an' flowan—
    As though it had never been.'

234

Orkney Crofter

Scant are the few green acres that I till,
But arched above them spreads the boundless sky,
   Ripening their crops ; and round them lie
    Long miles of moorland hill.

Beyond the cliff-top glimmers in the sun
The far horizon's bright infinity ;
   And I can gaze across the sea
    When my day's work is done.

The solitudes of land and sea assuage
My quenchless thirst for freedom unconfined ;
   With independent heart and mind
    Hold I my heritage.

ERIC LINKLATER   1899 –

from *Seven Years*

Beauty's a rose, a shining sword, a thief ;
   Beauty's a singing flute, the narrow flame
That lights the incense-smoke of all belief.
   Beauty was You, and You were beauty's name
When I was young : rose, thief, and cutting sword,
   The flute, the flame—I lost my peace to this,
Reached up for that, bled here, and there adored,
   Nor, thus bewildered, thought my state amiss.

Youth gives his heart away, for youth's ill fortune
   Is often to have nothing else to give :
Where others bargain he must still importune—
   You laughed, and found a fuller life to live.

You were not rich because of me, it's true,
But I was bankrupt quite because of you.

Soldiers and Guns

Soldiers and guns, soldiers and guns,
These for your daughters and those for your sons.
What if your children be lovely and tall ?
When soldiers and guns come, down they will fall.

Teheran

Here are white walls, and ease, and falling fountains,
  Obedient trees, and gardens neatly planned.
Beyond—why, mountains, desert, and more mountains,
  And the eternal road to Samarkand.

Here's chatter of bazaar.   Beyond the hills,
  Great Asian names, Bokhara, Khorassan—
Tumultuous, rough-singing syllables
  Like echoes of a brawling caravan.

ALICE V. STUART   1899-

The Clock in the Sick-room

The room was shrouded from the sun ;
Outside, the birds' rejoicing din
Mocked the uneasy peace within,
Where slow-drawn breaths came one by one.

More vitally, it seemed, than they,
The quick clock ticked the livelong day :
Tick-ticked, tick-ticked, the livelong day.

The groping fingers nerveless dropped,
Silent the fretful breathing ran,
The mechanism that was man
For ever with the heart-beat stopped.
The metal case of cunning springs,
Man-made, outlasted man's decay ;
Instinct with life beside the clay,
Tick-tick, tick-tick, the soulless thing
Reiterated all the day,
Tick-tick, tick-tick, the livelong day.

JOE CORRIE

The Image o God

Crawlin about like a snail in the mud,
   covered wi clammy blae,
ME, made after the image o God—
   Jings ! but it's laughable, tae.

Howkin awa 'neath a mountain o stane,
   gaspin for want o air,
the sweat makin streams doun my bare back-bane
   and my knees aa hackit and sair.

Strainin and cursin the hale shift throu,
   half-starved, half-blind, half-mad ;
and the gaffer he says, ' Less dirt in that coal
   or ye go up the pit, my lad ! '

So I gie my life to the Nimmo squad
  for eicht and fower a day ;
ME ! made after the image o God—
  Jings ! but it's laughable, tae.

When Bess was Badly

When Bess was badly and lain doun sae quait,
  the red gane frae her lip and frae her cheek,
  wi strength to smile a wee, but nane to speak,
a lily driftin helpless in the spate,
for three lang days I couldna eat a haet,
  I couldna rest, just wandert out and in,
  prayin to gray and empty skies abune—
a prayer frae a hert that was clean bate.

The turnin day, the day o life and daith,
  I watched the dawnin licht the country round,
  and heard a laverock sing as it had done
sae oft when we had lingered, happy baith,
  and doun I lay amang the dewy gress,
  and toomed my hert o tears for sake o Bess.

HAMISH MACLAREN   1901-

Little Sea House

Little sea house,
  when I found you,
the yellow poppies
  were nodding round you.

Your blue slate hat
    that the four winds
came to tug at
    over the tamarinds :

I remember it well :
    the salmon-nets drying—
Laugh, violin-shell,
    and cease crying !

For I will return,
    through the sea-haze :
I am sailing back there
    always, always.

Island Rose

She has given all her beauty to the water ;
    she has told her secrets to the tidal bell ;
and her hair is a moon-drawn net, and it has caught her,
    and her voice is in the hollow shell.

She will not come back any more now, nor waken
    out of her island dream where no wind blows :
and only in the small house of the shell, forsaken,
    sings the dark one whose face is a rose.

MARION LOCHHEAD   1902 –

Knight and Lady

Hath she beauty ?
    Yea, most fair.
Knows she wisdom ?
    Oh, so rare.

Is she holy ?
    As a prayer.

By that beauty
    I adore,
Of Thy wisdom
    I implore,
Keep her holy
    Evermore.

Fiddler's Bidding

Och, gin ye come to our toun,
    to our toun, to our toun,
Och, gin ye come to our toun,
    play up a rantin air.

Play like the verra deil, lad,
    be bauld, lad, be daft, lad ;
steer up the verra deil, lad,
    and fleg us aa sair.

For we're aa deid in our toun,
    in our toun, in our toun ;
we're deid and damned in our toun,
    and neither ken nor care.

ADAM DRINAN

from *The Ghosts of the Strath*

Long blue shadow of salmon lying,
    shot shell of leaping silver,
using the lull and the flies
    to practise for the rough river,

stay down on the salt sea stones,
   learn there, you yet-free fishes,
your sweet hope to come home
   was once on the hillside fishers.

Salmon may leap falls ;
   we deeps of the linn may master ;
but weeds grow up our walls,
   hearts whip in airy water.
Up in the rich meads
   such the rich men's power is,
only wrens are safe in streams
   and sheep in houses.

The great power had its magic !
   With strong spells of paper
money and law raised lairds ;
   burnt crops bewitched labour.
No cunning of fish-lore
   will conjure our safe return ;
but the same black arts be ours—
   from the need to burn to the burning.

HUNTER DIACK

Talk

Twa sarious men ae simmer nicht,
Walkin by the sea,
Nyattert awa about Wrang and Richt
And the best a man cwid dae
I the skelp o time atween birth and death
Tae mak his life warth while, but, feth,
Though Thocht set out at a gey-like spang
It cwidna catch up wi Richt and Wrang.

As seen as we spik, the meanins skail
Out o wir wirds, and it's jist the same
As combin the tanglet cloods wi a kaim,
Or catchin the lichtnin by the tail.

ALBERT D. MACKIE   1904-

Sea Strain

I fand a muckle buckie shell
   And held it to my lug,
And shurlan doun the stanie shore
   I heard the waters rug.
I heard the searchers at their wark,
   Waves wappan at the hull ;
I heard, like some dementit sowl,
   The girnin o the gull.
I heard the reeshlin o the raip,
   I heard the timmers grane ;
I heard the sab o a sailor's bride,
   Forever burd alane.

What's Aheid o's ?

The auld days are gane,
   The new days are to be,
But life changes nane
   For the likes o you and me.

This puirtith may devauld,
   Puir folk may win their share,
But herts will aye gang cauld
   And herts will aye get sair.

The contrar's true and aa—
    Hard times we'll see again,
But joy will aye can caa
    And hope we'll aye can hain.

Thunder Sky

It will be plowtan syne : the lift
Wad lopper the milk o aa the toun ;
But heedless o what cluds may drift,
What weet micht blatter doun,
Heedless o hou the simmer sky
Swithers atween the licht and gloom,
Twa bits o lassies wander by,
Twa bairns gaun for a soom ;
They oxter ither wi powes thegither,
Huggan ilk promise o delyte,
Their costumes, wraps—and buttered baps
Kept for a shiverie bite.
Guidsakes, man, I'd gie aa I hae
To see the warld wi een like thae.

A New Spring

The whins are blythesome on the knowe
    Wi candles bleezan clear,
Forsythia's lichtit lowe on lowe,
    But, lass, ye arena here.

Aside the dyke the catkins growe,
    The tulips are asteer,
The daffie wags its gowden powe
    Ahint its pale green spear.

Winter's lang gane, baith snaw and thowe ;
　　Bricht brairds anither year ;
Aathing comes back—my hert is howe !—
　　Aathing but you, my dear.

WILLIAM MONTGOMERIE　1904-

Glasgow Street

Out of this ugliness may come,
Some day, so beautiful a flower,
That men will wonder at that hour,
Remembering smoke and flowerless slum,
And ask—glimpsing the agony
Of the slaves who wrestle to be free—
' But why were all the poets dumb ? '

from *The Castle on the Hill*

('The still sad music of humanity')

I

When Norman knights came trampling from the south
In David's reign ; when men honoured the Bruce ;
And when the powerful words of an old man's mouth
Smashed the church images, and gave excuse
To double old estates—no castle stood
On yonder hilltop.　But when field and glen
Squeezed out their starving surplus, and for food
The mill took payment from the souls of men ;
When Scottish children lived the stunted years
Between a factory and city slum ;
When earth by smoke was curtained off from Heaven

244

—In that time, in the century of tears,
These towers rose up, far from the pitiful hum
Of the living souls by whom the price was given.

II

And if those souls by whom the price was paid
By tending dead machines come hither now
And look upon the towers their hands have made,
And ask fulfilment of the ancient vow
—If they ask leadership, will it be found
In him whose word will one day close the gate ?
If they ask service, will his heart be bound
To service of the people where they wait ?
Obedience they have given, but for a price,
Obedience they have paid, but pence for pence
They will demand repayment.   Will he pay ?
The people's will moves slowly, as the ice
Of glaciers, blind to whither and from whence ;
They cannot see an end, but know the way.

DOROTHY MARGARET PAULIN   1904–

Said the Spaewife

Said the auld spaewife to me—
    ' Never be humble !
Lads 'll tak' the rough o' your tongue
    An' never grumble ;
' But the thing nae man can bide,
    An' he be human,
Is that mim-moothed snivellin' fule,
    A fushionless woman.'

Prayer on Good Friday

We were in the frenzied mob, you and I,
When they shouted : ' Crucify Him !   Crucify . . .'

Once we'd realised The Way, it was we
Who, frightened, turned aside from Calvary.

We were the nation's counsellors who saw
In Him discord, and danger to the Law.

We are the timid common folk who choose
Seeming security ;   who compromise—and lose.

And ours the unlovely sins of self ;   the pride,
The heedlessness—neglect of Him Who died.

Still, year by year, His passion we renew
And darken Love with death.   O, grant us too,

Father, forgiveness.   Send to our hearts a sword—
Not peace—till we shall know Thy Word.

Sodger's Lass

Whiles, when frae the far clachan ayont the hill
I' the forenicht, the thin wild soun'
O' the pipin' rises, I've seen him look by me, his ear
Cockit to catch the tune.

I've felt the fierce fain kiss grow gentle ;   I've seen
Sic a far glisk come to his e'e,
As gin a bugle rang frae the Farawa'
Oot ower the sinderin' sea.

O, there's something ca's to me oot o' the mirk mid-nicht
Wi' the cry o' a wee lost wean,
An' aye I'm gaun blin' an glaikit aboot ma wark,
Think, thinkin' on nocht but the love I canna hain.

My ain lad !   Tho' the pibroch stound on the still nicht air
Wi' the wae lilt o' a sang
That's echoin' back frae the doors o' eternity,
He e'en maun rise an' gang.

Breaking Covert

Just one faint whimper below, but the mare's ears quiver
    And point ; there it is again.
Then one deep note ; a crash of tongues in the covert ;
    A plunge as we shorten rein.

No, they've lost it.   But look, look, look ! a red shadow
        stealing
    Up the hedge by old Gemmel's hay—
They're on ! Oh, damn those fools at the gate, they'll head 'im—
    No ! thank heaven, he's away !

The race for a start ; a gallop ; great choking heart-beats,
    And blinding, ridiculous tears ;
Can anything else in life infuse such well-being,
    Such delirious joys and fears ?

A light-hearted buck for the grass ; then some looming timber ;
    Up—over ; a glance behind
To be sure you're with me ; then after the streaming pack
    And away, away with the wind.

The White Rose

The breakers white and sorrowful
   In the long sea stray,
Sad as when they carry our people
   Far away.

When the clans sailed chiefless, when first
   The white Scots rose
Was scattered, this sea took the petals :
   White the wave goes.

ROBERT MACLELLAN·   1907-

Sang

There's a reid lowe in yer cheek,
Mither, and a licht in yer ee,
And ye sing like the shuilfie in the slae,
But no' for me.

The man that cam' the day,
Mither, that ye ran to meet,
He drapt his gun and fondlet ye
And I was left to greet.

Ye served him kail frae the pat,
Mither, and meat frae the bane.
Ye brocht him cherries frae the gean,
And I gat haurdly ane.

And noo he lies in yer bed,
Mither, and the licht grows dim,
And the sang ye sing as ye hap me ower
Is meant for him.

ROBERT KEMP   1908–

Last Judgment

When the warld is aa brunt duin,
Like a spunk that flaret in nicht,
And the starry een o heaven
Hae tint their sicht,
When there are nae fields tae ken
The chase o hairst and spring,
Nae howes tae kep the flood
And the snaw's on-ding,
Nae morn tae wauk nae hill,
Nae river, rock, nor sea,
Nae chant o storms, nae sun's
Saft clemencie,
When there's neither pipes for blawin
Nor yet the breath to blaw,
And aa that man has biggit
Is gane to the waa—
I care na wha my saul,
Hameless, is herdit wi :
It's the bonnie, broken hame
That dauntons me.

LAVINIA DERWENT

Traitor

She's weel respeckit i the kirk
(She's merrit til a clever birk,
Rowthy wi siller),
Singin the Psalms wi godly grace,
A smirk sae smug upon her face,
A perfect pillar.
She's decked wi furs and jewelled rings,
Ablow the counter buys her things,
And lauchs at laws.
And, while wi pleisure she is thrang,
The war can wage baith loud and lang ;
It's no *her* cause.
At nicht, when planes gang throbbin by
To brave the hardships o the sky
And fecht the Huns,
She'll coorie doun and sleep sae sound,
Her selfish hairt'll never stound ;
They're no *her* sons.

JANET MARY SMITH

The Fairm Quean to her Birl Pleuch
(The Land Girl to her Roto-tiller)

Thou doitert, donnert, deil's invention,
Was thou no fram't wi ae intention,
To gar me scunner at thy mention,
    Nor wish to mell
Wi tools whase maker draws his pension
    Frae Satan's sell ?

The day, I brocht thee oot, fu fain
To howk the yaird afore the rain ;
But stairting thee was fash and pain
    Wi routh o oil ;
A daylicht oor or twa was gane
    In clarty toil.

Whaur thou was biggit, yont the seas,
I daur be sworn thou'd rin wi ease,
Wi genty orra pairts to please
    And mend thee sune ;
Here, puir auld runt ! thou'll pinge and wheeze
    Till thou art dune.

But noo, praise be ! thou'rt rinnand weel ;
Straucht up and doon the brae thou'll speil,
And when thou goes, I'll say I'm real
    Set up aboot thee ;
It wud hae taen a week to sheil
    And dig 't wi'oot thee.

But whit has taen thee noo ? Tuts, tuts !
Thou spits and stops, and frae thy nuts
The petrol pours, and tho' I shuts
    It aff again,
Whit noo can ail thy creishy guts
    Is yont my ken.

O, ill befaa men's daft-like ploys,
Their wars and strikes and dearths' annoys,
That rob douce wemen-fowk o joys
    In hearth and weans,
And gar us guide thir deil's ain toys
    We caa machines !

The Fisherman

As he comes from one of those small houses
Set within the curve of the low cliff
For a moment he pauses
Foot on step at the low lintel
Before fronting wind and sun.
He carries out from within something of the dark
Concealed by heavy curtain
Or held within the ship under hatches.

Yet with what assurance
The compact body moves,
Head pressed to wind,
His being at an angle
As to anticipate the lurch of earth.

Who is he to contain night
And still walk stubborn
Holding the ground with light feet
And with a careless gait ?

Perhaps a cataract of light floods,
Perhaps the apostolic flame.
Whatever it may be
The road takes him from us.
Now the pier is his, now the tide.

Embro tae the Ploy

In simmer, whan aa sorts foregether
in Embro tae the ploy,
folk seek oot freens tae hae a blether
or foes they'd fain annoy.
Smorit wi British Railways' reek
frae Glesca or Glen Roy
or Wick, they come tae hae a week
o cultivated joy
                              or three
at Embro tae the ploy.

Americans wi routh o dollars
wha drink oor whisky neat,
wi Sassenachs an Oxford Scholars
are eydent for the treat
o music sedulously high-tie
at thirty-bob a seat :
Wop opera performed in Eyetie
tae them's richt up their street,
                              they say,
at Embro tae the ploy.

The tartan trade wuld gar ye lauch ;
nae trauchle is owre teuch,
your surname needna end in -och,
they'll cleik ye up the cleuch.
A puckle dollar bills will aye
prieve Hiram Teufelsdröckh
a scion o the Clan McKay,
it's maybe richt eneuch,
                              verfluch !
at Embro tae the ploy.

Furthgangan Embro folk come hame
for three weeks in the year,
an find Auld Reekie no the same,
fu sturrit in a steer.
The stane-faced biggins whaur they froze
and supped their puirshoose lear
o cultural cauld-kale and brose
see cantraips unco queer

at Embro tae the ploy.   thae days

The auld Hie Schuil, whaur mony a skelp
o Bunny's eydent tawse
hae gien a heist-up an a help
towards Doctorates o Laws,
noo hears, for Ramsay's cantie rhyme,
loud pawmies o applause
frae folk wha've peyed a pund a time
tae sit on wudden raws

at Embro tae the ploy.   gey hard

The Haly Kirk's Assembly-Haa
noo fairly coups the creel
wi Lindsay's *Three Estatis*, braw
devices o the Deil.
About our heids the satire stots
like hailstanes till we reel ;
the bawrs are in auld-farrant Scots,
it's maybe jist as weel,

at Embro tae the ploy.   hooch aye,

The Epworth Haa wi wonder did
behold a pipers' bicker ;
wi *hadarid* an *hindarid*
the air gat thick an thicker.

Cumha na Cloinne set for strings
inflames a piper quicker
tae get his dander up, by jings,
than thirty u.p. liquor,

we thocht,
at Embro tae the ploy.

The Northern British Embro Whigs
wha biggit Charlotte Square,
they fairly wad hae tined their wigs
tae see the Stuarts there,
the bleedan Earl o Moray an aw,
weel pentit an gey bare :
oor Queen an Princess, buskit braw,
enjoyed the hale affair

(see Press)
at Embro tae the ploy.

Whan day's anomalies are cled
in decent shades o nicht,
the Castle is transmogrifeed
by braw electric licht.
The toure that bields the Bruce's croon
presents an unco sicht
mair sib tae Wardour Street nor Scone ;
wae's me for Scotland's micht,

says I,
at Embro tae the ploy.

The Café Royal an Abbotsford
are filled wi orra folk
wha's stock-in-trade's the scrievit word
or twicet-scrievit joke.

Brains, weak or strang, in heavy beer,
or ordinary, soak.
Quo ane, ' This yill is awfie dear,
I hae nae clinks in poke,
                                nor foldin-money,
at Embro tae the ploy.'

The auld Assemblie-Rooms, whaur Scott
foregethert wi his fiers,
noo see a gey kenspeckle lot
ablow the chandeliers.
Tae Embro drouths, the festive club
a richt godsend appears ;
it's something new tae find a pub
that gaes on servin beers
                                fu late
at Embro tae the ploy.

They toddle hame doon mirky streets,
filled wi synthetic joy ;
aweel, the year brings few sic treats
an muckle tae annoy.
There's mony hartsom braw hy-jinks
mixed up in this alloy
in simmer whan aa sorts foregether
at Embro tae the ploy.

JOHN KINCAID   1909–

Citie

The nicht's duin wi daunce, the citie's wabbit oot.
The mune's settlan doun i the lap o the lift.
The folk ur aa skailan frae screen-ploy an pub
an gaean thur weys til sleep an til dwaum.

The nicht's duin wi daunce, ootstreicht on the flair ;
the citie is dowsan the gems i hir goun.
Ay, luke on the citie whaur she sleeps
wi luve on hir conscience an truth in hir airms,
wi ease i hir banes and weirds i hir bluid.
The staurs sclim the lift, burn brichter an brichter ;
the universe birls on its lang solemn wey.
Ay, sleep awa citie, ma douce smilan citie,
gaither strength fur the morn an the morn furbye,
an be it a daurk daw, or be it a bricht daw,
be it rain, be it sleet, be it blezzard wi claws,
yuir Setterday's lauchin wull ding doun the deils
that lowp frae the stanes as men bigg thur roads.
Ay, sleep awa citie, ma douce raucle citie,
sleep weel an sleep deep
wi yuir mirk-mockan een.

NORMAN McCAIG   1910–

I Remember You

The boat sits stuck in light, the water
lies heavy as honey ; and which
is stiller, the supple air or the grey
boulder lichened on the beach ?

Here, one would think, is a whole legend,
not to be added to, caught and held
in the still hallucination of summer
that honeys to blue the breathless wood.

But through the pine-tops slants the mallard
down to its gushing arrowhead ;
it makes a whole mountain tremble ;
it waves the arras of green shade.

257

So Many Make One

There are so many deaths that go
to make up death, as a grown man
is the walking grave of boy after boy.—
Sometimes we see in him the frown

of a forsaken ghost, or a dead boy
speaks suddenly in a petulant voice ;
six feet of blood have drowned so many.
But when death itself comes face to face

with us round that dreadful turning, will
all its ancestors be alive—
shall we, one moment, in its smile
see innocence and belief and love ?

The Last Week of the Year

The last week of the year's no time
for contemplating days like orchards.
They hide below ground their tot of bushels
and would spill over a million baskets.

For you below ground are hidden too
and overspill my every measure.
I with my buried hands will be
gathering you in all my future.

And in the last week of some year
I'll tell myself, ' O why remember
this toss and shine of flowers that all
the winter winds now fail to scatter ? '

Instrument and Agent

In my eye I've no apple ; every object
enters in there with hands in pockets.
I welcome them all, just as they are,
every one equal, none a stranger.

Yet in the short journey they make
to my skull's back, each takes a look
from another, or a gesture, or
a special way of saying Sir.

So tree is partly girl ; moon
and wit slide through the sky together ;
and which is star ?—what's come a million
miles or gone those inches farther ?

No Time, No Time

The day's impatient, but you sit still
with weeks to spend, as though no roses
ever yielded to a bitter air
and stepped out of their fallen graces.

The clouds go busily by ; the light
moves sideways, sniffing in every corner ;
the wind seeks what it never finds,
turning the glittering rubbish over.

And trees dance like children, roofs
wink and blink like exclamations.
The precious minutes go by ; and you
sit in the ring of four seasons.

But you've no season ; and on your hands
the loaded ships of days are stranded.
You prove no rose has ever died ;
you prove that no song ever ended.

GEORGE SCOTT-MONCRIEFF 1910-

The Toad

Lighten, Lord, my load ;
   I no beast of brawn
But tired and troubled toad,
   A simple son of spawn.

A harmless, foolish toad
   Whom dog disdains to clutch,
Who shuns the hurtful road
   But loves the lawn's touch.

Encourage me who creep
   With warted limb and back,
And send me gentle sleep
   When winter cometh back.

And I will worship well
   In manner of my mind,
Fold fingers, hunch, and tell
   The garden *God is kind*.

STUART HOOD   1910-

Du Rote Fahn'

Displenish sales and public roups
O auld, cohaiket, creesh-mairkt things—

The jummelt and forfauchen doups
That time aneth the mell-straik brings :
Ye mairk them a'.
Though tasht wi wind and splairged wi glaur,
You're aye unfurled,
Sune tae be mairkin—nane the waur—
' Roup o the Ragments o ae Warld,'
Lock, stock, and a' :
The auld een sauld, a noo een bocht ;
But no for nocht.

T. S. L A W

Lynes Scryveit til Henry P. Cameron

Cameron, whit's wrocht i the cleveralitie
  O weans whilk aye maun gar us byde kilhabbit
In oorsels whan raxin athort the years we dree,
  Undeemous in our grunshin darg, aye tholein the crabbit
Luiks o Tyme glowerin fae oor eternal bourne and queem ?

  Suddentlyke, amang the wandocht kanglin leid o the streets,
Twaa-fauldit i my ain mense for aa yae dream
  O a Scottis lawtithheid leal as the orrie gates
Bi whilk aa bairns i blytheheid haud thaem hame
  Whaur instinct is wi reason evendoon
Lik burds in haillhertheid sib til the wame
  O strussle, thaem aa yin aflocht i the luft whan soun'
Is tid wi feathers and the sugh or blast o air,

There, Cameron, i the hert o your leid I kent me there.

Epitaph

Yird him, yird snod the muckle nyaff o him.
Swith noo, hap him wi stoor an stanes, swith, owre
The sumph whause glinkin glisk o a sowl was dim
As tynt luve taivert wi a tüme luve's glower.

A hauflin bit craitur, noo een lat him be
Nocht haill avaa cep in yae weirdit nicht
Whilk has for truth yae kingheid honestie
We ken stravaigin ben nae-licht an licht.

A bittock span for dool as muckle's his ain
Dreams roost hissel, baith less nor sax füt tall ;
Lowsit fae blytheheid, sleekit inbye alane
His ain sel, yird him, eemage o us all.

Syne Resurrectioun, alane lat byde
Nocht else nor oors whan this paer corp maun hyde.

BERNARD FERGUSSON   1911 -

The Tryst

She was the lassie to redd the house
    And bake the scones on the fire ;
He was the laddie to tent the cows
    And bring them ben to the byre.
These were the twa ; and sure they swore
    To meet at the road-end late :
'Twas the lassie that never cam but the door,
    And the laddie that gaed his gate.

A sodger laddie that stands and daffs
    At the slock of a clarty close,
With a queyn o' the toun that lichtly laughs
    Wi' lips as reid as a rose ;
A farmer's lassie that dreams o' both,
    And greets, for she canna sleep
For the bitter thought of a broken troth
    And a tryst that she didna keep.

Bu tu camhanaich

Bu tu camhanaich air a' Chuilthionn
's latha suilbhir air a' Chlàraich,
grian air a h-uilinn anns an òr-shruth
agus ròs geal bristeadh fàire.

Lainnir sheòl air linne ghrianaich,
gorm a' chuain is iarmailt àr-bhuidh,
an òg-mhaduinn 'na do chuailean
's 'na do ghruaidhean soilleir àlainn.

Mo leug camhanaich is oidhche
t' aodann 's do choibhneas gràdhach,
ged tha bior glas an dòlais
troimh chliabh m' òg-mhaidne sàthte.

Cha do chuir de bhuaireadh

Cha do chuir de bhuaireadh riamh
no thrioblaid dhian 'nam chré
allaban Chrìosda air an talamh
no muillionan nan speur.

'S cha d' ghabh mi suim de aisling bhaoith—
coille uaine tìr an sgeòil—
mar leum mo chridhe rag ri tuar
a gàire 's cuailein òir.

Agus chuir a h-àilleachd sgleò
air bochdainn 's air creuchd sheirbh
agus air saoghal tuigse Leninn,
air fhoighidinn 's air fheirg.

Ye Were the Dawn

Ye were the dawn on the hills o the Coolin,
the bousum day on the Clarach arisan,
the sun on his elbucks i the gowden flume,
the whyte rose-fleur that braks the horizon.

Gesserant sails on a skinklan frith,
gowd-yalla lyft and blue o the sea . . .
the fresh mornin in your heid o hair
and your clear face wi its bonnie blee.

Gowdie, my gowdie o dawn and the derk,
your loesome gentrice, your brou sae rare . . .
albeid wi the dullyart stang o dule
the breist o youth's been thirlit sair.

[*trans.* Douglas Young]

I never kent sic glawmerie

I never kent sic glawmerie
nor stauchert frae sae stark a stound
at thocht o Christ's duil on the yird
or millions o the mappamound.

I hae taen nae sic tent o haiverel dreams—
mirk-wrocht mirligoes o glede—
as ma dour hert hankert for the smool
o her smile, and the glint o her gowden heid.

The shadow frae her beauty lay
owre poortith and a waesome scauth,
and the warld o Lenin's intellect,
his pouer o patience and his wrath.

[*trans.* Robert Garioch]

Ban-Ghaidheal

Am faca Tu i, Iudhaich mhóir,
ri an abrar Aon Mhac Dhé ?
Am fac' thu a coltas air Do thriall
ri strì an fhìon-lios chéin ?

An cuallach mheasan air a druim,
fallus searbh air mala is gruaidh ;
's a' mhios chreadha trom air cùl
a cinn chrùibte, bhochd, thruaigh.

Cha n-fhaca Tu i, Mhic an t-saoir,
ri an abrar Rìgh na Glòir,
am measg nan cladach carrach, siar,
fo fhallus cliabh a lòin.

An t-earrach so agus so chaidh
's gach fichead earrach bho an tùs
tharruing ise an fheamainn fhuar
chum biadh a cloinn is duais an tùir.

Is gach fichead foghar tha air triall
chaill i samhradh buidh nam blàth ;
is threabh an dubh chosnadh an clais
tarsuinn mìnead ghil a clàir.

Agus labhair T' eaglais chaomh
mu staid chaillte a h-anama thruaigh ;
agus leag an cosnadh dian
a corp gu sàmchair dhuibh an uaigh.

Is thriall a tìm mar shnighe dubh
a' drùdhadh tughaidh fàrdaich bochd ;
mheal ise an dubh chosnadh cruaidh ;
is glas a cadal suain an nochd.

Hielant Woman

Hae ye seen her, ye unco Jew,
ye that they caa Ae Son o God?
Thon trauchlit woman i the far vine-yaird,
saw ye the likes o her on your road?

A creelfu o corn upo her spaul,
swyte on her brou, saut swyte on her cheek,
a yirthen pat on the tap o her heid,
her laigh bouit heid, dwaiblie and sick.

Ye haena seen her, ye son o the vricht,
wi 'King o Glory' fowk roose ye weel,
on the staney westland machars thonder
swytan under her wechtit creel.

This spring o the year is by and gane
and twenty springs afore it spent,
sin she's hikeit creels o cauld wrack
for her bairns' meat and the laird's rent.

Twenty hairsts hae dwineit awa,
she's tint her simmer's gowden grace,
while the sair trauchle o the black wark
pleud its rigg on her clear face.

Her puir saul is eternallie tint,
as threeps aye your kindly Kirk;
and endless wark has brocht her corp
to the graff's peace, lown and derk.

Her time gaed by like black sleek
through an auld thaikit hous-rig seepan;
she bruikit aye sair black wark
and gray the nicht is her lang sleepin.

[*trans.* Douglas Young]

bho *An Cuilthionn*

Có seo, có seo, oidhche dhona ?
Có seo ag coiseachd air a' mhonadh ?
Ceumannan spioraid ri mo thaobh
agus ceumannan ciùin' mo ghaoil,
ceumannan, ceumannan, air na sléibhtean,
monmhar cheumannan ag éirigh :
ceumannan fiadhta, ceumannan ciùine,
ceumannan èalaidh, socair, mùinte.

Có seo, có seo oidhche dunaidh ?
Có seo ag coiseachd air a' mhullach ?
Tanasg eanchainne luime nochdta,
fuar ri aognuidheachd an torchairt.

Có seo, có seo oidhche 'n spioraid ?
Chan 'eil ach tanasg lom cridhe,
manadh leis fhéin a' falbh a' smaointinn,
cliabh feòil-rùisgte air an aonach.

Có seo, có seo oidhche 'chridhe ?
Chan 'eil ach an nì do-ruighinn,
an samhladh a chunnaic an t-anam,
Cuilthionn ag éirigh thar mara.

Có seo, có seo oidhche 'n anama
a' leantainn fiarachd an leòis fhalbhaich ?
Chan 'eil, chan 'eil ach am falbhan
a' sireadh a' Chuilthinn thar fairge.

Có seo, có seo oidhche 'chinne ?
Chan 'eil ach samhladh an spioraid,
anam leis fhéin a' falbh air sléibhtean,
ag iargan a' Chuiltinn 's e' g éirigh.

Finale of *The Coolin*

Who goes there on an evil night ?
Who goes marching across the height ?
Steps of a spirit here at my side,
the gentle steps of my love, my pride :
steps, steps on the hills ascending,
the thud of steps swelling and blending :
steps gentle and steps wild,
stealthy steps, disciplined, mild.

Who's there on a night of unrest ?
Who goes marching on the summit crest ?
The wraith of a bare naked brain,
cold with agony's chilling pain.

Who goes there on the spirit's night ?
The wraith of a heart, naked and slight,
a phantom alone with its thoughts and hopes,
a fleshless skeleton on the stone-slopes.

Who goes there on the night of the heart ?
A thing unreachable by any art,
the ghost seen by the soul's devotion,
a Coolin rising beyond the ocean.

Who goes there on the soul's night,
following the shifts of the wandering light ?
Only the voyager, travelling free,
seeking the Coolin over the sea.

Who goes there on the night of humanity ?
The spirit's ghost, a thing of vanity,
a lone soul on the peaks contending,
yearning for the Coolin and it ascending.

Thar lochan fala clann nan daoine,
thar breòiteachd blàir is strì an aonaich,
thar bochdainn, caithimh, fiabhrais, àmhghair,
thar ana-cothrom, eucoir, ainneart, ànradh,
thar truaighe, eu-dòchas, gamhlas, cuilbheart,
thar ciont is truaillidheachd, gu furachair,
gu treunmhor, chithear an Cuilthionn
's e 'g éirigh air taobh eile duilghe.

Coin is Madaidhean-allaidh

Thar na sìorruidheachd, thar a sneachda,
chì mi mo dhàin neo-dheachdte :
chì mi lorgan an spòg a' breacadh
gile shuaimhneach an t-sneachda ;
calg air bhoile, teanga fala,
gadhair chaola 's madaidhean-allaidh,
a' leum thar mullaichean nan gàradh
a' ruith fo sgàil nan craobhan fàsail,
ag gabhail cumhang nan caol ghleann,
a' sireadh caisead nan gaoth-bheann ;
an langan gallanach a' sianail
thar loman cruaidhe nan àm cianail,
an comhartaich bhiothbhuan na mo chluasan,
an deann-ruith ag gabhail mo bhuadhan ;
réis nam madadh 's nan con iargalt
luath air tòrachd na fiadhach,
troimh na coilltean gun fhiaradh,
thar mullaichean nam beann gun shiaradh ;
coin chiùine cuthaich mo bhàrdachd,
madaidhean air tòir na h-àilleachd,
àilleachd an anama 's an aodainn,
fiadh geal thar bheann is raointean,
fiadh do bhòidhichid chiùin, ghaolaich,
fiadhach gun sgur, gun fhaochadh.

Beyond mankind's blood in lakes,
the battlefield's rotting, the climb's aches,
poverty, consumption, fever, stress,
brutality, fraud, violence, distress,
misery, despair, malice, meanness,
crime and filth, rising in keenness
the Coolin is seen, with heroic glow
rising on the far side of woe.

[*trans*. Douglas Young]

Dogs and Wolves

Across eternity, across its snow,
   I see my unborn poems ; the paw-marks breaking
The harsh white of the snow ; fur starting,
Bloody-tongued lean dogs and wolves, mad chasing
   Across the dykes, mad racing
Beneath the wild tree shadows, parting
The pass of the narrow glens, taking
   The sweep and the gale-blow
Of the hills ; their throaty howls rending
Across the stark bareness of this time,
   Their eternal baying in my ears,
   Their hot rush taking my bounds
Of mind ; a race of wolves and ghostly hounds,
Swift chase of the hunt through the tiers
Of words without turning, across the sheer climb
Of the tops of the mountains unbending ;
   Mad gentle dogs of my songs, lean wolves in chase
   Of beauty, the beauty of soul, the beauty of face,
   White deer across hill and desolate space,
   Deer of gentle loved loveliness ; and my songs wolves, wending
   A chase without waiting, a chase without ending.

[*trans*. J. M. Russell]

An Trom-Laighe

Oidhche de 'n dà bhliadhna
'N uair shaoil mi gun do chreuchdadh
Mo luaidh le giamh cho miosa
'S a bh' air mnaoi bho linn Eubha,
Bha sinn comhla am bruadar
Ri taobh a' bhalla chloiche
Tha eadar cluich ghart ghillean
Is nighean mo cheud sgoile,
Bha i eadar mo lamhan
'S mo bheul a' dol g'a bilibh
'N uair straon an ceann oillteil
Bho chul a' bhalla 'n clisgeadh,
Is rinn na cràgan ciara
Fada bréine mo sgornan
A ghlacadh an greim obann
'S lean briathran an eu-dochais :
' Tha thu ghloic air dheireadh.'

Calbharaigh

Cha n-eil mo shùil air Calbharaigh
no air Bethlehem an àigh
ach air cùil ghrod an Glaschu
far bheil an lobhadh fàis
agus air seòmar an Dun-éideann,
seòmar bochdainn 's cràidh
far am bheil an naoidhean creuchdach
ri aonagraich gu 'bhàs.

The Widdreme

Ae nicht o thae twa year
Whan I thocht ma luve
Was strak wi a skaith as dure
As wumman's had sen Eve,
We were thegither in a dwaum
By the stane dyke that stauns
Atween the loons' and lassies' yairds
O ma first schuil.
                              Ma airms
Were round her an ma lips
Seekan her mou
Whan the laithlie gorgon's heid stuid up
On a sudden frae hint the waa,
And the lang mirk ugsome fingers graipt
Ma craig wi a sidden grup—
An than the words o weirdless dule :
' Owre blate, ye fuil ! '

[*trans.* Sydney Goodsir Smith]

My een are nae on Calvary

My een are nae on Calvary
or the Bethlehem they praise,
but on shitten back-lands in Glesga toun
whaur growan life decays,
and a stairheid room in an Embro land,
a chalmer o puirtith and skaith,
whaur monie a shilpet bairnikie
gaes smoorit doun til daith.

[*trans.* Douglas Young]

J. F. HENDRY

from *The Orchestral Mountain*

(A Symphonic Elegy)

Drums thinner than dreams—
Trumpets fainter than streams—
Songs unsung in a speechless tongue,

Are louder for love than cymbals,
Clearer than bugles.
No rifle ranges the distance of eagles.

Out of the light of the night
Of love, into the day's sharp doom
Only the white dove flies

Frightened by sun whose eyes
Start hardened shapes and bright
Breaking into sacrificial bloom,

A cloud, both touch and sight
In one ; a death, whose parting breath
Frees the spirit's lightning.

DOUGLAS YOUNG   1913-

Last Lauch

The Minister said it wald dee,
   the cypress-buss I plantit.
But the buss grew til a tree,
   naething dauntit.

It's growan, stark and heich,
    derk and straucht and sinister,
kirkyairdielike and dreich.
    But whaur's the Minister ?

Love

Gie aa, and aa comes back
    wi mair nor aa.
Hain ocht, and ye'll hae nocht,
    aa flees awa.

For the Old Highlands

That old lonely lovely way of living
in Highland places,—twenty years a-growing,
twenty years flowering, twenty years declining,—
father to son, mother to daughter giving
ripe tradition ; peaceful bounty flowing ;
one harmony all tones of life combining,—
old wise ways, passed like the dust blowing.

That harmony of folk and land is shattered,—
the yearly rhythm of things, the social graces,
peat-fire and music, candle-light and kindness.
Now they are gone it seems they never mattered,
much, to the world, those proud and violent races,
clansmen, and chiefs whose passioned greed and blindness
made desolate these lovely lonely places.

For a Wife in Jizzen

Lassie, can ye say
    whaur ye ha been,
whaur ye ha come frae,
    whatna ferlies seen ?

Eftir the bluid and swyte,
    the warsslin o yestreen,
ye ligg forfochten, whyte,
    prouder nor onie Queen.

Albeid ye hardly see me
    I read it i your een,
sae saft blue and dreamy,
    mindan whaur ye've been.

Anerly wives ken
    the ruits o joy and tene,
        the march o daith and birth,
            the tryst o love and strife
    i the howedumbdeidsuinsheen,
        fire, air, water, yirth
            mellan to mak new life,
        lauchan and greetan, feiman and serene.

Dern frae aa men
    the ferlies ye ha seen.

Winter Homily on the Calton Hill

These chill pillars of fluted stone
shine back the lustre of the leaden sky,
stiff columns clustered on a dolerite hill
in solemn order, an unperfected vision

dimly gleaming.   Not at random thrown
like old Greek temples that abandoned lie
with earthquake-riven drums.   Rigid and chill
this still-born ruin stands for our derision.

A fine fantasy of the Whig literati
to build a modern Athens in our frore islands,
those elegant oligarchs of the Regency period,
Philhellenic nabobs and the Scots nobility.
As soon expect to meet a bearded Gujerati
stravaiging in a kilt throu the uttermost Highlands,
or in Princes Street gardens a coy and blushing Nereid.
Athens proved incapable of such mobility.

Is the thing meaningless, as it is astonishing,
a senseless fantasy, out of time and place ?
Aping foreign fashions is always derisible,
and mimicry, for Plato, was the soul's unmaking.
The ruin is symbolic, a symbol admonishing
Scottish posterity.   Seekers after grace
must not imitate the outward and visible.
The culture of Athens was a nation's awaking.

Simplon Tunnel

The bens are nae ayebydan.   Frost and sun,
   rain and the winds fret doun the proudest hicht.
   See thonder Monte Rosa's massy micht,
whas spelderan snaws skinkle tae mak ye blin'.
Its thretteen thousand feet that rise abuin
   the Val d' Anzasca like a touer o licht
   sall aa ligg laigh and level.   Time sall dicht
the hale warld epple-round or aa be duin.

But Nature's forces wark owre slaw for Man,
    whas life is brief, whilk gars him mak mair speed.
    He terraces his roadweys up the glens,
    wins out their ores for steel, brings til ae heid
        their water-pouer, and tunnels throu the bens.
Sall warld-wide peace owretax his hairns tae plan ?

G. S. FRASER   1914-

Lean Street

Here, where the baby paddles in the gutter,
    Here in the slaty greyness and the gas,
Here where the women wear dark shawls and mutter
    A hasty word as other women pass,

Telling the secret, telling, clucking and tutting,
    Sighing, or saying that it served her right,
The bitch !—the words and weather both are cutting
    In Causewayend, on this November night.

At pavement's end and in the slaty weather
    I stare with glazing eyes at meagre stone,
Rain and the gas are sputtering together
    A dreary tune !   O leave my heart alone.

O leave my heart alone, I tell my sorrows,
    For I will soothe you in a softer bed
And I will numb your grief with fat to-morrows
    Who break your milk teeth on this stony bread !

They do not hear.   Thought stings me like an adder,
    A doorway's sagging plumb-line squints at me,
The fat sky gurgles like a swollen bladder
    With the foul rain that rains on poverty.

Meditation of a Patriot

The posters show my country blonde and green,
Like some sweet siren, but the travellers know
How dull the shale sky is, the airs how keen,
And how our boorish manners freeze like snow.
Romantic Scotland was an emigrant,
Half-blooded, and escaped from sullen weather.
Here, we toss off a dram to drown a cough
And whisky has the trade-mark of the heather.
My heart yearns southwards as the shadows slant,
I wish I were an exile and I rave :
      With Byron and with Lermontov
      Romantic Scotland's in the grave.

In Glasgow, that damned sprawling evil town,
I interview a vulgar editor,
Who, brawny, self-made, looks me up and down
And seems to wonder what my sort is for.
Do I write verse ?   Ah, man, but that is bad. . . .
And, too polite, I fawn upon this tough,
But when I leave him, O my heart is sad.
He sings alone who in this province sings.
I kick a lamp-post, and in drink I rave :
      With Byron and with Lermontov
      Romantic Scotland's in the grave.

In the far islands to the north and west
Mackenzie and MacDiarmid have their peace.
St Andrews soothes that critic at her breast
Whose polished verse ne'er gave his soul release.
I have no islands and no ancient stone,
Only the sugary granite glittering crisp
Pleases the eye, but turns affection off,
Hard rhetoric, that never learned to lisp.

This town has beauty, but I walk alone
And to the flat and sallow sands I rave :
    With Byron and with Lermontov
    Romantic Scotland's in the grave.

ANN SCOTT-MONCRIEFF   1914-43

A Night in the Country

Oh, what a glister's to the wintry night !
Whan aa the company are gleg and bien.
In the fank o silence made by mountains
They're birlan wi an oorie quean.

They're birlan doon a yellow wine
Far glintier nor her hair,
And aye their sauls are gashant wi laughter,
And aye she laughs the mair.

Oh, whativer maks the anaphrodisiacal
Wine sae sig and warm ?
Tyned fleurs gie their deemless pouer
Wi lees o love for barm.

Up raves the fire more roary than the host,
It rouchles in the lum, and
Glims in gawsy glass, and luely in their een
Mid brash and bummand !

ALEXANDER GALLOWAY   1914-

The Ploughman

The tank had grund him to the yirth,
    And trailed him through the mire :

His bonnie flesh has dunged a land
   Far frae his native shire.

And, whan his brithers plew at hame,
   The love-fraught hour 'll see,
Within the dulse broon o the yirth
   The glintin o his ee.

R. CROMBIE SAUNDERS   1914–

The Panthers

Within the confines of this room
My thoughts like hunting panthers roam.
In fields outside grey figures sow
Their furrows while the gulls pursue.

The clamour on the mountain slope
Threatens the immemorial sleep
That guards this valley, as the sheer
Rock-cliffs of the island shore

Guard the small fields.   But time will get
Its own revenge.   The rotting gate
Swings in the wind.   And the disdained
Slow waves will be victors in the end.

And where a mountain stood will rise
The white gulls in their old carouse,
And in my room the panthers drowse
Till on each claw the red blood dries.

Sonnet

Dear, nou, gin sic response were aa I kent
As micht intern my life in povertie,

Lackan but luve, I wud be weel content ;
I hadna then this sair perplexitie.
An though fordelyd langin rocht my hert
Wi thinkin o that happy ither day,
I hadna fund in treason sae apert
Ane servitour wha staw my traist away.

Or gin mysel an luve had ches to flee
Out o thy hert thegither, I wud dree
Mair lichtly though my gledness suld be skaith.

But, ach, the ghaist that glowers in our bed
Is o a bairn that lang embraced us baith
An nou is rengan in his faither's stead.

DAVID MARTIN   1915-

Lament for the Gordons

I sing of the Gordons,
  Lament to young soldiers,
Who never came back to the land of their kin.
  O Lowland and Highland !
  On Singapore Island
Your sons fell for freedom and bonny Prince Tin.

Be silent now, Greenock,
  Dundee and Auld Reekie,
And silent the winches on Forth and on Clyde,
  When Scotland is sleeping,
  Sweet lassies are weeping
For lads who will never lie down by their side.

How far from Malaya
To snowy Ben Doran ?
How far from Johore to Saltcoats or Ross ?
No pipes and orations
On rubber plantations,
O chimes of Saint Andrew, how far Glasgow Cross ?

The Gordons are children
Of shipwrights and crofters,
Strong like the stormwind and tender as rain,
O that our cherished
Young eagles have perished,
And none of the gin-sodden planters was slain.

I sing of the Gordons,
Lament to brave soldiers,
They will not come home to their land and their wives.
O Lowlands and Highlands
And all the small islands—
Don't wait for the transport that never arrives.

DERICK THOMSON

An Loch-a-Tuath

Tha 'n iarmailt ciùin, 'san Loch-a-Tuath
'na laighe suaint' fo bhrat na h-oidhch',
's cha ghlac mo bhreithneachadh a chaoidh,
ged shiubhladh i air iteig luath,

cion-fath an aoibhneis a tha 'falbh
mar airgiod-beò air leac mo smuain,
no cobhar bàn air clàr a' chuain,
no soillseadh reuil 'san anmoch bhalbh.

GEORGE CAMPBELL HAY   1915-

Grunnd na Mara

' Tha iad ann an grunnd na mara,
is cha b' e sud an rogha cala '—
rug sud orm o dh'fhalbh mo mhacan,
an cuilean a bhithinn 'ga thatadh,
a dheanadh gàire 'na mo ghlacaibh.

Thàinig an seann sgeul air a chasan.
Tha 'n speur ag ciaradh mu fheasgar,
goir aig na h-eòin air na sgeirean,
geumnaich a' chruidh a' teachd dhachaidh,
éigheach nan giullan anns a' bhaile,
s mi'm thurraman leam fhéin mu'n chagailt,
a' smuaineachadh air na bh' agam.

Chì mi do chòta air an tarran,
is, och ! an tigh gun fhuaim, gun fhacal,
an stairsneach nach bi fuaim chas oirr',
an seòmar fàs s an leabaidh fhalamh.

The Loch o the North

The loch o the North i the quaet air
Liggs happit sleepan ablow nicht's coat,
And ma thochts canna rax til the haudin o't
(Tho fleean on swithest wings they were)—

The maik o thon ecstasie that's roaman
Quicksiller ower the stane o ma notion
Like whytest faem on the briest o the ocean
Or skinklin o starns i the quaet gloamin.

[*trans.* Alexander Scott]

The Grund o the Sea

' Thonder they ligg on the grund o the sea,
nae the hyne whaur they wald be.'
Siccan a thing has happenit me
sin my son's been gane. When he was wee
I dannlit the bairn like a whelpikie
and he leuch i ma airms richt cantilie.
It's the auld weird nou I maun dree.
The luft grows derk, the sun gangs laigh,
atour the skerries the sea-maws skreigh,
the rowtan kye come shauchlan doun,
the laddies rant out-throu the toun ;
but here I rock at the fire my lane,
mindan o him I had that's gane.
I see your jacket on the heuk,
but the hous is lown in ilka neuk,
never a sound or a word i the room,
nae sclaffin o buits on the threshart-stane,

285

Ma's e an osna théid fada,
cluinnear m'osnaich far an laigh thu
'nad chadal luasganach san fheamainn,
s na fuathan a' sìor dhol seachad,
cruthanna aognaidh na mara !

(*Am marbh a' bruidhinn*)
' Eisd, a bhean, is na bi rium,
is truimide mo dhìol do bhròn ;
sgàin is leagh an long fo 'r buinn—
thriall an cuimhn' an cois an deò.
Lunnainn a mharbh mi,
a mhill an tsùil nach fhaca i.
Theagamh gu'm b' aithne dhomh thu,
sgùr an sàl mo chuimhne nis.
Tha mi air sabhd sa' chuan mhór ;
Bu Domhnall mise an dé.
Laigh do ghul orm 'na lòd,
ge b' e có thu, a bhean, éisd.'

Mo losgadh, mhuinntir nan Eilean,
is daor a phàigh sibh mórachd Bhreatainn !

Aonarain na Cille

Ochan, aonarain na cille,
gach aon 'na ionad fhéin fa leth,
'na thighearna air tigh gun tathaich
far nach dèanar farraid air.
Cha n-éirich grian ann no reul,
cha tig neul no fras no gaoth,
gormadh an là no 'n dùthrath,
sìth no ùspairt, gràin no gaol.

the bed cauld and the chalmer toom.
Gin it's the sech that traivels far,
ye'll here my sechin whaur ye are,
sleepan i the wrack, jundied aye,
wi ugsome ferlies sooman by,
the ghaistlie monsters o the sea.

' Wheesht, woman, wheesht, and deavena me.
My wae's the mair to see ye greet.
The ship brak doun under our feet,
life gaed aff, and memorie wi't.
London slew me, weary faa't,
connacht the een that never saw it.
Aiblins I was acquent wi you,
the saut has reengit my memorie nou.
Here I stravaig i the merchless faem,
yestreen Donald was my name.
The wecht o your wae liggs sair on me.
Woman, wheesht, whae'er ye be.'

Sair the price maun be dounpitten
by the island-fowk for the greatness o Britain.

[trans. Douglas Young]

The Solitaries

Wae for the lanely kirkyaird fowk,
ilk ane in his place pit past for aye,
maister o a hous whaur nane chaps,
nane ettles to speir gin he's inby.
Sun risesna nor starn thonder,
clud nor shouer nor wind move,
bluein o day comesna nor derkenin,
peace nor tulzie, grame nor love.

[trans. Douglas Young]

To a Certain Loch Fyne Fisherman who Keeps to the Old Ways

Calum thonder, long's the night to your thinking,
nightlong till dawn and the sun set at the tiller,
age and the cares of four and a boat to keep you
high in the stern, alone for the winds to weary.

A pillar set in the shifting moss, a beacon
fixed in the wandering sea and the changing waters,
bright in the midnight waves and the hidden terrors ;
the ancient yew of the glen, not heeding the ages.

Set among men that waver like leaves on the branches,
still among minds that flicker like light on the water ;
those are the shadows of clouds, the speckled and fleeting,
you are the hill that stands through shadow and sunlight.

Little you heed, or care to change with changes,
to go like a broken branch in the grip of a torrent ;
you are your judge and master, your sentence unshaken,
a man with a boat of his own, and a mind to guide her.

The Three Brothers

Thon nicht the three pit the sails ty her,
    cheerily, heidin home from Ayrshire ;
a gale o southerly wund cem on them
    by the Coomra Licht, but they werena carin.

Oot thonder by Garroch Heid she trevelled,
    runnin like smok, and her daicks streamin ;
when the rip was risin roon her gunnel,
    seas that wad swalla, she didna heed them.

288

West she trampt, and the white ridges
  like bochkans oot o the nicht cem breengin
agenst her quaarter.   Slack they werna
  thon nicht, but the nicht had a sore endin.

It wasna the wave that the wund wekkent,
  a steep-faced sea brekkin aboard her,
nor a white lump shaken over her shouthers
  that fillt her, so that she sank below them.

Ootside o Laggan Heid it struck her.
  Doon from the home hills cem boondin
a livin squaal that whuppt the watter.
  Her mast bent lik a rash, and over it threw her.

To ther folk's hoos cem the hann o somethin,
  thro the derk to the door, and clasht upon it,
three times.   At thon uncanny knockin
  they couldna speak for the thochts that wer in them.

Ther eyes stood in ther heid, starin,
  and they wisht they couldna hear the howlin
that the wund med, and the soonn o the brekkers
  doon on the shore.   But it aye was louder.

They gazet in the fire wi gash faces,
  and nivar talkt, for they couldna speak it.
They werna for lyin doon or sleepin,
  and they darna say for why they werna.

Afore the brekk o day in the moarnin,
  when it wasna derk and it wasna dawnin,
from the rocks on the rhu they heard a cryin,
  a *céinteach's* keenin.   They kent ther story.

They kent what thon sore cry was sayin,
 and whose lair was laid in the wrack and seaweed,
and they sat there wi the day brekkin,
 grey face on the men and the wummen greetin.

JOHN SINGER

Smooth on the Aftermath

Smooth on the aftermath came an iron law,
And each man, turning to his neighbour, saw a truth,
Saw truth, saw a furtive and fearful truth
In the averted eye and astonished jaw.
It is I, it is us, it is all of us,
It is we who are responsible for this.

Smooth on the aftermath came an iron law,
And a shudder rolled like a wave and a warning through masses,
Through the sudden collective body and blood of the group,
Like a trapped animal guilty of animal sin,
Guilty of betraying its inmost moving and meaning,
It is I, it is us, it is all of us.

Smooth on the aftermath came an iron law,
And a knowledge trickled and crept like the source of a torrent,
And a wisdom and power was born in the womb of submission,
Burning and growing, O quick with the stamen of freedom,
It is I, it is us, it is all of us,
It is we who will change, who will tower above this.

The Mither's Lament

What care I for the leagues o sand,
The prisoners and the gear they've won ?
My darlin liggs amang the dunes
Wi mony a mither's son.

Doutless he deed for Scotland's life ;
Doutless the statesmen dinna lee ;
But och tis sair begrutten pride
And wersh the wine o victorie !

Largo

Ae boat anerlie nou
Fishes frae this shore,
Ae black drifter lane
Riggs the crammasie daw,
Aince was a fleet, and nou
Ae boat alane gaes oot.

War ir Peace, the trawlers win
And the youth turns awa
Bricht wi baubles nou
And thirled tae factory ir store ;
Their faithers fished their ain,
Unmaistered ;—ane remains.

And never the clock rins back,
The free days are owre ;
The warld shrinks, we luik
Mair t'oor maisters ilka hour—
Whan yon lane boat I see
Daith and rebellion blinn ma ee !

Sahara

Inexorable on ye stride,
Fate, like a desart wund ;
Agin yir vast unpassioned pride
I pit ma saul and haund,
As the wild Bedouin
Tykes gowl at the muin.

March, ye luveless Cailleach, blaw
Til the dumbest mirkest end,
And whan the yerth's a blastit skau
As toom Sahara brunt and blinnd
Thare, daft and damned wi raivan ee,
Adam, greinan tae be free.

Ye Mongers aye Need Masks for Cheatrie

Delacroix pentit Chopin's heid
No lik ithers a jessie hauf deid
But true, wi a neb lik a eagle's beak,
Een lik levin frae the thunner's crack,
His rasch face sterk wi pouer and daith
And aa the agonie o Poland's skaith.

Wha'll pent trulie Scotland's heid
Nae couthy gloam but mirk and reid ?
Skail yir myth o the Union year
Saw mob and riot but deil a cheer ?
Syne an Empire's biggit wi Scottis bluid
—But wha'd hae gane gin hame was guid ?

Ye mak a myth o a cheated land
As Chopin's made a lilly man ;

But truth wull screich and Scotland rid
Ye mongers as the Irish did ;
The bluid ye drave til ilka airt
Sall feed its ain reid sleepan hert.

For my Newborn Son

Blythe was yir comin,
Hert never dreamt it,
A new man bydan
In warld whan I've left it.

Bricht was yon morn,
Cauld in September,
Wi sun aa the causey
Glentered wi glamer,
Sclate roofs lik siller
Schire-bleezan yon morn.

Hert in my kist lep,
Joyrife its dirlin,
Bairn, whan oor lips met
Yir mither's were burnan,
Weet were oor een then,
Puir words downa tell it.

As hert never dreamt on
Was joy in yir comin,
Maikless wee nesslin,
Ma sleepan reid Robin.

from Under the Eildon Tree   VIII

I had a luve walked by the sea,
The waterfront at eenin,

Sol was a gowden pennie at our side
A bare league awa.
A wee boat wi a broun sail
Left the pier juist at our feet
And sailed awa intil the sunset
Silentlie, the water like a keekin-glass.
We spak nae word ava.
My luve turned til me wi her een
Owre-rin wi greit, and mine
Were weet wi the like mysterie.
We stude by the Pharos there
A lang while or the sun dwyned doun
And the gray-green simmer humin
Closed about the hyne.
Syne it grew cauld, and in my airms
I felt her trummlan
Wi the like undeemous mysterie did steek
My craig, sae's I couldna speak.

The Moment

The gaslicht flichtered on the stair,
The streaman cobbles black wi rain,
I held the auld warld's glamerie there
—And aa the greinan years were lain.

In our braith did past and future mell
And aa was as it aye had been,
I the nicht o space the globe was still
—Was't birth or daith we breathed yestreen?

Fowr year fleered up like paper then
And in the bleeze the future burned,
Your black een wild i the stacheran flame
As the wings o Fate abune us turned.

from *The New-rigged Ship*

Fou tid it was ;
the harr was gane ;
a gray-green smirr
flushit the bottom step o nicht,
whan,
quately,
forouten fuff,
forouten shoot,
forouten ony ceremonie,
the wee ship
slippit her cables
and lea'd the hyne.
A wee ship,
haudan oot til sea,
heidan fur the haaf,
a wee ship,
nae Leviathan,
trim and tait o sail,
and snod o graith,
and gleg for ony wather ;
gled,
tippie on the green-tapt swaws,
lichtsome on the purpour chirn o seas,
a wee ship
sails
awa, awa, frae daurkniss,
till,
abune the shooglan proo,
a new-born sun cam up,
encramasiean aa her sails,

mirlan aa her ropes wi gowd,
   and makan her
      intil
   a wee glore.

W. S. GRAHAM   1917–

from *The First Journey*

Launched three windy neptunes high from a gargoyle scree
My birth in a spittle of glass like the death of a lark
In a settling largo falls from the crucified height
Or in motion fearfully loves the rainbow waterspout
And climbs the myth, the tented miracle.
Born in a diamond screeched from a mountain pap
My faith with a hoof in myrtle considers the jig
Of the rowans and brambles rocked in the beanstalked moon.
Amen to the dark medusa freezing in air
With the plough in sparstone like the eyes of idols.
Without a song backward since spring bleeds the peat at my shin
My balancing giant so strideful of farewell words
Leads the tenderly mimicing feet of my wormward heart
On a weaving hair path gouged by a roving seal
Through mauve seas tasselled and trellissed in emerald.

Fourth Sonnet (1940)

  Sometimes the whisky-balanced miner sings
  On Saturday's bus-top swinging in the night,
  Brings through his pit-hoarse voice his lea rig heart
  And lifts from slag his fierce young poet's head.
  Sometimes a tear starts from the evervoid
  Threading from soul to time through time to soul.

296

And this love-kernel tear of Burns has forked
Out from the star-soul-splintering fields of time
And found this pit-shift-guarded centre prince.
Crumble the coal-bent hours.   The heart is here
Breaking in trees of song between the slags,
Rearing through spectrum voids in grains of time.
Sometimes the whisky-balanced miner sings
And brings through his dark voice the lea rig heart.

ANTONY ROSS   1918 –

Christ ran stumbling

Christ ran stumbling down the street
on little twisted feet ;
small blue hands over the place
where someone had bruised his face.
His starved, thin body shook with tears
and quick short gasps of fear.

Bitter the December day,
streets and sky an equal gray ;
no brightness, but the neoned pub
where city men with Christmas grin
forgetfully went out and in.

When did we see you ? folk will say,
at the last day.

To love, and more to love

To love, and more to love,
Is all the heart's desire ;
So springs the white fire
In which I burn.

I wandered far, dear Lord,
Before at last I came,
Wild, weary and in shame
Before Thy Word.

Come quickly ! Oh, consume
All that can hide Thy Face,
And in Thy loving grace,
Lord, keep me still.

TOM SCOTT   1917-

To X

Not because your body is lovely or your hair,
Nor those wombs of light where love suffers openly,
Nor only for the sphere our bodies make at night,
Though these contribute, dear, and flow toward.

But because of the tears and our human needs,
Because we met in the dark and bred a flame
That kindled in the ribs of each, though never together,
Fires that joined light across the seas that severed.

Because love is not ours to command or commend
But a wreath of fulfilment offering us
Ourselves through the gift of surrender :
Not to be treated coldly ever but made at home.

And because the heart mumbling over its isolation
Rehearses death in desiring all its fears
Till love unlocks its tethered floods
Unfolding slowly the humble mother and compasses.

298

Hurlygush

The hurlygush and hallyoch o the watter,
a-skinklan i the moveless simmer sun,
harles aff the scaurie mountain wi a yatter
that through ten-thoosand centuries has run.

Wi cheek agains the ash o wither't bracken,
I ligg at peace, and hear nae sound at aa
but yonder hurlygush that canna slacken,
through time and space mak never-endan faa.

As if a volley o the sound had caught me,
the saul o me gaes dounward lik a lynn
towards some faur, timeless pool whaur endless faain
wi ilka ither force is gethert in.

The Tunnel

(A Bairnsang)

I wuldna gae near thon tunnel gin I was you,
for losh, it's a muckle great dragon's gantan mou !

Frae faur and near, it sooks in screaman trains ;
and eftir it's swallow't them haill, you can hear its pains.

It burps oot smeik and soot when it's jist had its fill,
but when it gets hungry, it liggs that quate and still.

I wuldna gae near thon dragonish tunnel the nou,
for it's no had a train for hours, and it micht eat you !

299

John Knox

Who in his heart broke churches and burnt fugues,
walking across sprung heather in the sun,
darkness his head, his long gray beard like God's,
held virtue on an edge of ugliness,
stripped windows with a fanatic's delight,
raved bitter sermons to the baffled poor.

Who in his hand hurled an appalling Hell,
ground into atoms Grace beneath his staff,
hung preachers' plenty from his pulpit's pit,
brought stolid strength that stunned the source of love,
a fiery terror and the Lord of War !

THURSO BERWICK   1919-

Brig o Giants

(Fur Goodsir Smith an Mayakovsky)

An oot o aa calamitie there cam
Ane laverock, a-lowan wi the bleeze,
Thit anerlie the sangs o wund can gie,
Thit anerlie the wund frae oot the trees,
An sang ti me.

An wi his sang ane trummlin tuik ma hauns :
The Brig o Giants thit lowps acorss the Forth,
The Eiffel Tour thit pirouettes Paris,
The Dniepro Dam inheritan the Yerth,
Aa bowed ti me.

Frae Ferry owre ti Ferry ah hae lowpt
This mony a year, an watcht the workers dee ;

An watcht thir bairns luikan up at me,
Ti catch the siller, thit the tourists drappt,
And tears wur in ma ee.

Whilst war-ships, battle-in and battle-oot,
Hae sneakit oot an in ablowe ma knees,
Hae reekit roun an roun the Seevin Seas,
Pertectan ane nobilitie o loot,
Defendan lees.

Athout ane dout, the hauns thit gien me braith
Wur workers' hauns, wur hauns juist like yuir ain ;
An, och, ah'm eager, eager fur the passin o yuir pain.
Yuir hauns are worth ane rebirth on the Forth.
—Ah'm eager fur yuir gain.

Yuir Scottish passport's music in ma ears.
Ah'll radio yuir visit roun aa France.
Hou gled they'll be ti ken the Auld Alliance
Is fact again !   Ti mak up aa arrears,
Oor streets wull daunce.

Attention La France !   Attention all !
Til neus thit ye're onwytan lang lang years ;
Re-signed wi Scotland, Laund o Engineers,
The Auld Alliance !—Nae need ti mak ane call
Fur carnival.

The reid bank o the river's aa alowe,
Wi colourt fire, the fire o workers' een.
Bit Bourse is black.—Ah'll tap him wi ma paw.
Ah'll no hae ony insults ti ma freen.
Ma word is law.

Ay, France is no a circuit free o faults,
Bit wi ma voltage there's the dugs a-bark !

301

An there's the dauncers breengean oot the Park !
An freen—Pardon, La Concorde wants a waltz
—Ah'll suin be back.

Tovarisch Scotland !—Vodka richt awa !
Ah'm, proud ti tak yuir haun, an hou's the Clyde ?
Ah wish ye'd send some Clydesmen here ti bide,
Fur, gin it's true whit aa the warld says,
They'd patch ma pride.

Ye see, tovarisch, twis ane muckle clour
Ah got ; it damn near liquidated me.
Bit Bolsheviks are awfu sweirt ti dee.
An weel—the health o convalescence pouer
Til you and me !

O, Brig o Giants ! thit lowps acorss the Forth.
O, Eiffel Tour ! thit pirouettes Paris.
O, Dniepro Dam ! Inheritan the Yerth,
Ah thank ye fur yuir solidaritie :
Ah ken yuir worth.

An, whin yuir steel is alloyed wi the sang
O laverocks ; whin lords hae lost thir loot ;
Whin Bourse has gin the way thit Bourses gang ;
An Bolsheviks, thir convalescence oot,
Jyne in oor sang :
Athout ane dout,
Yuir steel wull shout, til ilka leaf,
Ane blithe salute.

HAMISH HENDERSON

from *The Highlanders at Alamein*

They move forward into nomans-land, a vibrant sounding-
board.

                    As they advance
the guns push further their murderous music.
Is this all they will hear, this raucous apocalypse ?
The spheres knocking in the night of heaven ?
The drummeling of overwhelming niagara ?
No !   For I can hear it !   Or is it ? . . .
                    Tell
me that I can hear it !   Now—listen !
                    Yes, hill and sheiling,
loch and sea-island, hear it, the yell
of your war-pipes scaling sound's mountains,
guns' thunder drowning in their soaring swell !
—The barrage gulfs them :   they're gulfed in the clumbering
      guns,
gulfed in gloom, gloom.   Dumb in the blunderbuss black—
Lost—gone in the anonymous cataract of noise.
Now again !   The shrill warsong :   it flaunts
aggression to the sullen desert.   It mounts.
                    Its scream
tops the Valkyrie, tops the colossal artillery.
Meaning that many
German Fascists will not be going home—
Meaning that many
will die, doomed in their false dream.
We'll mak siccar !
Against the bashing cudgel,
against the contemptuous triumphs of the big battalions,
mak siccar against the monkish adepts
of total war, against the oppressed oppressors,
mak siccar against the leaching lies,
against the worked out systems of sick perversion,
mak siccar against the executioner,
against the tyrannous myth and the real terror,
mak siccar.

Calvinist Sang

A hunder pipers canna blaw
   Wir trauchled times awa,
Drams canna droun them out, nor sang
Hap their scarecraw heids for lang.

Gin aa the warld was bleezan fou
   Whit gowk wald steer the plou ?
Gin chiels were cowpan quines aa day
They'd mak, but niver gaither, hay.

Pit by yir pipes and brak yir gless,
   Gie ower yir gallusness,
The day ye need a hert and harns
Dour as the diamant, cauld as the starns.

Coronach

(For the Dead of the 5/7th Battalion, The Gordon Highlanders)

Waement the deid
I never did,
Ower gled I was ane o the lave
That somewey baid alive
Tae trauchle my thowless hert
Wi ithers' hurt.

But nou that I'm far
Frae the fechtin's fear,
Nou I hae won awa frae aa thon pain
Back til my beuks and my pen,
They croud around me oot o the grave
Whar luve and langerie and blyness grieve.

Cryan the cauld words :
' We hae dree'd oor weirds,
But you that byde ahin,
Ayont oor ugsome hyne,
You are the flesh we aince hae been,
We that are bruckle brokken bane.'

Cryan a drumlie speak :
' You hae the words we spak,
You hae the sang
We canna sing,
Sen daith maun skail
The makar's skill.

' Maker, frae nou ye maun
Be singan for us deid men,
Sing til the warld we loo'd
For aa that its brichtness lee'd,
And tell hou the sudden nicht
Cam doun and made us nocht.'

Waement the deid
I never did,
But nou I am safe awa
I hear their wae
Greetan greetan dark and daw
Till I their biddin dae.

R. L. COOK   1921–

Bothwell at Malmo (1578)

The flowers are fled : they say that I am mad
    So often that I have begun to think

That they are right and I have reached the brink
　　That overlooks the pit where monsters pad,
Howling, and thirst to suck my ticking brain ;
　　To claw me down into oblivion :
It will be hard to fall from grace alone,
　　Without her lips to lull me out of pain.
The heavy castle presses like a tomb
　　Upon my mind, yet I can still remember
The delicate, proud lily of her face :
　　The breath of her last kiss kindles the gloom
　　　　To searing light, and then my heart's black ember
　　　　Springs into flame—and I recover grace.

Thocht on a Winter E'en

　　The mirk shaws teeth o steel-cauld ice ;
　　The glitterin' sun gangs birlan doun
　　Agin the velvet sky ; the gloam
　　Draps its grey feathers on the toun.

　　And nou the snawflakes daunder doun
　　And pouther owre the nekkid tree ;—
　　I wonder wull the wide warld end
　　Sae quiet-like, sae bonnily ?

GEORGE KAY　　　　　　　　　　　1924-

Rome

　　Last mercy to see,
　　In our mortal failing,
　　A Message flowering

306

(Through massive gloom,
Passage-roots of catacomb)—
Envy itself would give up the ghost.
    Rome's leaf is stone
    About the crown
    Of lonely columns
    Not yet down.

What could come to Rome
By way of history
Once the columns fell,
And all the men
(But the dead were raised through time !)
Tall columns silent, men bitterly ?
    Temples are worn
    To white-ash bone,
    And thought in sleeping
    Turns to stone.

Exile

1

Where will I return ?
To the bell-tower town ?
—Cypress and sun,
Colours flaring up
To the point of flame,
Burning brick, black green—
Where Adige spins
In his gasping strength—
Will I return ?

2

Or will I go back
To that dark-browed land,
To my rich-of-heart
Where the streams sing dark,
But the green may break
Into lilting heights,
To a purpling wave
Where the beech lifts wild—
Where I may go ?

O let the traveller
Lie at length
And lose his dust
And lose all sense
Of painful days.
There, in the water,
Silver-blank,
He'll see his rest,
Will see new life
In the stream that glides away.

A. H. EMSLIE-SMITH

Scottish Renaissance

Now is the yaird kail boiled and hashed
  While Muses feed in slums ;
The Ball of Kirriemuir has smashed
  The window-pane of Thrums.

NOTES

page 1

CHARLES GRAY'S verse letter is chosen to start the selection because it is a good example of the couthy, pawky, kailyard style of Scots verse that dominated at the opening of our period. A Fife man, he served as Lieutenant of Marines in the blockade of Venice and addressed this pleasing utterance to a well-known correspondent of Robert Burns. The popularity of Gray is well attested by a round-robin, signed by some forty noted versifiers of the day, which runs :

Sir, We, whose names are attached to this Round Robin, earnestly and affectionately prefer to you our humble petition. For some time past it has been a source of great gratification to have read, in various periodicals, the effusions of your Lyric Muse, and other esteemed productions, which, we know, have afforded no less delight to others than they have done to ourselves. This feeling has now increased into a strong desire to see these effusions collected into a volume, to save them from the fate of the productions of those kind-hearted sons of Song, who have, in various periods of our Country's history, lent the efforts of their genius to enrich the periodical literature of their times, nobly regardless of name and fame, to both of which they were justly entitled. We do not presume to dictate, but would affectionately solicit your consideration of this our petition, and earnestly entreat you would comply with the same.

Signatures include those of Henry Scott Riddell, author of ' Scotland Yet ' ; Robert Chambers, of ' Young Randal ' ; Allan Cunningham, of ' The Sun Rises Bright in France ' ; Alexander Rodger, who wrote ' My mither men't my auld breeks, And wow ! but they were duddy ' ; James Ballantine, of ' Ilka blade o gress keps its ane drap o dew ' ; Alexander Smart, John Mitchell, David Vedder and James Hedderwick, whose poems are here ; Thomas C. Latto, who wrote ' The School Examination ' and ' The Country Sacrament ' and other *Memorials of Auld Lang Syne* ; William Thom, Robert Gilfillan, Evan McColl, George Thomson, J. S. Burns and others who were once kenspeckle figures in Scottish letters. *Lays and Lyrics* (2 ed., Edinburgh, 1841) was dedicated to Prof. Tennant, author of *Anster Fair*.

page 2

DAVID SHAW, from *The Bards of Angus and the Mearns*, p. 408.

page 3

DAVID VEDDER. An Orkneyman active in Edinburgh journalistic circles. See his *Poems and Sketches* (Wm. Peace, Kirkwall, 1878).

page 5

THOMAS LYLE is best remembered for his song 'Let us haste to Kelvingrove,' but in his day he was known as the collector of *Ancient Ballads and Songs* (London, 1827).

page 6

HEW AINSLIE made his name by *A Pilgrimage to the Land of Burns*, 1822, reissued with other poems and a memoir by Thomas Latto in 1892 (Gardner, Paisley), from which comes the song here, which is 'supposed by some to refer to Burns's unfortunate amour with his dear Highland Mary.' Ainslie emigrated to the United States, where he voiced republican sentiments :

> Owre aft hath Labor sown, boys,
>   The crap that ithers reap ;
> Seen grain that he hath grown, boys,
>   But fill a landlord's heap.
> But stent or tax or tythe, boys,
>   Our girnals daurna spill ;
> These burdens were bought aff, boys,
>   Langsyne at Bunker's Hill.

Ainslie was a perfervid patriot, linguistically and otherwise, as is well seen from his piece 'Stands Scotland where it did ?'

> Do Southern loons infest your touns
>   Wi' mincin' Cockney gab ?
> Hae *John* and *Robert* taen the place
>   O' plain auld *Jock* and *Rab* ? . . .
>
> Gang lovin' sauls in plaids and shawls
>   A-courtin' to the bent ?
> Has gude braid lawlans left the land ?
>   Are kail and crowdy kent ?

Amusing in a rather Irish way is his ballad of a rustic courtship, ' The Dogs o Drumachreen,' which ends :

> It's first they reft my wylie coat,
>   And then they reft my breek ;
> And syne they fastened on a bit
>   'bout whilk I maunna speak ;
> 'bout whilk I maunna speak,
>   Tho' it watters baith my een.
> Oh, the Deil tak my dear
>   And the dogs o Drumachreen.

page 8

JANET HAMILTON was a Lanarkshire woman of Covenanting stock, fifth in descent from John Whitelaw, executed at the Old Tolbooth of Edinburgh for his part in the battle of Bothwell Brig. Self-taught, she was unable to write till she was over fifty, but poured out pithy verses in Scotch and English on a great range of religious, social and political topics, and prose sketches.

page 12

WILLIAM KENNEDY, born near Dublin, died in Paris, was joint editor with William Motherwell of the *Paisley Magazine*, secretary to Lord Durham in his famous Canadian inquiry, and British Consul in Texas. This piece from *Fitful Fancies* (Oliver & Boyd, 1827) recalls James Hogg's *Confessions of a Justified Sinner* and Stevenson's *Dr Jekyll and Mr Hyde*. He also published *The Arrow and the Rose, and other poems*, 1830, and *The Siege of Antwerp*, a verse play, 1838.

page 14

JAMES NICOL, a weaver at Luthermuir in Angus, studied the Bible at his loom and while walking abroad, and composed a *Life of the Apostle Paul in Metre*, extending to eighty close-printed pages, of which I quote the start, as a specimen of verse influenced by Tate and Brady's version of the Psalms, and by the Paraphrases used in Scottish worship. The influence is not exhausted in our own time, as was seen from Willie Soutar's *But the Earth Abideth*, 1943. Hardly less absurd than Nicol was John Gemmel, for whom Maclehose published in 1881 *The Tiberiad : or the Art of Hebrew Accentuation. A Didactive Poem, in Three Books*.

page 14

LORD NEAVES was a judge, with something of the eighteenth-century quality of Kames and Monboddo. His remarks on Hyper-Calvinism recall that as recently as a few years before our period opens the Established Church of Scotland had expelled as heretical a minister who preached that Christ died for all men. As to drunkenness, on 22 May 1850 *The Scotsman* newspaper editorially commented thus :

> SCOTTISH INTEMPERANCE.—That Scotland is, pretty near at least, the most drunken nation on the face of the earth is a fact never quite capable of denial. It may seem strange that Edinburgh, the headquarters of the various sections of a clergy more powerful than any other save that of Ireland, should, in respect of drunkenness, exhibit scenes and habits unparalleled in any other metropolis, and that Glasgow, where the clergy swarm, should be notoriously the most guilty and offensive city in Christendom. . . . The Causes of the disease . . . appear to consist in the state of physical and moral degeneration in which the lowest class of our labouring people habitually exist. They live in crowded dirty houses, and they are ill-fed. Mentally they are ignorant, strangers to thrift, and untrained to self-restraint.

Remember this background in reading some of the working-class poems that follow.

page 16

The Barnyards o Delgaty is one of those excellent *corn-kisters* which flourish best in the north-east, ballads sung by farm servants drumming their heels on the wooden corn-bin. My text comes from the Carswells' *The Scots Week-End* (Routledge, 1936).

page 17

EDWARD L. SLOAN published *The Bard's Offering* at Belfast in 1854. He is a specimen of the Ulster Scot whose dialect is closely akin to those of south-west Scotland. The Burns cult early took root among small farmers and weavers in Ulster. Among the more cultivated classes the Universities of Edinburgh and Glasgow were common places of resort for higher education, at a time when only Episcopalians were allowed into the Universities of Ireland and England. Welsh and English Nonconformists also came to Scotland. At that time, too, Scottish intellectual periodicals, pioneered a couple of generations earlier, retained something of their dominance.

page 19

THOMAS AIRD carried on the Blackwood circle's chief tendencies, but with rather more anglicisation. Being rather indifferent to blank verse I owe this passage to John Hewitt : it comes from *Frank Sylvan* (Fitte the Third).

page 19

GEORGE OUTRAM, son of a manager of the Clyde ironworks, entered the Faculty of Advocates in 1827, but in 1837 became Editor of *The Glasgow Herald*, chief organ of the North British capitalist class, which he conducted with a good infusion of liberal, humanist and patriotic spirit. His *Legal Lyrics* (a good illustrated edition, T. N. Foulis, 1916) is full of fun. Notable too is the invitation, in Scotch prose, he sent for a select dinner to commemorate the 138th anniversary of the Treaty of Union, 1844, which included not only an indigestible accumulation of ancestral viands but a great series of nationalist toasts, such as ' The Cassin o the Wanchancie Covenant ' (annulment of the Treaty) and ' A Speedie Parliament in the Parliament House ' (a policy which *The Glasgow Herald* is now, in 1951, almost alone among Scottish newspapers in opposing). Lord Cockburn wanted to interdict the dinner as treasonable.

page 24

WILLIAM LIVINGSTONE, Uilleam MacDhunLeibhe, is commended to me by competent authorities as the highest-ranking Gaelic poet of the nineteenth century, both for his seriousness of purpose and for his accomplishment. While others were content with low-flying singable ditties or pietistic platitudes, he addressed himself to great historical and literary themes, and identified himself with the struggle of the crofters alike in Scotland and in Ireland to retain their land and their way of living. He has a better poem than the one given here, called ' Fios thun a' Bhaird ' (Message to the Poet) ; but I do not have a version of it.

page 25

WILLIAM MILLER, cabinet-maker in Glasgow, was one of the most popular contributors to the series of anthologies called *Whistle-Binkie, A Collection of Songs for the Social Circle* (first issued in 1832 ; a neat enlarged issue in two volumes in 1890 by David Robertson & Co., Glasgow). His orally current ‘ Wee Willie Winkie ’ sits nicely beside his moving lines to Victor Hugo ; and the two pieces may serve to exemplify a great deal of verse writing to be found in *Whistle-Binkie* and in the four volumes issued by the Glasgow Ballad Club (Blackwood, 1885 to 1924), most of the better pieces too long, and not quite good enough, to quote. Some of those by David Wingate, a coal-miner, appeal particularly.

page 27

T. T. STODDART, head of an old Border family, started off in a mood like Byron or Beddoes with a curious, furious effusion called *The Death Wake*, published in 1830, the year of Victor Hugo's *Hernani*. Christopher North damned it in Blackwood's *Maga* ; after seventy copies had been sold the publisher failed ; the cook burned the rest ; but in 1842 Louis Fitzgerald Tasistro pirated it in *Graham's Magazine* in America, under the title *Agatha : A Necromaunt, in Three Chimeras*. Stoddart took to writing hearty angling songs, like :

> A birr ! a whirr ! a salmon's on,
> A goodly fish ! a thumper !
> Bring up, bring up the ready gaff,
> And if we land him we shall quaff
> Another glorious bumper !

He also printed, privately, an idyllic romaunt, *Yarrow*, ‘ the larger proportion of which [he says] is written in the Scottish language,’ not without orthographical troubles.

page 27

LADY JOHN SCOTT is best known for ‘ Annie Laurie.’

page 28

W. E. AYTOUN, Professor in Edinburgh and a leading light of *Blackwood's*, joined with Sir Theodore Martin in *The Bon Gaultier Ballads*, from which this mock-Gaelic piece is taken, in a style that had a vogue for about half a century. Spellings vary in his own editions of it.

page 30

JAMES HEDDERWICK, editor of the Glasgow *Evening Citizen*, was a generous patron of struggling talent.

page 31

JOHN MITCHELL expressed the mentality of Liberal industrialism in its heyday, as in this piece from *My Grey Goose Quill*, 1852, the year after the Crystal Palace Exhibition (Caldwell & Son, Paisley). The Tennant family referred to, who for their chemical works built the greatest chimney in Glasgow, sprang from an Ayrshire neighbour of Robert Burns, and have since figured in London politics with such distinguished ladies as Margot Asquith and Mrs Walter Elliot.

page 33

JOHN CRAWFORD published *Doric Lays* at Alloa, 1850, containing some delightful bairns' rhymes.

page 34

HUGH MACDONALD was enormously popular on the Clydeside, and his funeral was the occasion of an impressive concourse.

page 36

GEORGE MURRAY, laird of Troquhain and minister of Balmaclellan in the wilds of Galloway, was not disconcerted by the great Disruption of the Kirk in 1843, and varied a life of sport and drinking by the production of sets of verses, mostly too long and dull to read now.

page 37

NOEL PATON was best known as an artist and patron of the arts.

page 37

DOROTHEA OGILVY, grand-daughter of an Earl of Airlie, and sprung from one of the few Scottish clans ancient enough to have a name with the Irish-type prefix O, instead of the customary Mac, showed in her poems a sympathy and insight into the lives of countryfolk comparable with what one finds in the work of a more recent and better-known Angus writer, Violet Jacob.

page 39

GEORGE MACDONALD was a best-selling novelist in his day.

page 40

WALTER SMITH, D.D., a great Churchman, was one of the most successful exponents of a Scottish style of verse-making in the English language. His *Poetical Works* (Dent, 1902) fills 624 octavo pages in double columns, and is worth reading for sketches of character. His verses in *The Scotsman* on the distress of the gentlewomen ruined by the failure of the City of Glasgow Bank made considerable impact politically.

page 43

Sheriff ALEXANDER NICOLSON's *Verses* was issued with a memoir by Dr Walter Smith (David Douglas, Edinburgh, 1893), showing in some detail the incompatibility of the Celts with English bourgeois civilisation. Amusing is his song on ' The British Ass,' to the air ' The British Grenadiers ' :

> Some men go in for Science,
> And some go in for Shams ;
> Some roar like hungry Lions,
> And others bleat like Lambs :
> But there's a Beast that at this Feast
> Deserves a double glass,
> So let us bray that long we may
> Admire the British Ass !
>   With an Ass-Ass-sociation, &c, &c.

page 46

ALEXANDER SMITH's prose book, *A Summer in Skye*, retains its interest ; and his poem ' Barbara ' is fine. As a personality he is much more sympathetic than John Davidson or James Thomson, but his *Poetical Works* as a whole (ed. Wm. Sinclair, Edinburgh, 1909) puts him in a class below even Thomson, though neither much excelled his best poem, ' Glasgow.'

page 50

SIR WILLIAM TOPAZ McGONAGALL, Poet and Tragedian, Knight of the White Elephant, Burma, as he styled himself on the broadsheets he hawked about, was born of Irish parents in Edinburgh, but lived mainly in Dundee, as a handloom weaver. He tells us : ' The most startling incident in my life was the time I discovered myself to be a poet, which was in the year 1877. During the Dundee holiday week, in the bright and balmy month of June, when trees and flowers were in full bloom, while lonely and sad in my room, I sat thinking about the thousands of people who were away by rail and steamboat, perhaps to the land of Burns, or poor ill-treated Tannahill . . . I seemed to feel as it were a strange kind of feeling stealing over me, and remained so for about five minutes. A flame, as Lord Byron has said, seemed to kindle up my entire frame, along with a strong desire to write poetry : and I felt so happy, so happy, that I was inclined to dance. . . . Then all at once a bright idea struck me to write about my best friend, the late Reverend George Gilfillan.' His second poem was ' The Railway Bridge of the Silvery Tay,' ' which caused a great sensation in Dundee and far away. In fact, gentle readers, it was the only poem that made me famous universally. The reading of the poem abroad caused the Emperor of Brazil to leave his home far away *incognito* and view the bridge as he passed along *en route* to Inverness.' There is an enormous McGonagall apocrypha, but I believe a competent stylistic criticism could establish what is genuine. The current edition, *Poetic Gems*, published by David Winter & Son, Dundee, 1947, is not critical ; and I resorted for a text to the volume of broadsheets in the National Library where are manuscripts by the Poet and Tragedian, with his own corrections and glosses. McGonagall is strangely superior to his imitators, but the tendencies he manifests have been further instantiated by more esteemed poets in recent days, not excluding T. S. Eliot and Hugh MacDiarmid, and the London literary Left of the Thirties.

page 54

JAMES EASSON issued in 1856 a *Select Miscellany of Poetical Pieces* (Park, Sinclair & Co., Dundee), with a preface by McGonagall's ' best friend,' the Rev. George Gilfillan, a dominating figure in the religious and literary life of a considerable region at that time. One can see why local mill-owners subsidised Gilfillan's church when one finds him specially commending the piece by Easson which I print, and remarking : ' A poet should avoid the currents of scepticism which are at present flowing in our land, and engulphing so many minds of the imaginative order. Let him not be seduced by the fascination which genius has given to the pantheism of Shelley, the mysticism of Bailey, and the sentimental and untangible faith of Tennyson. Let him remember that the manliest, healthiest, highest and most permanent poetry has been inspired by profound belief in Christianity.' Easson's verses, preaching acceptance of the existing industrial system, found ready

317

publication in *The People's Journal*, published in Dundee and circulating in hundreds of thousands all over Scotland, whose proprietors erected a tombstone for the poet in the Dundee Eastern Necropolis, ' in memory of a working man [he was a painter to trade] who had rare literary gifts, and whose writings are his best memorial.'

page 55

ADAM LINDSAY GORDON, of the soldierly Hallhead branch of the clan, became the favourite poet of Australia, partly because of his intrepid horsemanship, but also because he expressed the spirit of the pioneer settlers. See Edith Humphries and Douglas Sladen's life and letters (Constable, 1912). On hearing that, through the breaking of an entail, he would not inherit the Esslemont estate in Aberdeenshire, and suffering from head injuries through falls while steeplechasing, he shot himself, leaving this poem.

page 56

JAMES THOMSON shocked the Mid-Victorians by his equivalent of *The Waste Land*, which he published under the name ' Bysshe Vanolis,' or the initials B.V., in *The National Reformer* of Charles Bradlaugh, the Atheist M.P., between March and May 1874. A commentator remarked that ' It is really very generous of Mr Thomson to consent to live at all.'

page 62

' MOSES PEERIE,' D.D., ' Minister of the united parishes of Benstaggers and Glenstodgie,' was one of the pseudonyms of the Rev. Principal Story of Glasgow, who issued through Blackwood in 1884 *Nugae Ecclesiasticae*, from which I take this passage. He advertises as in the Press also *Kneaded Dough for Needy Duffers*, and *De Pulice Celtico ; or, Lees on Fleas. A Chapter of Highland Entomology*. There are numerous volumes of facetious stuff by professional men, but little of it so near any worthwhile mark as this piece. The ironmaster, I believe, was Mr Baird of Gartsherry, founder of the noble family of Stonehaven.

page 65

ELLEN JOHNSTON is known to me only from *The Bards of Angus and the Mearns*, where one learns that she was born at Hamilton, received £50 from the Royal Bounty Fund, and died in the Barony Poorshouse at Glasgow.

page 65

DAVID GRAY, who had attracted the patronage of Lord Houghton, was thought of as a Scottish Keats, not only for his early death. But his most popular poem, ' The Luggie,' is scarcely Keatsian, and hardly interests today.

page 66

THOMAS DAVIDSON, born of English parentage in Oxnam, Roxburghshire, the parish of James Thomson, the eighteenth-century Anglo-Scottish poet, was bred for the Scottish Kirk. Worth reading is the memoir of him by the Rev. Dr James Brown, *The Life of a Scottish Probationer* (3rd ed., enlarged, Maclehose, Glasgow, 1889).

page 67

ROBERT BUCHANAN, close friend of the ill-starred David Gray, long survived him, became a big man in London journalism, and issued a *Poetical Works* in 534 octavo pages, double-columned (Chatto & Windus, 1884). I was surprised to find nothing worth printing, except a stanza of ' The Wedding of Shon Maclean,' to which nothing is added by the rest of the piece. In general, Buchanan, like his contemporary Tennysonian, the 9th Lord Southesk, never seems to give birth to more than a small idea, and then suffocates it with poeticising. The poems that survive this treatment best are ' Up in an Attic ' ; ' London, March 1866 ' ; and ' O'Murtogh,' a ballad on the hanging of a Fenian, of which, however, I doubt if the Irish would think much.

page 71

ALEXANDER ANDERSON, seventh child of a quarryman at Kirkconnel in Nithsdale, taught himself French, German, Italian, Spanish, Latin and Greek while working on the railway, and published poems in Scotch and English under the pseudonym ' Surfaceman,' in the garb of which office you may see his photograph in *Songs of the Rail* (Simpkin Marshall, 1878). Patronised at first by the editor of *The People's Friend,* Dundee, and then by Lord Rowallan, who took him touring as far as Italy in 1879, he became assistant librarian of Edinburgh University in 1880. See his *Later Poems*, with memoir by A. Brown, 1912 (Fraser, Asher & Co., Glasgow & Dalbeattie). His bairns' poem ' Cuddle Doon ' is orally current.

page 72

JOHN YOUNG GRAY, of Letham, Angus, was prominent in the cultural life of Dundee. He begat Sir Alexander Gray (see below).

page 73

HUGH HALIBURTON (James Logie Robertson), of Milnathort, was a close friend at Edinburgh University of the last distinguished man of the Ferrier family, grandson of Christopher North, and thus a strong link with the *Noctes Ambrosianae* tradition, which Robertson carried on, but with less robustness and more linguistic refinement. I quote from his *Poems* of 1878 his attitude to the Scotch language itself, rather than from the kailyard idylls he began sending to *The Scotsman* in 1881 over the signature 'Hugh Haliburton,' which had a tremendous vogue as 'Hughies.' According to the memoir in *Horace in Homespun* (Blackwood, 1925), farmers greeted one another with 'Anither Hughie oot the day,' and ploughmen pasted their bothy walls with the press cuttings. I choose this poem, rather than any of his delightful sketches in the manner of Horace *via* Allan Ramsay, because Hugh himself strove to publicise it by reprinting it, entitled *Lament for the Language*, in his collection of polemical essays *For Puir Auld Scotland's Sake*, dedicated to Robert Burns Begg, grandson of Burns, and published in the same year, 1887, as Robert Louis Stevenson's *Underwoods*, two years after the institution of the Scottish Office under a Secretary for Scotland, one year after the founding of the first Scottish Home Rule Association, and a year before Keir Hardie and Cunninghame Graham started the Scottish Labour Party : in fact, in the midst of a 'Scottish Renaissance' movement.

page 75

ROBERT LOUIS STEVENSON'S poetry has been revalued at a higher level in recent years, and there are dozens of pieces one could print as good as the eight I have chosen. In English verse his contributions were seminal : in what he called Lallans he did not pioneer, but his interest and approval undoubtedly helped the movement to develop the tradition. Those who know his works and life will see more in the pieces I select than can briefly be explained here, but I mention the occasion of 'A Portrait.' The Savile Club was founded on the novel principle that all members should be ready to talk without introduction : R.L.S. accordingly went over to greet a distinguished *littérateur*, recently elected, whom he saw lunching alone : rebuffed, he sat down to write 'A Portrait,' wherein the offender is made to speak in the first person (Sir S. Colvin, *Memories and Notes*, 120). Janet Adam Smith found for it the title 'Mannock *Loquitur*.'

page 83

JAMES YOUNG GEDDES I have been unable to find much information about. He seems to have spent his life between Dundee and the pleasant Perthshire burgh of Alyth. Also notable is his satirical poem, ' Thrift ! Thrift ! Thrift ! ' on the lines of the famous ' Song of a Shirt ' (" Stitch, stitch, stitch . . .') by Thomas Hood (1798–1845), whose family had connections with Tayside (Errol, Dundee and Tayport : since possessing myself of the house next door to that in which Hood stayed with his aunt I have discovered that I am myself related to him). See *In the Valhalla*, by J. Y. Geddes, author of *The New Jerusalem, The Spectre Clock of Alyth*, etc. (Leng, Dundee, 1891).

page 87

THOMAS GIVEN, farmer at Cullybackey, Co. Antrim, descended from the Givens of Drumochrein, Ayrshire, wrote a poem on a pilgrimage to the Burns country. See *Poems from College and Country* (W. & G. Baird, Belfast, 1900).

page 88

ROGER QUIN, born of an Irish father and Scottish mother at Dumfries, at the age of seven held in his hands the temporarily unearthed skull of Burns, and later served the great Thomas Carlyle in a shop : which contacts set his mind on literature. Giving up his clerking he took to tramping the Borders with flute and concertina in summer, spending the winters in a Glasgow model lodging-house. See *The Borderland* (Walker, Galashiels) and *Midnight in Yarrow* (Gowans and Gray). He has a strong long poem on an Irish eviction, ' Glenbeigh ' ; an interesting allegory, ' The Butterfly and the Rose,' about a Glasgow ' model ' ; a longish ribald rhyme, ' The First Operation ' ; and a good many sets of verses in Lallans. But this sonnet is surely his best utterance.

page 89

ADAM WILSON was known as ' The Factory Muse ' (see *The Bards of Angus and the Mearns*).

page 90

SIR DONALD MACALISTER, Principal of Glasgow University, wrote verse in about twenty languages besides his native Gaelic. George Campbell Hay, also from Tarbert, has the same gift, and poetic power besides.

page 91

ROB WANLOCK (Robert Reid) published *Moorland Rhymes* (Anderson & Son, Dumfries, 1874) and *Poems, Songs and Sonnets* (Gardner, Paisley, 1894), with the well-known recitation piece 'Kirkbryde.'

page 91

RONALD CAMPBELL MACFIE's preoccupation with scientific themes or their implications was shared by John Davidson, on whom he wrote an obituary poem. 'A Moral' is from *New Poems* (Lane, 1904); 'Man in Evolution,' from *War* (John Murray, 1918).

page 92

W. A. MACKENZIE's poem is known to me from *The Scottish Students' Song-Book*. The tale it tells was only too common before Andrew Carnegie's transatlantic millions began to aid Scottish students. Nowadays they do not 'grind' so much, and their health is better. 'Tertians' are third-year students.

page 93

JAMES KEIR HARDIE's poem originally appeared in *Life and Work*, organ of the Church of Scotland, and was chosen for me by Emrys Hughes, M.P. for South Ayrshire, son-in-law of the founder of the Labour Party. It exhibits more poetry than Marxism. Hardie wrote it with reference to a picture he saw in the studio of a painter to whom he was sitting. (*Re* Marxism, I asked Willie Gallacher, long the Communist M.P. for West Fife, for one of his poems, but he was too modest to let me print any.)

page 94

PITTENDRIGH MACGILLIVRAY, whose name is a poem in itself, was a good sculptor and a zealous Scot in every way. In the Foreword to the beautifully printed *Pro Patria* (1915, on hand-made paper, for private circulation) he writes: 'If behind these things any discern a true love-militant for Kin-folk and Country—a love which is yet so based in heart and kindness that it would gladly overflow in friendship with other Peoples: then, the printing of them may be a little service at this time, when the sword of the spirit—The Word—is as needful at the Nation's Front as the tools of steel.' He prints there also his 'Memories of "The 45",' a toast given at a Jacobite dinner in the Caledonian

Hotel, Edinburgh, in 1911, celebrating what he termed ' a defeat which was yet a Victory in kindness, loyalty, and many things chivalrous.' For poems in certain moods he affected an archaic spelling.

page 96

JOHN DAVIDSON has not yet been fully reassessed. Probably the best short discussion of his work is that by R. M. Wenley, introducing a selection of *Poems* put out by Boni and Liveright, New York, 1924. In his bibliographical note Prof. Wenley expressed the hope that Mr Grant Richards, Davidson's literary executor, would issue a complete edition of the poems ; but there is also a wealth of other material to be re-examined by an enterprising critic. Davidson's town is Greenock, on a steep rain-drenched hillside towards the mouth of the Clyde. His parents adhered to a small Calvinist sect, James Morison's Evangelical Union, which had hived off from the United Secession. Rebelling under various influences in Glasgow, Davidson took up journalism in London (1890), and was strongly influenced by James Thomson, to whom he ascribed ' passion and intellect second only to Shakespeare.' See *The Scots Review*, Dec. 1950 and Jan. 1951, for controversy on the relative influence of Thomson and Davidson on Hugh MacDiarmid compared with that of Ezra Pound. Always remember that, while English literary influence is omnipresent in the Scots poets of this period, as of most periods, English influence is almost confined to literature and has to compete with all sorts of influences, literary and non-literary, emerging from the Scottish inheritance and environment of the poet. Words quite often mislead one in trying to grasp what is Scottish and what is not : but I hope some bold spirit will venture an exhaustive book on Davidson. Meantime this selection may help to change views of him derived from English anthologies based on the taste shown by a reviewer of his *New Ballads* who wrote, in 1897, ' We do not want Mr Davidson's moralizings, we prefer his lyrics.' So too many reviewers of MacDiarmid grudge him his poetical adventures after *Sangshaw* and *Pennywheep* (1925-6).

page 107

WALLACE MARTIN LINDSAY, Professor of Humanity in the University of St Andrews, the greatest Latinist of his age and my very dear teacher, manifests in these verses the same desire for precision and finality that characterised his work on ancient texts.

page 109

DUGALD SUTHERLAND MACCOLL, a son of the manse from Glasgow, won the Newdigate Prize for verse at Oxford, became Keeper of the Tate Gallery and later of the Wallace Collection, and was a polemical man of letters to editors on art and other matters.

page 110

BASIL RAMSAY ANDERSON, grand-uncle of Willa Muir, was a Shetlander who died young in Edinburgh, where R. & R. Clark published in 1888 a memorial volume, *Broken Lights*.

page 111

DR DAVID RORIE, born at Edinburgh but with Aberdeen and Fife connections, published in 1920 *The Auld Doctor* (Constable). Orally current is his quatrain :

> Aberdeen and twal mile round,
>   Fife, and aa the lands about it,
> Taen fae Scotland's runklet map,
>   Little's left, and wha's tae doubt it ?

page 114

J. J. HALDANE BURGESS, editor of *The Shetlander*, wrote *Rasmie's Muddie*, 1891 ; *Young Rasmie's Kit*, 1929 ; and other popular books.

page 114

ROBERT FULLER MURRAY issued in 1891 *The Scarlet Gown : Being Verses of a St Andrews Man* (A. M. Holden, St Andrews, N.B. ; Simpkin, Marshall, Hamilton & Co., London), with the prefatory hope that they would be found ' pleasant, if not over exciting.' Many of them have endeared themselves even to the under-privileged, i.e. students of other universities, and enjoy a vocal currency. The Greek motto is that of the University.

page 115

MARY SYMON published *Deveron Days* (D. Wyllie & Son, Aberdeen, 1934), from which I take this, to me, rather moving piece as representing a good deal of minor but honest utterance in good north-eastern dialect, such as one finds in J. G. Horne's *Flooer o the Ling*, 1936, Lewis

Coutts' *Scotch Hotch Potch*, 1923, or George P. Dunbar's (' Stoneywood ')
A Guff o Peat Reek, 1920, and *A Whiff o the Doric*, 1922.

page 123

NEIL MUNRO was primarily a novelist and short-story writer.

page 125

CHARLES MURRAY left his native Aberdeenshire for South Africa but
grew up with the Donside dialect, and when he put out his *Hamewith*
in 1900, during what was called the ' Great South African War,'
attained at once world-wide popularity, chiefly for his long character-
sketches for recitation.

page 126

DR JOHN F. FERGUS published *The Sodger and Other Verses* (Gowans
& Gray, Glasgow, 2 ed., 1915).

page 127

WALTER WINGATE published *Poems* (Gowans & Gray, 1919).

page 133

DOUGLAS GRANT DUFF AINSLIE'S *Chosen Poems* (Hogarth Press, 1926)
has a preface by G. K. Chesterton, who comments thus on Ainslie's
varied and cosmopolitan activities, displayed in his versions from
Sanskrit, his translation of Benedetto Croce's *Philosophy of the Spirit*,
his book of *Adventures Social and Literary*, etc. : ' And yet I have happy
doubts about all this universality of culture. I suspect Mr Ainslie of
being something better than a citizen of the world. I suspect him of
secret nationalism, and of wearing, so to speak, a plaid under his
pilgrim's gown. Nobody ever yet got Scotland out of a Scot ; and I
do not believe that the author, in his heart, allows Scotland to descend
to an equality with trifles like Athens and India and China.' For permission to print I am indebted to his literary executrix Mrs Quinton.

page 136

MARION ANGUS in her eightieth year greatly altered ' The Wild
Lass ' for the worse. I print an eclectic text, using the four-line stanza
Miss Angus sent to Dr John Oliver (*A Scots Anthology*, Oliver & Boyd,
1949), with the original words as retained by Miss Helen Cruickshank,
with her habitual discrimination, in the *Selected Poems* edited by her
and Mr Maurice Lindsay (Serif Books, Edinburgh, 1950).

page 138

GEORGE DOUGLAS BROWN wrote *The House with the Green Shutters*, leading novel of the 'Stinkin Fush' school of Scottish literature, which arose as a reaction from the 'Kailyard.' This poem came out in *The Ayr Advertiser*.

page 139

ROBERT MURRAY, Co-operative M.P. for East Renfrewshire, published *The Deil and John Knox* (Moray Press, 1936).

page 146

HAMISH HENDRY, of Alloa, published *Red Apple and Silver Bells*, 1896, *A Scots Dominie*, 1924 (Gowans & Gray), and other collections. For an insight into the different aims of the 'Kailyard' and the 'Scots Renaissance' you may compare Hendry's effort here with MacDiarmid's *A Drunk Man Looks at the Thistle* (Blackwood, 1926).

page 156

ROBERT CRAWFORD's poem is from 'Coalscapes,' a sonnet sequence in *Poems* (Blackwell, 1924). Born at Dalry, he worked as railwayman there, being crushed in a shunting accident in 1902, and as coal-miner at Hamilton Palace and Plean, where his spine was crushed in 1919. In three years off work he wrote much under the influence of Milton and Burns. See his *In Quiet Fields* (Porpoise Press, Edinburgh, 1929) for contrasting work in Scots and English (to which Charles Graves drew my attention after my selection had been made).

page 157

A. W. MAIR, Professor of Greek at Edinburgh, was an Aberdonian, like his successor W. M. Calder (see below). Though resolved not to admit translations I could not resist his adaptation of *Palatine Anthology*, vii, 309, or Professor Calder's of the Roman inscription, as showing the lapidary quality of Scots.

page 158

JOSEPH LEE's war poems, illustrated by himself, had a considerable vogue. His best is probably *The Green Grass*, but I have not printed it because you can find it in the companion volume to this, John Buchan's *The Northern Muse* (Nelson). For the same reason I have omitted a good many other excellent poems of considerable length, notably the

'Address to the German Gun' by the Rt. Hon. W. S. Morrison, most of the sporting poems chosen by Buchan, and those Victorian favourites, Principal Shairp's 'The Bush Aboon Traquair' and William Bell Scott's 'The Witch's Ballad.' While on omissions I mention that some living writers declined to be represented by the pieces I chose, e.g. Miss Muriel Stuart by 'Lady Hamilton'; and some of the well-known dead proved most disappointing on a reperusal, notably Sir George Douglas and William Sharp, *alias* 'Fionn MacColla.' Some refused to disclose the year of their birth.

page 161

JOHN MACDOUGALL HAY, minister of Elderslie, Sir William Wallace's parish, wrote a first-rate novel about Tarbert, Loch Fyne, *Gillespie* (Constable, 1914), and begat the poet George Campbell Hay (see below).

page 168

IVO MACNAUGHTON CLARK, D.D., minister of Farnell, Angus, published mainly in *The Scotsman*. This poem appeared also in *The New Athenian Broadsheet* (57 Newington Road, Edinburgh) for Christmas 1949.

page 170

A. M. DAVIDSON's poem, first quoted to me by Dr J. B. Salmond, comes from his *The Weaver's Loom*, of which 120 copies were printed by hand, with designs by James Guthrie, at the Pear Tree Press, Flansham, Bognor Regis, Sussex, England, 1932.

page 177

DR W. H. HAMILTON's allusion in v. 2 is to C. H. Sorley (see below).

page 177

EDWIN MUIR's poem, 'Scotland's Winter,' I long ago copied from some periodical, which neither he nor I can now trace. The rest are from his accessible collections, except 'The Stronghold' which came out in *The Modern Scot*, autumn 1934.

page 187

ANON. I owe this admirable piece, like much else, to Miss Helen Cruickshank, who found it in *The People's Friend* of 2 April 1917.

page *188*

JAMES BRIDIE's verses are from *Tedious and Brief* (Constable, 1945).

page *190*

WALTER ELLIOT's piece is from *University Verses*, from the Glasgow University Magazine (of which he was editor), 1903–10, with illustrations by OH ! (O. H. Mavor, *alias* James Bridie). ' Sauchie ' is Sauchiehall Street. Though now (1951) seated on the Front Bench of the Conservative Opposition, Colonel Elliot was in those days a Socialist and used the pseudonym *Parvus*.

page *193*

G. BRUCE THOMSON's comic verses I copy from *The Scots Week-End* (Routledge, 1936), where Wm. Kemp's tune to them is printed.

page *195*

GEORGE BUCHANAN-SMITH's ' Fragment ' was published in a privately printed memoir by his father, Sir George Adam Smith, Principal of Aberdeen University, 1916.

page *195*

WILLA MUIR was blackmailed into giving me a poem by my threat to print one of her Juvenilia from *College Echoes*, the St Andrews University magazine.

page *197*

NEIL GUNN's excellence in the novel lends interest to this piece from *The Modern Scot*, 1930.

page *200*

HUGH MACDIARMID's treatment of Cophetua contrasts with a piece by a pre-' Renaissance ' Scottish songstress, Maria Steuart's ' Cophetua aud the Beggar-Maid ' (*A Garland of Lyrics* : A. H. Bullen, London, 1907), which goes :

> HE   What though I am a king upon a throne ?
>   Only in worldly rank I am above you,
>   All greater gifts are yours and yours alone,
>   Only—I love you !

SHE   And though you are a king both brave and wise,
As all your words and deeds do truly prove you,
A beggar I accept your sacrifice
Because—I love you.

Likewise one may glimpse the difference between ' Renaissance ' ideas and the ' Kailyard ' by comparing the Rev. T. S. Cairncross's poem ' Tarras ' in his *The Scot at Hame* (Constable, 1922), dedicated to the Glasgow Ballad Club, which starts :

> Oh it's fine to be in Tarras
> When the leaves are comin' oot,
> Where the saughs and elders trimmle,
> And there's mony a peat-broun troot,

with MacDiarmid's ' Tarras,' in *Scots Unbound* (Eneas Mackay, Stirling, 1932), which starts :

> This Bolshevik bog !   Suits me doon to the grun' !
> For by fike and finnick the world's no run.

Interesting, too, would be to contrast Somhairle Maclean's treatment of the bog Mararabhlainn in *An Cuilthionn*. MacDiarmid's *Lucky Poet* (Methuen, 1943), a self-study in literature and political ideas, may stimulate or exasperate, but is useful for the understanding of the poet.

page 217

WILLIAM JEFFREY'S poem is taken from *The Modern Scot*, winter 1934 (reprinted in *Towards a New Scotland*, Maclehose, 1935). Jeffrey worked in both Scots and English, and here has devised a mixed Anglo-Scots dramatically appropriate to John Knox. Mr Alexander Scott's collected edition of Jeffrey will prove a revelation to many.

page 221

C. H. SORLEY, son of one of the Aberdeen Professors of Philosophy, started writing at Marlborough, and his posthumous volume was entitled *Marlborough and Other Poems* (Cambridge University Press, 1916).

page 222

JAMES PEACOCK, a Galloway man, sometime editor of *The Rangoon Gazette* and colleague on *The Times of India* of Eric Linklater, who deals with him as 'McOstrich' in *The Man on My Back*, wrote a verse play, *The Nazarene*, which the Lord Chamberlain bans because it makes Christ appear as a character on the stage (see *The New Scot*, vol. xi, no. 4).

page 223

A. F. McGLASHAN published *St George and The Dragon* (Selwyn & Blount, 1931).

page 223

ANON. This piece appeared in *The College* (St Andrews), vol. iii, no. 1, 1905, entitled *Aus einem kleinen Wirtshaus* and signed *Potztausend*.

page 226

NAOMI MITCHISON's 'Westminster' comes from *The Tribune*, 2 June 1950. The 'Lament' came out in *The Laburnum Branch*, 1917. I should like to have printed a swatch of her long poem, *The Knife*, written in the 1939–45 war.

page 227

WILLIAM SOUTAR's 'The Auld House' is from *The Voice of Scotland*, vol. i, no. 1, 1938. The rest come from his various collections.

page 234

ROBERT RENDALL, crofter and merchant in Kirkwall, is an eminent theologian and conchologist, as well as an enthusiast for the making and translation, collection and criticism of verses in various tongues.

page 237

JOE CORRIE is best known now as a playwright, but when he started publishing poems after the 1914–18 war, some of them immediately won a wide oral currency, especially in the Scots mining communities. For some time in the 1920s the wage for a shift was eight shillings and four-pence, and a high proportion of miners could not get work for more than three or four shifts a week. Sir Adam Nimmo was a colliery owner.

page 240

ADAM DRINAN's identity is variously conjectured.

page 241

HUNTER DIACK published this in *Outlook*, Nov. 1936.

NOTES

page 242

ALBERT MACKIE, editor of the Edinburgh *Evening Dispatch*, chaired a representative committee of contemporary poets in the drawing up of a better spelling for Scotch, which has to some extent been adopted since 1947. You should read his *Sing a Sang o Scotland* (Maclellan, 1944).

page 248

ROBERT MACLELLAN'S poem came out in *Poetry Scotland, 2*. He is primarily a playwright, as also is

page 249

ROBERT KEMP, whose poem appeared in *Verses from New Kings*, poems by Aberdeen students since 1913 (Wyllie & Son, Aberdeen, 1938).

page 250

LAVINIA DERWENT'S wartime piece appeared in the Glasgow *Evening Times* and in *Scots Writing*, no. 2.

page 250

Dr JANET MARY SMITH wrote *The French Background of Medieval Scots Literature*.

page 253

ROBERT GARIOCH'S admirable *jeu d'esprit* on the Edinburgh Festival is here printed for the first time, I believe. Usually he sets up and prints and publishes his own work at the Chalmers Press, e.g. *Seventeen Poems for Sixpence* (with Somhairle Maclean, an epoch-making booklet), 1940, and *Chuckies on the Cairn*, 1948. Apparently a reincarnation of Robert Fergusson, like him R. G. Sutherland is partly of Aberdeenshire stock.

page 256

JOHN KINCAID'S piece comes from *Setterday Nicht Symphonie* (dedicated to Hugh MacDiarmid) in the group publication, *Fowrsom Reel*, published by the Caledonian Press, Glasgow, for 'The Clyde Group,' 1949, and dedicated to John Maclean, Soviet Consul in Glasgow in the 'Red Clydeside' days, and the nearest Scottish counterpart to James Connolly in Ireland. A far cry from the 'Kailyard' now!

NOTES

page 257

NORMAN MCCAIG allowed me my pick from a selection of manuscript pieces.

page 260

STUART HOOD's juvenile piece aroused a good deal of interest when it came out in *The Modern Scot*, winter 1936. His prose work, *The Circle of the Minotaur*, 1950, was accorded great praise, and I do not doubt that here he is rather under-represented, as are a good many other contemporaries who have not put out collections in book form. I apologise to him and others concerned.

page 261

T. S. LAW's poem to Cameron appeared in *The New Scot*, Feb. 1947, with a translation into English, and an invitation to ' note the vigour of the Scots tongue.' (Henry P. Cameron, M.A., author of *A History of the English Bible* etc., an Australian Scot, published through Gardner of Paisley in 1913 a revised edition of his Scots version of Thomas à Kempis's devotional work *De Imitatione Christi*. My copy was given me by Andrew Tannahill, great-grand-nephew of the poet Tannahill.) Mr Law's translation runs :

> Cameron, what is wrought in the cleverness of children which must always compel us to stay encharmed in ourselves when reaching across the years we endure, years incalculable to us in our rasping struggle, bearing hardly the soured looks of Time glaring ill-naturedly from our eternal overwhelming bourne ? Suddenly, among the petty-fogging speech of the streets, with duplicity in my own discretion in spite of a dream of a Scottish total-faithfulness as true as the extraordinary means by which all children joyfully arrive at understanding where instinct is confirmed with reason like birds in complete selfness one with the source of action, all of them one in movement in the sky when sound is in right accord with feathers and the sough or blast of air, there, Cameron, in the heart of your speech I knew myself there.

To me these *Lynes* communicate deeply and fully, and seem to have a true spontaneity for all their superficial self-consciousness. Mr Law is not a dilettante bourgeois academic, as some opponents think devotees of the Scots Renaissance movement must be, but a very wide-awake and highly competent skilled man working in the coalfields of the Lowlands.

The other piece of his I print is a version of Edwin Muir's *Epitaph* in this collection, which shows again Mr Law's resource and workmanship. For his own developing original powers in poetry I can only refer the reader to his booklet, *Whit Tyme in the Day*, with foreword by Mac-Diarmid (Caledonian Press, Glasgow, 1948), and advise that an eye be kept open for later work.

page 262

Lt.-Col. BERNARD FERGUSSON's little poem, taken in conjunction with his *Beyond the Chindwin*, *The Black Watch and the King's Enemies*, etc., indicates that the old *mither tongue* remains the right medium of expression for certain matters even for a high-ranking officer who is also a master of English prose.

page 278

G. S. FRASER's two pieces here are early, and show his Scottish affiliation ; he has done better things since, though mostly too long for this anthology, and will do better yet if his exile in Japan proves as fruitful as those he endured in Egypt and London. The allusion to Lermontov is to his descent from the Learmonths of Dairsie. Compton Mackenzie has abandoned Barra, MacDiarmid Whalsay, and Muir St Andrews ; nor is it now true that ' He sings alone who in this province sings,' though the chorus is not always in unison.

page 280

ANN SCOTT-MONCRIEFF's poem appeared in *The New Alliance* and in Ernest Marwick's *Anthology of Orkney Verse* (The Kirkwall Press, 1949).

page 281

R. CROMBIE SAUNDERS gave me my pick of a manuscript selection.

page 282

DAVID MARTIN's *Battlefields and Girls* (Maclellan, 1942) made some impact on Scottish literary circles during the last war, particularly this piece, originally printed in *Forward*. (I do not associate myself with the remark about the ' gin-sodden planters,' but it was common enough at the time.)

page 284

GEORGE HAY's ' Aonarain ' has been beautifully set to music by Mrs Oliver Brown, and ' To a certain Loch Fyne Fisherman,' by Francis

George Scott. The fisherman was Malcolm Johnston, Tarbert, a descendant of a MacIain who survived the massacre of Glencoe ; I recall his normal conversation as sheer poetry, in a mixture of Gaelic, Lallans and Biblical English. ' The Three Brothers ' was written more or less in that synthetic or eclectic speech.

page 290

JOHN SINGER exerted a lively influence in Scottish letters during the war, editing *Million : The People's Review* (Maclellan, Glasgow). Dr Mary Ramsay pointed out this poem particularly as having what R.L.S. termed ' a Scottish accent of the mind.' Indeed, Singer and Martin, though not Scots, seem closer in these pieces to Scottish literary traditions than are some of those of Scots blood assimilated to English culture, including such good poets as Ruthven Todd, Lilian Bowes-Lyon and Patrick Hore-Ruthven. It appeared in *The Voice of Scotland*, June 1946.

page 291

SYDNEY GOODSIR SMITH is unquestionably *il miglior fabbro* among the younger Lallan Makars in 1951, though others may do better by 1961 ; but he suffers more than most from being served up in the *hors-d'œuvre variés* to which an anthologist must confine himself. Yet can anyone show me a finer poem of paternity than *For My Newborn Son*, unless perhaps the elaborate effort of Yeats ?

page 295

ALEX DOW's piece comes from *Bricht Mortalitie*, described as ' a diversity of major poems,' to be published by New Lang Syne (Kenneth McLaren, 50 Park Road, Glasgow C 4), a co-operative poetic venture.

page 296

W. S. GRAHAM's pieces here are early ones, written while he was in Scotland, and may interest the many admirers of his more recent work, such as *The White Threshold* (Faber, 1949). ' Fourth Sonnet ' appeared in *Contemporary Poetry* (Baltimore), spring 1946.

page 297

Father ANTONY ROSS, editor of *The Innes Review*, kindly made available to me some rare volumes of Father John Gray's work, as well as manuscripts of his own, on being told that I was looking out for religious verse, in which Scotland seems never to have been very fertile, certainly not proportionately to the output of controversial ecclesiastic prose.

page 298

TOM SCOTT'S poem came out in *Poetry Scotland, 3*. He has received an Atlantic Award for a novel and a long narrative poem, *The Bight o' Benin*, and tells me he thinks it easier to write an epic than a lyric.

page 300

THURSO BERWICK (Maurice Blythman) comes from Inverkeithing, near the north end of the Forth Bridge, on crossing which many passengers make it an article of religion to throw coins out of the windows. Above the bridge is the naval base of Rosyth. Originally printed in *The Voice of Scotland*, June 1947, it reappeared, with variants as here, in *Fowrsom Reel*, 1949.

page 302

HAMISH HENDERSON'S poem came out in *The New Alliance*, June–July 1943, from which version I excerpt. The same material was worked up afresh for his *Elegies for the Dead in Cyrenaica* (John Lehmann, 1948), a most moving document, which well deserved its award of the Somerset Maugham Prize. I regret not having room for the political and other ballads by him and by others, or for such specimens of the *Musa Proterva* still proliferating in Scotland as *The Ball o Kirriemuir*, now current all over the world in almost epic abundance and variety (including a Latin metrical version concocted between Balliol and New College, Oxford, by graduates of Glasgow and St Andrews). Indeed, while this collection goes through the press I become more aware how many worthwhile contemporaries are omitted and how many others under-represented. I offer them my humblest apologies and hope to do them all justice in another decade or two in another anthology with a different scope. Meantime I trust that this interim report on the past century will prove interesting and stimulating alike to producers and to consumers of Scottish verse.

GLOSSARY

THIS glossary is designed mainly for those familiar with standard King's or American English, but unacquainted with Scots. A great many words of standard Scots are forms of common Germanic words found also in German, English, Dutch, Frisian, etc., and can readily be recognised if a few frequent changes are remembered, e.g. v tends to disappear in Scots, as in *gie* for *give*, *loe* for *love*, *ser* for *serve*, *hae* for *have*; terminal d is often lost, as in *blin(d)*, *fin(d)*, *han(d)*, *lan(d)*, *caul(d)* for *cold*, *aul(d)* for *old*; ll is lost, as in *fu(ll)*, *ca(ll)*, *a(ll)*, *fa(ll)*, often written *caa*, *aa*, *faa*, or changed to w or we, as in *howe* for *hollow*, *pow(e)* for *poll*, *rowe* for *roll*. Long o often appears as ae or ai, thus, *bane* for *bone*, *gae* for *go*, *haill* for *whole*. Scots may have oo or ou for English ow, as in *toon*, *hoose*, *doun*, *nou*. Short a appears for English short o, e.g. in *lang*, *sang*, *strang*, *wrang*. In the Aberdeen and north-east dialects of Scots, initial wh tends to become f, e.g. *fa* for English *who*, *fan* for *when*, *faur* for *where*, *fite fulpie* for *white whelp*. All but the most obvious words are listed in this glossary, together with phrases and words other than Scots that may not readily be found in an ordinary dictionary. The best Scots-English dictionary is that being issued by the Scottish National Dictionary Association, King's College, Aberdeen; the best complete one now (1951) available is Jamieson's, revised by Longmuir, with supplement by Metcalfe (Alex. Gardner, Paisley, 1927). The glosses given here are restricted to the meanings employed in the anthology; the need for brevity seldom admits of more than an approximate explanation of a word.

ABLOW : below
abradit : worn smooth
abstraklous : cross-tempered
abune, abuin, abeen : above
acquent : acquainted
ae, ane, yae, yin : one
afa, afu : awful
aflocht : flying
afore : before
afore the face : over the precipice
aftergait : later course
agley : squint, awry
ahin, ahint : behind
aiblins : perhaps
aiglet : tagged point ; any jewelled or ornamental part of clothing

aik : oak
aiker : surface ripple or underwater track made by trout
ain : own
airnstane : ironstone
airt : direct ; direction
ait : oat
ajee : aside, squint, in disorder
albeid : although
allemand : in formal courtly style, like a slow German dance
allevolie : at random, in a volley
aluinn : beautiful (Gaelic)
amene : pleasant, having amenity
amow : excite, arouse, stir

GLOSSARY

amplefeyst : restive humour, unnecessary talk

an, an', and : if

aneath, aneth : beneath

anerly : only

aneuch : enough

anoraq (Eskimo) : blouse

anse : else

anterin, antrin : occasional, rare

apert : open, manifest

appliable : pliant, complaisant

archin : hesitating

areird : backward, reluctant

arnut : earth-nut, edible tuber

arrachin : winding forward

ashypet : dirty drudge, Cinderella

a'smither : to smithereens, in little bits

aspate : in a flood, overflowing

asteer : stirring

Atchison : low-grade silver coin, two-thirds of a penny sterling

athort : across

athout : without

atour, attour : around, above, beside

attercap : spider ; cross-grained person ; a bit of a fool

atweesh, atween : betwixt and between, so-so

auchimuty : paltry, parsimonious

aumry : cupboard, wardrobe

austerne : austere, severe-looking

ava, avaa : at all

averins : cloudberries

aweel : ah well !

awfie, awfu : awful ; awfully

a-whummle : overwhelming, pouring furiously

ayebydan : everlasting

BACK-END : autumn

back-lands : blocks of slum houses built on the back-greens of older blocks

backthraw : resiling, drawing back (from bargain, promise, etc.)

bade, baid : stayed, abode

bailie : magistrate and town councillor

bairn, bairnie, bairnikie : child

bajan : first-year student at Aberdeen University (*bec jaune*, yellow bill)

balas : a sort of ruby

ballant : ballad

ban : curse

bannock : a round flat thickish cake of oat-, barley-, pease-meal or wheat-flour, baked on a girdle

bap : a thick roll made with yeast, baked in an oven

barm : yeast, fermenting agent

barmybrained : giddy, flighty, mad

barritchfu : harsh, stern

bate : beat ; beaten

bauch : dull

bawbee : halfpenny

bawr : joke

be, bi : by

bead : form small drops or bubbles

beaver, cock his : set his cap, assumed a self-assured air

bebble : bubble

begane, wi gowd : overlaid with gold

beggar's broon : light brown snuff made from stem of tobacco plant

begrutten : tear-drenched

bell : bubble, swell up

bell, bear the : win the prize

bellox : belly

bellwaverin : straggling, moving aimlessly

belth : whirlpool

ben : inside, to the inner part of the house ; between ; a mountain

bent, gang to the : flee from danger (especially creditors) ; take to the wilds

beschacht : distorted

besom : sweeping-broom ; mischievous or slovenly female

betide : befall

bewis : boughs, branches

bezant : brilliant, like a gold coin of the Byzantine Empire

bick and birr : cry like grouse

bicker : beaker, wooden vessel for drinking ; competition, quarrel

bide, byde : await, endure

bield : shelter

bien : comfortable, well off

bigg : build

bightsome : easily and lightly active

billie : fellow, companion, mate, chap

bin, bind : bind (e.g. sheaves)

binna : be not, are not

338

binnae : except, but not

birk : birch-tree ; smart fellow

birkie : smart fellow

birl : whirl ; carouse, pay for rounds of drinks

birn : load, quantity, burden

birth : subsidiary and contrary current

birze : press (of setting small turnips after singling or thinning the rows of seedlings)

bittock : little bit

bitty : small piece

bizz : buzz

blad : leaf; large swatch or lump

blae : blue ; blueish hard clay or soft slate, carbonaceous shale, mudstone

blaeberry : bilberry

blare : dim and deceptive sheen ; howl, shout

blate : belated, shy, retiring

blatter : blow, bespatter

Blawin Beelie : blowing billie, boastful fellow

blawp : watery patch like a blister

blear : dim, damp

blee : complexion, hue

bleeze : blaze

blether : frivolous chat

blocher : gurgle, guggle in coughing

bluffert : squall

blyness : joy, happiness

blythe : merry

blytheheid : merriment, joy, happiness

bochkan : hobgoblin, spectre

boddle : copper coin, valued at one-sixth of a penny sterling

body, buddie : person, friend

boich : emit short difficult coughs

bonnet-laird : small landowner cultivating his own ground and wearing a bonnet rather than a hat

bonnie : beautiful

boo, bou : bow, bend down

bool : bowl, bend, curve

boon-tree : elder-tree

borne-heid : headlong

botheration : pother, teasing

bouk : bulk

bourtree : elder-tree (planted at boundaries to keep off evil spirits)

bousum : gracious, cordial

boutgate : roundabout

bow : a boll, dry measure of weights varying by locality and substance ; of meal usually 140 pounds avoirdupois

brade-up : springing up

brae : hill slope

brae-hag : steep bank with overhanging turf edge

brag : boast, boost

braid : broad

braird : growing crop ; spring up from seed

brak : break ; broke

bramble : branch of blackberry plant

brash : effort, excitement

braw : fine

bree : broth, gravy, any liquor

breeks : trousers

breenge : rush forward recklessly

brent : steep, prominent

brent on : precipitously onward

brim : swelling, violent

brod : board

broo, brou, bree : forehead ; eyebrow

broozled : smashed, bruised

brose : pottage made by pouring boiling water (or milk, or the liquid in which vegetables have been cooked) on to oat- or pease-meal, and mixing with salt and butter

bruckle : brittle

bruik : use, enjoy, endure, brook

brunstane : brimstone

buckie : convoluted shell ; perverse person ; fellow, chap, creature

buckie-beads : strings of small shells

buddie : person, friend

buird : board

bukser (Eskimo) : trousers

bum : hum

bummand : hubbub

bummie : bumble bee, or any bee

burd alane : a solitary bird, absolutely alone

burdies : young people, especially lower-class women

burnet : dark brown, brunette

burnie : small stream

burp : belch

busk : adorn, equip, prepare, trim

339

buss : bush, shrub

but : along in the direction of the best room or towards the house door

but(t) and ben : two-roomed house

butterie : butterfly

bydand : abiding (motto of the Gordon Highlanders)

byke : bee-hive, wasps' nest

byllie : cattle-man

by-ordinar : extraordinary

byre : cowshed

by-rinnins : arrears ; side-runs

byspale : marvel, person or thing of wonderful qualities (often said in irony) ; illegitimate child (side-play, by-speel)

CA', *caa* : call ; drive

cadger : travelling hawker

cailleach : Gaelic word meaning an old woman ; the last week of spring-time equinoctial gales

cairney : hillock

cairtin : playing cards

cakes : primarily oatcakes

callan, callant : boy, stripling, young man, fellow, chap

caller : fresh

canny : careful, safe, handy

cantie : cheerful, contented, comfortable

cantraips : antics, magical or mischievous sleights

carle doddie : ribwort plantain, used by girls to discover the fidelity of lovers, and by children in duels (Charlie-Geordie, Jacobites *v.* Hanoverians)

carritch : catechism

carse : moist lowland

cast : put off ; cut peats and expose them to dry

cast, gied a : gave myself an air

cater-cousins : kinsfolk in a quarrelsome family

causey : causeway, main street

Ceinteach : *Caointeach* (Gaelic), female water-kelpie, who warned of death in the family by wailing at the kitchen door

cep : except

certies, my : by Heaven, I assure you

chackit : checked, clipped

chalmer : private room

chap : strike, knock

chappit : having skin cracked by cold

chauve : sallow, pale swarthy, black mixed with dirty white

cheep : feeble sound

chemie : chemise

ches : chose

chiel : fellow, chap

chirn : churning

chitter : shiver

chumley-cheek : chimney-side

clachan : village

claith : cloth

clap : throw ; embrace, caress

clart : dirty, befoul

clarty, clorty : dirty, messy

clash : scandal, tittle-tattle

clavers : prattle, nonsense

claw : scratch

cleed : clothe

cleg : gadfly

cleik up the cleugh : hook up the ravine, lead up the garden, cheat

clerk : scholar, man of learning, expert

cleveralitie : cleverness

clim : climb

clinks : coins

clort : dirt, muck

close, closs : courtyard, usually narrow, in city or farm

clour : blow, wound

clyak : the last sheaf at harvest, cut by the youngest on the farm and dressed as a maiden (Gaelic *caileag*), carried home in triumph, and given on Yule Eve to a valued animal ; the period after completion of harvest

clype : tell tales, tattle

coble : rowing-boat, ferry

cockernony : high-set coiffure

cockit : perky

cock-o-the-north : upstart

cohaiket : damaged

coinyelled : agitated, disturbed

collady-stane : cowlady (ladybird)-stone, river-worn quartz boulder

collyshangie : dog-fight, squabble

connach : destroy, ruin

coorie : snuggle, cower, crouch

coronach : dirge, lament (for voice or bagpipes)

corp : dead body

corrie : cauldron-shaped hollow in hillside

corrieneuchin : conversing intimately, usually of lovers

cosh : cosy, snug, comfortable, smug

cottar, cottier : small-holding tenant

cougher : cough continuously

coulter : ploughshare

counter-lowper : male shop assistant

coup, cowp : overturn

coups the creel : upsets the applecart, causes a sensation

couthie : sympathetic, familiar, hearty

cow, cowe : cut, trim, outdo, surpass

cowes the cuddy : polls the donkey, beats the band, takes the cake

crabbit : bad-tempered

crack : crack a whip ; talk

craig : throat, neck

cramasie, crammasie : crimson

craturie : small creature

craw : crow

craw-steps : projecting stones on house-gables

creashy, creeshy : fat, greasy

creel : basket ; *in a creel* : in a mix-up

crine : shrink

critters : creatures

croichle : have a dry husky cough

cronie : intimate friend

crook : hook and chain for hanging pots over fire

croon : crown, five-shilling silver piece

cuddie : donkey, inferior pony or horse

cuddle : sit close by, talk intimately with, embrace

cuddle ba' : comfortable bed

cuits : ankles ; shins

cushat : wood-pigeon, ring-dove

cutter, rin the : fetch or carry beer or spirits on the sly

cutty : short ; saucy

cwa : come away (call to arrest attention)

DAE, DEE, DIV : do

daff : sport, converse frivolously

daffie : daffodil

damakie : young dame

dambrod : draught-board

da(u)nder : stroll ; cinder ; wrath

dang : damn

dannlit : dandled, fondled

darg : task

daunt : depress, intimidate

daunton : discourage

daur : dare

daw : dawn

deave, deeve : deafen, tire out

decreet : a judge's final sentence

deemless : incalculable

deid-set : setting in death

deil : devil. An otiose oath, e.g. *whaur deil . . .*

dell : delve, dig

dene : narrow deep valley

depone : testify, give evidence on oath

dern : hide ; hidden

devaal, devauld : cease ; cessation

dhubrack : dark-coloured trout

dicht, dight : wipe

diligence : legal execution

dilly-dally : move in a lazy slovenly way

ding : strike, defeat ; stroke

dirk : dagger carried by Highlanders

dirl : thrill, piercing pain ; strike

dishielogie : coltsfoot, *Tussilago farfara*

disjaskit : dejected, exhausted

dispitefull : envious

displenish : selling off of farm-stock, implements, etc.

divot : sod, turf

dochter, dother : daughter

Dod : God (in a non-serious context)

dodder : totter

doited : doting, confused in mind

doitert : feeble-minded

dokkin on da scroo : dockweed on the cornstack

dominie : schoolmaster

donnert : dazed, stupid

doo : dove, pigeon

doonby : downhill nearby

doon on : down with !

Doric : journalistic nickname formerly applied to the Lowland Scots language (as if the King's English dialect were classical Attic)

341

dorty : pettish, saucy, fastidious
douce : gentle, pleasant, dulcet
dounpitten : put down, paid out
doup, dowp : bottom, backside ; residue
dour, dure : hard, severe, unyielding, sullen
dowie : sad, drooping
downa : cannot
downie : subdued
dowse : extinguish, dim
dozened, dozent : asleep, dozing
dozy breet : stupid slow brute
draigon : kite
dram : small drink of whisky or other distilled liquor
drappie : little drop, small drink
dree : endure
dreetle : dribble
dreich : melancholy, lugubrious
drouth : dryness, thirst
drumlie : turbid, obscure
dub : rainwater puddle
dud, duddie : rag
duddie : ragged
dule, duil : sorrow
dullyart : dull, dreary
dulse : dull, heavy
dung : knocked
dunnlan : dully reverberating
dunt : blow
durst : dared
dwaiblie : enfeebled
dwaum : swoon
dwine, dwyne : dwindle
dyke : stone wall or turf bank

EEMIS : balancing precariously
een : eyes ; one ; even, just
e'en : evening
eerie : depressing, fearful ; sad, frightened
ee'st : used
eident, eydent : diligent, eager
elbuck : elbow
eldhood : old age
Embro : Edinburgh
emerant, emerod : emerald
encramasiean : crimsoning
epple : apple
etin : giant
ettle : aim, try

evendoon : confirmed in friendship on an equal footing and without reserve

FACK'S DEATH : as sure as death
faem : foam
fain : eager ; eagerly
fank : sheepfold
farrant ; auld-farrant : old-fashioned, sagacious
farrer : further
fash : vex, perplex
faught, fecht : fight
feart : afraid
fecht : fight
feckless : undependable, resourceless
fee : engage for a wage
feeze about : turn, twist, screw around
fegs : faith (a petty oath)
feiman : in violent diffused heat or emotion
fere, fier : companion
ferly : marvel, miracle
feth : in faith !
fey : infatuated, under an evil doom
feynd : devil
fidge : fidget, be restless
fient a : the devil a ; no
filies : occasionally
filius nullius : no-one's son, illegitimate child
fin, find : find, grope
firet : blistered
fit : what
fit, fuit : foot
flair, fleer, flure : floor
fleg : scare
fleitch : wheedle
fleur, flour, flouer, flure : flower
flichter : flutter ; flicker
fling : dancing or kicking motion
flume : flow, flood, outpouring
flype : turn inside out
flyte : quarrel in words
fock, fowk : people, folk
fog, fug : moss, lichen
folk o peace : fairies
fooge : escape, play truant
for aa : in spite of, for all
forbye : besides
forcey : energetic, go-ahead
fordele : destroy, spoil

fordelyd : wasted
fore, tae the : forward, to the fore
forenicht : evening
forfochen, forfauchen : exhausted, worn out
forjeskit : tired out
forkytail : earwig
forouten : without
fou : full of liquor, drunk
fowin peats : filling peats into baskets or carts to stack for household burning
foziness : sponginess, obtuseness
fraise : make a crashing noise ; cajole with phrases
fraught : freight, load
freen : friend
fremmit : alien, strange, hostile
fret : agitate, excite ; eat, devour
fuff : blast
Fullarton : winner of Fullarton scholarship for Greek and Latin at Aberdeen University
fulp : whelp, puppy
fummart : polecat, foul marten
fun' : found
funder : demolish
furr : furrow
fushionless : insipid, useless, without energy or capacity
fusome : foul, unpleasant
futtled : whittled, carved

GAB : talk
gaed : went
gaet, gait : road, way
gaffer : overseer, foreman
gairten : garter
gale : gable, end of building
gallusness : gallows-bird ways, unvirtuous propensities
gang : go
gangrel : vagabond
gant : yawn, gape
gar : cause, make
gash : distorted, writhing with emotion
gashant : fluent, insolent
gate : way, road, method
gaud : showy ornament ; meretricious custom, trick
gaun, gyaun : going

gaup : stupid person
gawcie : massive and cheerful
gean : wild cherry-tree or its fruit
gear : possessions
gentle : genteel
gentrice : gentle and well-bred elegance
genty : elegant
gerss : grass
gesserant : sparkling like armour
gey : very ; considerable, frightful
gien : given ; gave
gin : if ; against ; by, before
girn : grin ; complain
girnel : granary, meal chest
glacket, glaikit : foolish, capricious
glamer, glamerie : glamour, dazzlement
glaur : mud
glawmerie : glamour
gled : glad, bounding
glede : fire
gleg : brisk
Glenlivet : brand of whisky
glenter : flash
glinkin : sidelong, transient
glisk : glimpse, view ; passing ray
glister : lustre, radiance
gloam : twilight
gloamin : evening twilight
glore, gloir : glory
glower : glare
gorcock : male grouse
gove : wander stupidly
gowan : any whitish daisy, especially the ox-eye
gowand swaird : daisy-covered turf
gowdie : jewel
gowk : fool, cuckoo
gowkit : cuckoo, scatter-brained
gowl : hollow between hills ; howl
graip : grip
graith : equipment, harness, tackle
grame : anger, hate
gramest : most warlike, grandiose
grane : groan
grat : wept
gree : agree
greet, greit : weep ; tears
grein : yearn
griddle : girdle
grieve : farm overseer
grit, grite : great, big

343

groff-write : large-lettered

grunshin : grunting, grumbling, tedious, harsh

gude, guid : good ; God

gudeman, guidman : husband ; small proprietor

guide : manage ; help

guidsake, guidsakes : for God's sake !

guidwyfe : mistress of household

gushet-neuk : gusset, strip of cloth at armpit or elsewhere

gype : simpleton

gyte : mad

HAAF : open sea

haar, harr : chill sea mist

haddie : haddock

haet : small bit

haggis : a dish of minced sheep's lungs, heart and liver, mixed with toasted oatmeal, onions, suet, salt and pepper, and boiled in a sheep's stomach

haill, hale : whole

haillhertheid : whole-heartedness, entire self-possession

hain : keep, save

hairns, harns : brains

hairse, hearse : hoarse

hairst : harvest ; autumn

haiverel : foolish

halflins : partly, by half

half-stockit : defective

hallyoch : noise of water on shingle

hannie : little hand

hantle : handful, quantity

hap : wrap ; bury

harle : trail, drag

harra : harrow

hartsom : hearty

hashin throw : hurrying through a job

haud : hold

haud thaem : direct themselves

hauflin : half-grown or half-witted person

havers : chatter

hazelraw : lichen

hech mon : eh man ! (amused cry)

heddles : small cords through which the warp is passed after going through the reed

Heelanters : Highlandmen

heicht, hicht : height

heist : hoist

herd : shepherd or other watcher of domestic animals

Hieland, Hielant : Highland

hikeit : lifted and carried

hillfoot : from an upland farm

hing in : hang on, stick in

hinmaist, hinmost : hindmost, last

hint : hinder part, back-end

hirple : hobble

hoast : cough

hodden : clownish, rustic, rough, homespun

hodge : jerk irregularly

holine : dark green like holly leaf

hoodie-craw : hooded crow

hoot ay : ho, yes ! (amused cry)

hotch : jerk suddenly

hous-rig : house roof

how-dumb-deid : stillest period of night

howdumdeidsuinsheen : midnight sunshine

howe : hollow

howk : dig

humin : evening twilight

humphy : humped

hup : cry ' Gee-up ' to horse

hurkle : contract the body, crouch ; limp

hurl : drive or be driven in a wheeled vehicle ; whirl, tour

hurly : small-wheeled truck

hurlygush : outburst of water

hushaba : lullaby

hyne : haven, harbour

hyow : hoe

hypothec : concern, affair

IJJIT : idiot

ilk, ilka : each, every ; same

inbye : inside, within

ingle : fire

JAD, JAUD : jade (contemptuous term for female)

jessie : effeminate man

jilp : dash of liquid

jings : Jesus ! (mild oath)

jizzen : childbed

344

GLOSSARY

jock : joke

jorum : a drinking-vessel for a social company, a loving-cup

jouk : dodge

joukery-pawkery : dissembling, cunning

jow : roll violently with swinging motion

jummelt : miscellaneous, jumbled

jundie : jog, rock, shove sideways

jyne : join

KAIL : cabbage ; vegetable broth

kail throu the reek, send ane his : give one a raw deal

kailyaird : cabbage-patch

kaim : comb for hair

kame : cell in honeycomb

kamiker (Eskimo) : sealskin boots

kanglin : wrangling, cavilling

kankert : morose

kebbick : cheese

keek : peep

keekin-gless : mirror

keel : ruddle, coloured chalk or clay

kelpie : water-spirit

ken : know ; knowledge

kenna-what : unknown thing

kennet : hunting hound

kenspeckle : conspicuous, distinguished

kep : catch, hold

kilhabbit : enchanted

Kilmarnock : broad bonnet

kingheid : sovereign, supreme

kintra : country

kipper : fish salted and cured by hanging in air or smoke

kist : chest

kist o whistles : church organ

kittle : tickle, titillate, stimulate

kittlie : tickling

kittok : a wanton woman

knir : knot ; tough and dwarfish person

knock : clock

knowe : knoll, hillock, mound

kyaak : (oat)cake

kyanised : treated with Cayenne pepper

kye : cows

kyloe : small black or Highland cattle-beast, especially a young black bullock

LACE INTIL : lash into

lade : channel leading water to a mill

laich, laigh, law : low

lair : site for digging ; grave ; section of peatmoss

laird : landowner

lairdie : young laird ; degenerate laird

laithlie : loathsome

Lallan : Lowland (Scotch)

Lammas : loaf-mass, feast of first-fruits, 1st August

lane, his (*her* etc.) : on his own, by himself

langer, haud fowk oot o : keep people from boredom

langerie : yearning

larach : site of a building ; ruined foundation ; corpse, skeleton

lassock : girl

lave, the : remainder, the rest

laverock : lark

laverock's hoose, there was nae reek in the : it was a dark, stormy night

law : hill

lawtithheid : loyalty, trueness

leal : loyal, trusty

leal, land o the : kingdom of heaven

lea-lang, leelang : livelong

lear : learning

leavin, leevin : living

lee : tell lies

lee : lonely ; live (as in *leelang*)

leese: leeze me on : I am grateful for (lief is me)

leet : list of nominees

leid : language ; lay, song

lench : launch

lep : leaped

let be : not to mention

leuch : laughed

levin : lightning

ley : lea, grass pasture

lichtlie : depreciate, slight

liefer : rather

lift, luft, luift, lyft : sky

ligg : lie, be couched

like : likely ; similar to

likes o you, the : people like you

lilt : sing in a lively way ; limp about

limb, the auld deil's : imp of Satan

limmer : wench

345

ling : heather
links : windings of road or river ; sandy flat meadows by seashore
linn : waterfall
lint in the bell : growing flax in bloom
lippen tae : depend on, trust to
lirk : wrinkle, fold, hollow
list : listen ; enlist
lithe : warm shelter
loesome : lovable, winsome
loof : palm of hand
loon, loun : lad
loonie, loonikie : little lad
lopper : turn sour
losh : Lord ! (mild oath)
louch : sinking into liquid depths
loup, lowp : leap
lowe : flame
lown : calm
lowse, lowsen : loose ; loosen
luely : softly
lug : ear
lum : chimney ; top-hat

MAE : more
machar : seaside pasture
maik : match, equal
maikless : matchless, unrivalled
maist : most ; almost
mak : make ; matter
mallimaks : fulmar petrels
maltalent : malice, mischief
Manse : official residence of parish minister
mappamound : world, universe
march : boundary
marra, marrow : match, equal, companion
mate : equal, peer, match
maun : must
maunner : maunder, mutter
mavis : song-thrush
mear, meer : mare
meat : food (flesh or other)
meen, muin, mune : moon
mell : mix ; meddle
mell-straik : hammer-stroke
mense : discretion, measured conduct proper to a *Mensch* (German) with a *mens* (Latin)
men't : mended

merchless : without boundaries
merrit : married
mew : seagull
mickle, muckle : much
midge : small gnat-like insect
mim : prim, prudish, affected
mimp : be shy, reserved ; speak affectedly
mind : bear in mind, consider ; remember
mirk : gloom, darkness
mirl : speckle
mirligoe : small spinning-wheel ; any upright whirling thing
misdoot : suspect, doubt
mongers : intriguers, racketeers, warmongers
mools : clods of mould
morn : morrow
moss : bog
mote : small piece of extraneous matter
mou, mouthie : mouth
moulter : fee for grinding grain
moyne : procure, convey
Mulciber : Vulcan, god of metallurgy
murlack : crumb

NATHELESS : nevertheless, in spite of that
near haun' : nearly
neb : nose
neebor, neepur : neighbour
neep : turnip
neep'rin : neighbouring
neist : next
neoned : embellished with neon lighting
nesslin : nestling, baby bird
neuk : nook, corner
nick : cut ; nickname of the devil
nieve : fist
niffer : exchange
none : noon
noo : now ; new
nor : than
Norland : North Country, northern
nowt : cattle
nyaff : poor feeble stupid person
nyattert : argued in a pettifogging way

OCHT : aught, anything
oe : grandchild, youngest descendant

GLOSSARY

on-ding : downpour
onkent : unknown
onwytan : waiting for
'oo' : wool
oorie : melancholy, languid, shivering
with cold and damp
ootbye : outside yonder
or lang : ere long
orra, orrie : odd, extraordinary, queer
Osnaburg : coarse linen cloth, of a type
copied from the town in Hanover
ourhailet : subdued
outowre : all over and around
ower, owre : over
oxter : armpit ; take under the arm

PADDIES : immigrants from Ireland
paer, pair, puir : poor
paitricks : partridges
pandrop : hard peppermint-flavoured
sweet
parritch : porridge
partan's tae : crab's toe, a sort of clay-
pipe
pat : pot
pavone : peacock
pawkie : sly in a venial way
pawmies : beatings of palms, clappings
peat-moss : peat-bog
pech : pant
peekie : pining, thin
peenged : reduced to misery
peez : dry peas, inserted in shoes by
pilgrims to obtain greater merit
pertectan : protecting
pibroch : bagpiping ; classical variation
music of the great Scots bagpipe
pickle, puckle : small amount, a few
p'ind, poind : seize, distrain upon
pinge : whimper, make miserable
sound
pit past : put aside, stored away
plash : heavy fall of rain
plowt : fall plump, rain heavily
ploy : frolic
plunk : plunge ; disappear, play truant
from
podduck : frog
poke : bag, pouch, purse
polysemous : seminal and having meanings on many levels (a coinage like

some of those by James Joyce in
Anna Livia Plurabelle and elsewhere)
ponnage : pontage, ferrying-point
poortith, puirtith : poverty
pooshan : poison
poother, pouther : powder
pot : deep pool in river
pow, powe : head
powet : tadpole ; *powet's creels* : toy-
baskets
pree : sample, taste, enjoy
preen : pin
prett : artifice
prieve : prove
primp : act affectedly, primly
provand : provender, provisions
provost : chief magistrate of town,
mayor
pudden : pudding-like
purpour : purple
pushion : poison

QUAET, *quaiet, quait, quate* : quiet
quat : quitted, ceased
quean, queyn, quine : girl
queem : complete, finalised
quey : two-year-old cow
quhilk : which
quick : alive
quicksiller : mercury

RAGMENTS : residues of an estate
raipit : roped
randle-tree : (rowan-tree) beam sup-
porting chimney
randy : quarrelsome, debauched
rant : frolic, sing gaily
rasch : bold, impassioned, energetic
rash : rush
rashion : ration, portion of food
rauch, reoch, reuch, roch, rouch, rogh :
rough
raucle : vigorous, bold, loud
rax : stretch, reach, pass
reaper : machine for cutting grain crop
reck, what : what does it matter ?
redd : arrange, tidy up
rede : advise
reed : frame for warp in loom
reek : smoke
Reekie, Auld : the Old Smoke, Edinburgh

347

reem : cream, froth

reenge : scour, scrub

reese : praise

reeshle : rustle, disturb(ance)

reest, reist : roast

remed : remedy

rengan : reigning

rhu : promontory

rid : get rid of

rig, rigg : ridge, ploughland, any division of a field

ripe, rype : search

rocht : treated roughly

roop, roup : cry hoarsely

roose : praise, extol

rotten : rat

rouchled : ruffled

roup : auction

routh, rowth : abundance

rowan : mountain ash

rowe : roll

rowt : moo, low, bellow

rowthy : abounding

rubbin-bane : rubbing-bone

ruck : heap of corn or hay, stack

rugg : pull

rung : staff, cudgel

runt : stalk, stump

ryall rone : royal crest

ryve : tear in bits

SAIR : sore ; sorely ; strongly, hard

sair, ser' : serve, supply

sairin : serving, enough to serve their turn

sake : self

sans : without

sanshach : sly, saucy

sark : shirt

Sassenach : Saxon, English(man)

saul, sowl : soul

saut : salt

Sawbath : Sunday

scailt : spilt

scart : scratch

scaurie : with scree-slopes bare of turf

scauth : injury, distress

scheid : shed

schire : clear, sheer, vivid

sclafferin : shuffling

sclaffin : scraping

sclarrie : shower promiscuously

sclim : climb

scone : thin round cake of meal

sconsit : ensconced (but with association from context with *scomfished*, suffocated)

scoogie : apron

scough : catch

scraap : scrape (of hoeing out turnips to thin the rows of seedlings)

scrieve, scryve : write, inscribe

scrimply : scarcely

scruntit : stunted, niggardly

scunner : disgust

scutter : trivial, messy or incompetent work

sech : sigh

seelfu : pleasant

seep-sabbin : oozing with a sobbing noise (of water trickling through peat)

selie : silly, simple

selvedge, the blessing with the black : the Union of the Scots and English Parliaments in 1707, by the international treaty constituting the United Kingdom of Great Britain

sen, sin : since

set her up : expression of contempt or resentment against undue advancement or pretension

shaavin : sowing

shauchle : shuffle, trail the feet

shaver : wag, joker

shaw : wood

sheemach : matted

sheen, shuin : shoes

sheep-shank : falsely pretentious person

sheet : shoot

sheil : clear turf and weeds

sheiling : summer hut in upland pasture

sheltie : pony, small or poor horse

shilpet : sickly, timorous, meagre

shitten : befouled with ordure

shoggly : unsteady

shooglan : joggling

shool : shovel

shortsome : lively, entertaining

shouther, shooder : shoulder

shuilfie : chaffinch

shuin, suin, sune : soon

shurlan : murmuring
sib : akin, related
siccan : such a
siccar : sure
siclike : so, in such a way
sig : cordial
siller : silver, money
silly : simple
sindry : asunder
sinsyne : in the past ; since then
skail : disperse, scatter
skailie : pencil for writing on slate
skaith : harm
skau : scene of havoc
skeel : skill
skelp : stroke, slap ; beat of a clock, portion (of time etc.)
skep : straw-hive
skerry : rock exposed at low tide
skian-dhu : black knife (Gaelic)
skilpin on : plunging ahead
skimmer : large flattish ladle for skimming cream etc.
skinkle : shine, glitter
skirl : make a shrill noise
skreel : cry shrilly
skreigh, screigh : shriek
skreigh o day : first daylight
skutch : scoot, slip, dodge, loiter
slae : sloe, blackthorn
sleek : sleet, slush
sleekit : fawning, moving slily
sliddery, slithery : slippery
slock : entrance
sloke : slake, quench
smeddum : mettle, bold vigour
smeek, smeik : smoke
smirr : anything clammy and close-clinging, e.g. butter or fog
smool : steal unperceived ; transient apparition
smorit : smothered, suffocated
sneckit : fixed by latch or snib
snell : chill
snod : trim ; trimly
snoot-cloot : handkerchief
snoul : tamely submit
snowk : sniff
sodger, sojer : soldier
sones : sun's
soo : sow, female pig

sook : suck
soom : swim
soop : sweep
sort : arrange ; chastise
sou : large oblong stack
sough : sound, breath, sigh, rumour, whisper
souple : supple, subtle
spaewife : female fortune-teller
spang : leap, spring
spate : flood
spaul : shoulder, back
speak : speech
speel, speil : climb, ascend
speen, spuin, spune : spoon
speer, speir : ask
spelder : spread, sprawl
splairged : bespattered, sodden
splatterdashes : gaiters, leggings
sporran : leather or fur pouch or purse worn with kilt
spout-gun : hollow piece of stalk for spitting or blowing through
sprang : variegated stripe or patch
sprot : sprout, withered end, stump
spunk : spark ; spirit, mettle
spunkie : mettlesome ; will-o'-the-wisp
spurkle : wooden stick for stirring porridge
stacher : stagger
stairheid : at the head of a common staircase in a ' land ' or block of flats
stang : sting
stark, sterk : strong, powerful
starn, starnie, sterne : star
staucher : stagger
staw : surfeit, disgust ; stole
steek, steik : stitch, close, shut
steer : stir
stem-mill : itinerant threshing-mill propelled by steam
stend : spring, extend
stey : steep, vertical
stieve : stiff, stubborn
stilpert : long-legged, stepping as on stilts
stockie : person who stands stiffly
stook : set of corn sheaves propped together on end
stoor, stour : dust

349

stoorie : restlessly active
stot : bounce
stound : ache, astonishment
stoup, stowp : large mug
stoury : dusty
stousie : strong healthy child
strath : wide valley
strathspey : a kind of dance, or the type of tune for it
straucht : straight
stravaig : wander
streik : stretch
strussle : struggle, effort
stumpie : squat, walking as on stumps
sturrit : stirred, upset
sugh : whistling sound
sumph : softie ; stupid dolt
swa : so
swap : exchange
swaw : form waves, ripple, undulate
sweelin : swilling, washing
sweir, sweirt : unwilling, reluctant
swig : whirl, rock
swith : quick
swither : hesitate ; agitate oneself, put on airs
swound : swoon, sleep
swyte, sweit : sweat
syne : then, later, since ; *lang syne* : long ago

TACK : lease
tade : toad
tae : to ; too ; toe
tait : gay
taivert : tired, bewildered
tammie : round bonnet with central knob, called ' tam-o'-shanter '
tane, the : the one (of two)
tap : top
tasht : spotted, stained, spoiled
tattie : potato
tawse : leather strap
tchyauv : work, especially at something tough and tangled
teem, toom, tuim : empty
tene : grief, passion
tenement : block of flats
tent : attend ; *tak tent on* : pay attention to
tenty : attentive, careful, competent

terraneezed : tyrannised
tether's fu, if the : if you already have a husband tied up
teuch : tough
thack, theek : thatch
thae : those
than : then
thegither : together
thir : these
thirl : pierce ; enthrall, enslave
thole : endure
thon : that there, yonder
thorter : thwarting
thowe : thaw
thowless : without energy or ability
thrang : busy ; a throng
thrangety : close-thronging multitude
thrapple : throat
thraw : throw, twist ; frustration ; wrestle, resist
threep, threip : say repeatedly and emphatically
threshart-stane : threshold
throu'ther, throwther : confusedly
thrum : loose end of thread ; *grey thrums* : soft purrings
Thrums : nickname of Kirriemuir, birthplace of Sir James Barrie, sentimental anglicised author, of whom a philosopher has said that he ' wrote as though there had never been a Ball in Kirriemuir ' (alluding to a popular bawdy ballad)
tid : tide, time, mood ; *tid wi* : properly adjusted in mood and occasion to
timmer : timber
tine, tyne : lose
tirl, tirrl : twirl
tirl a pin : rasp a plectrum against a metal spiral on a door
tither, the : the other (of two)
tnock : clock
tocher : dowry
toddy : warm drink of diluted and spiced spirits
toukin : pulling
toun, toon : farm ; town
toure : tower
tousie : dishevelled, untidy
tovarisch : comrade

GLOSSARY

tove : chat

tow : rope

tow-gun : fibre gun, made from elder shoot by extracting pith, used for firing paper balls (larger sizes as bellows for fire)

towsie : shaggy, unkempt

trachle, trauchle : wearisome work ; to weary by working

trackie : small tract, pamphlet

traist : trust

transmogrified : transformed, metamorphosed

trauchlit : tired and harassed with work

treddles : foot levers for loom

trephine : trepan

trow : believe

truff : turf, peat

trummle : tremble

trump : trumpet

tryst : market for animals ; any assignation

tulzie : brawl, quarrel

tup : ram

turn-gree : winding stair

Tusitala : Samoan nickname for R. L. Stevenson

twaa-fauldit : two-fold, double ; characterised by duplicity, schizophrene

twalmonth : year

twa-three, a : two or three, a few

tyaav : work at something tough and tangled

tyke : dog, cur

UGSOME : ugly, horrible

unco : extraordinary

undeemous : incalculable

unken'd : unknown

U.P. kirks : United Presbyterian churches

usquebae : whisky, *aqua vitae*

VAIGAN : wandering

viduity : widowhood

vivand : vital, vivid, lively

vow : cry of surprise or alarm

vricht : carpenter

WAB : web

wabbit : tired

wad : wager, bet

wae : woe ; woeful

waement : lament

waesome : woeful, sad

waft : woof, the threads going from the shuttle through the web

wag : waver, sway

wa-gang : away-going

wale : choose ; choice, selection

wall : spring of water

wamble : move wavily

wame, wime : belly, womb ; point of origin, centre

wan : dark, gloomy, dirty

wandocht : puny, contemptible

wane : little one, small child

want : lack

wanworth : unworthy one, ne'er-do-well

wap : wrap ; wrestle

warl, warlt : world

warsle, warssle, warstle : wrestle, struggle

wastrey : wasting, devastation

watchet : greyish-brown

watergaw : fragment of rainbow ; bright interval in bad weather ; something not to be expected, however much desired

waucht : draught

wauken : staying awake ; awaken

waukrife : wakeful

waur : worse

wean, waen : wee ane, small child

weary faa't : a curse befall it

wecht : weight

wede : finished, effete

week : corner

weel : well

weird : fate, destiny

wersh : insipid ; bitter

wey, wye : way

weyve : weave

whammle, whummle : overwhelm, turn upside down

whang : fly, cut away

whaup : curlew

wheen, a : a few

wheeng : whimper

wheesht : hush

whiles : sometimes

whilk : which

whin : gorse, furze

whitemaa : seagull
wicht, wight : person
widdreme : sudden raving ; nightmare
widin : wading
wife : woman, married or not
wilyart : wild
wimple : wind, meander
winnock : window
wir : our
wiselike, wycelike : sensible, proper
witter : throat
wizen : windpipe, throat
wode, wud : mad
wow : cry of surprise
wrack : seaweed (used as manure)
wrocht : wrought, made
wud, wuid : wood
wun : wind, breeze
wyte : blame

YAAVIN : awn of barley
yae, yin : one
yaird : garden
yammer : continually yell, whine ; chatter, yatter
yerk : engage busily
yestreen : yesterday evening
yett : gate
yill : ale, beer
yird : earth ; bury
yirthen : earthenware
yoke : set to work (of horses, farm servants, etc.)
yoky : itchy
yont : beyond
yowdendrift : down-driving gale
yowl : yell, howl
yow-trummle : ewe-tremble, cold spell after midsummer shearing

ALPHABETICAL LIST OF AUTHORS AND PSEUDONYMS

AINSLIE Douglas Grant Duff · 133
AINSLIE Hew · 6
AIRD Thomas · 19
ANDERSON Alexander · 71
ANDERSON Basil Ramsay · 110
ANGUS Marion · 136
ANON. (various) · 16, 187, 223
AYTOUN William Edmondstoune · 28

BERWICK Thurso · 300
BRANFORD Frederick Victor · 198
BRIDIE James · 188
BROWN George Douglas · 138
BROWN Ivor John Carnegie · 198
BROWN James B. · 51
BRUCE George · 252
BUCHAN John (1st Lord Tweeds-
  muir) · 151
BUCHANAN Robert · 67
BURGESS J. J. Haldane · 114

CAIE J. M. · 159
CALDER William Moir · 162
CARLYLE Thomas · 10
CLARK Rev. Dr Ivo MacNaughton · 168
COCKER W. D. · 163
COOK R. L. · 305
CORRIE Joe · 237
CRAIGIE Sir William · 138
CRAWFORD John · 33
CRAWFORD Robert · 156
CRUICKSHANK Helen Burness · 170

DAVIDSON A. M. · 170
DAVIDSON John · 96
DAVIDSON Thomas · 66
DERWENT Lavinia · 250
DIACK Hunter · 241
DOUGLAS Lord Alfred · 143
DOUGLAS George · 138
DOW Alex · 295
DRINAN Adam · 240

EASSON James · 54
ELLIOT Walter · 190

FERGUS Dr John F. · 126
FERGUSON John · 144
FERGUSSON Lt.-Col. Bernard E. · 262
FRASER G. S. · 278

GALLOWAY Alexander · 280
GARIOCH Robert · 253
GEDDES James Young · 83
GIVEN Thomas · 87
GORDON Adam Lindsay · 55
GRAHAM W. S. · 296
GRAY Sir Alexander · 166
GRAY Captain Charles · 1
GRAY David · 65
GRAY Father John · 134
GRAY John Young · 72
GRIEVE Christopher Murray · 200
GUNN Neil M. · 197

HALIBURTON Hugh · 73
HAMILTON Janet · 8
HAMILTON Rev. Dr W. H. · 177
HARDIE James Keir · 93
HAY George Campbell · 284
HAY Rev. John MacDougall · 161
HEDDERWICK James · 30
HENDERSON Hamish · 302
HENDRY Hamish · 146
HENDRY James Findlay · 274
HOOD Stuart · 260
HUTCHISON Dr Isobel Wylie · 191

JACOB Violet · 118
JEFFREY William · 217
JOHNSTON Ellen · 65

KAY George · 306
KEMP Robert · 249
KENNEDY William · 12
KERR Roderick Watson · 225
KINCAID John · 256
KIPLING Rudyard · 129

LAMONT Dr Archie · 248
LANG Andrew · 67

353

LIST OF AUTHORS AND PSEUDONYMS

LAW T. S. 261
LEE Joseph 158
LINDSAY John Maurice 299
LINDSAY Wallace Martin 107
LINKLATER Eric 235
LIVINGSTON William 24
LOCHHEAD Marion 239
LOCKHART John Gibson 7
LYLE Thomas 5

MAIR A. W. 157
MARTIN David 282
MAVOR Dr O. H. 188
MENZIES G. K. 141
MILLER William 25
MITCHELL John 31
MITCHISON Naomi 226
MONCRIEFF Ann Scott- 280
MONCRIEFF George Scott- 260
MONRO Harold 160
MONTGOMERIE William 244
MUIR Dr Edwin 177
MUIR Willa 195
MUNRO Neil 123
MURRAY Charles 125
MURRAY Rev. George 36
MURRAY Robert 139
MURRAY Robert Fuller 114

MACALISTER Principal Sir Donald 90
MACARTHUR Bessie J. B. 192
MACAULAY Thomas Babington,
   Lord 13
McCAIG Norman 257
MacCOLL Dugald Sutherland 109
MacDHUNLEIBHE Uilleam 24
MacDIARMID Hugh 200
MACDONALD George 39
MACDONALD Hugh 34
MACFARLAN James 51
MACFIE Ronald Campbell 91
MACGILLIVRAY James Pittendrigh 94
McGLASHAN Alan Fleming 223
McGONAGALL William 50
MACKENZIE W. A. 92
MACKIE Albert D. 242
MACKINTOSH Ewart Alan 215
MACLAREN Hamish 238
MACLEAN Somhairle 264
MACLELLAN Robert 248

NEAVES Lord 14
NICOL James 14
NICOLSON Sheriff Alexander 43

OGILVIE William 196
OGILVIE Will H. 142
OGILVY of Clova, Dorothea Maria 37
OUTRAM George 19

PATON Sir Joseph Noel 37
PAULIN Dorothy Margaret 245
PEACOCK James 222
PEERIE D.D., Moses 62

QUIN Roger 88

REID Robert 91
RENDALL Robert 234
RIVERS Gabriel 225
ROBERTSON J. Logie 73
RORIE Dr David 111
ROSS Father Antony 297

SAUNDERS R. Crombie 281
SCOTT Alexander 304
SCOTT Lady John 27
SCOTT Tom 298
SELKIRK J. B. 51
SHAW David 2
SHEPHERD Nan 217
SIMPSON Margaret Winefride 198
SINGER John 290
SLOAN Edward L. 17
SMART Alexander 10
SMITH Alexander 46
SMITH A. H. Emslie- 308
SMITH George Buchanan- 195
SMITH Dr Janet Mary 250
SMITH M. C. 140
SMITH Sydney Goodsir 291
SMITH Rev. Dr Walter Chalmers 40
SORLEY Charles Hamilton 221
SOUTAR William 227
SPENCE Lewis 148
STEVENSON Robert Louis 75
STODDART Thomas Tod 27
STORY Rev. Principal R. H. 62
STUART Alice V. 236
SURFACEMAN 71
SYMON Mary 115

354

LIST OF AUTHORS AND PSEUDONYMS

TAYLOR Rachel Annand	154	WANLOCK Rob	91
THOMSON Derick	284	WELLS Nannie K.	53
THOMSON G. Bruce	193	WILSON Adam	89
THOMSON James	56	WINGATE Walter	127
V., B.	56	YOUNG Rev. Canon Andrew	169
VEDDER David	3	YOUNG Douglas	274

ALPHABETICAL INDEX OF FIRST LINES

A BITTER meditation in the mirk it is 217
A digger he digs in the dark 225
A hunder pipers canna blaw 304
A hundred pontiff hills entomb 198
A hunner funnels bleezin, reekin 9
A little while, O Love, and thou and I 157
A million stars decide the place 91
A rosary of stars, love ! we'll count them as we go 27
Across eternity, across its snow 271
Ae boat anerlie nou 291
Ae müneless nicht in a blear October 146
Ae nicht o thae twa year 273
Ae weet forenicht i the yow-trummle 201
Afore that I'd be terraneezed as I this file hae been 193
Aifter the war, says the papers, they'll no be content at hame 151
Alas ! the people's hearts are now full of sorrow 50
All through that summer at ease we lay 183
Allan Ian Og Macleod of Raasay 124
Am faca Tu i, Iudhaich mhóir 266
Among the twelve Apostles whom 14
An oot o aa calamitie cam 300
Ane by ane they gang awa 39
Arise ! ye sons of labour, artisans of every grade 89
Arouse ! all ye true-hearted Scots 10
As he comes from one of those small houses 252
As I cam in by Netherdale 16

Beauty's a rose, a shining sword, a thief 235
Blin' ! an I'll hae to fin' for the face o my wife an wean 126
Blows the wind to-day, and the sun and the rain are flying 82
Blythe was yir comin 293
Bu tu camhanaich air a' Chuilthionn 264

Calum thonder, long's the night to your thinking 288
Cameron, whit's wrocht i the cleveralitie 261
Cauld, cauld as the wall 217
Cha do chuir de bhuaireadh riamh 264
Cha n-eil mo shùil air Calbharaigh 272
Christ ran stumbling down the street 297
Clouds of smoke on the hill 175
Có seo, có seo, oidhche dhona ? 268
Could I have sung one song that should survive 37
Courage, faint heart, press forward to the hill ! 195
Crawlin about like a snail in the mud 237
Cwa een like milk-wort and bog-cotton hair ! 203

357

INDEX OF FIRST LINES

Day in and day oot in his auld farrant loom   87
Daytime and nicht   119
Dear, nou, gin sic response were aa I kent   281
Delacroix pentit Chopin's heid   292
Did iver ye see the like o' that ?   122
Dir üsliss deevils here an dere   114
Displenish sales and public roups   260
Doon at Nether Dallachy there's neither watch nor knock   159
Drums thinner than dreams   274

Ever to be the best. To lead   114
Every bullet has its billet   158

Fair angels will sing tae ye   225
Far 'yont amang the years to be   78
Fhairshon swore a feud   28
Fou tid it was   295

Gie aa, and aa comes back   275
Gin I was God, sittin' up there abeen   126
God, give us the grace to hate   153
Green graves in the Southland. My heart it is sair   226
Gude guide me, are ye hame again, and hae ye got nae wark ?   65

Hae ye seen her, ye unco Jew   267
Hameward ye're travellin' in the saft hill rain   136
Hath she beauty ? Yea, most fair   239
He cam tae mend the broken wheels o life   168
He caught a chill in Leicester, he came here   144
He lay outstretched upon the sunny wave   184
' He was aye vaigan b' the shore   234
Here are the shores you loved   174
Here are white walls, and ease, and falling fountains   236
Here I, Jock Scott, frae Peterheid   158
Here in the land of *Würste* (*id est* sausages   223
Here in the uplands   166
Here lies Rob Allan's bonny Bell   163
Here, where the baby paddles in the gutter   278
Hing it up aside the chumley-cheek, the aul' glen's Muster-Roll   115
His father's house looked out across a firth   96
His mither sings to the bairnie Christ   201
Ho ! for the blades of Harden !   142
Hold not the hour   233
Homeward by other paths Frank never fails   19

I am a kind of farthing dip   77
I am pure, because of great illuminations   156
I canna dee, tho' I fain wud dee   138
I couldn't touch a stop or turn a screw   103
I fand a muckle buckie shell   242
I gaed to spend a week in Fife   19
I had a luve walked by the sea   293

INDEX OF FIRST LINES

' I had three tykes,' the silly old Man saith   189
I have a friend,—a faithful friend   12
I ken the ploys that ye had planned   26
I'm a puir man, I grant   39
I met a man when I was drinkin' ale   171
I met ayont the cairney   202
I mind o' the Ponnage Pule   172
I never kent sic glawmerie   265
I saw the Bairn in a city car   139
I sing of the Gordons   282
I speak of ebon tracts, whose sullen gloom   156
I' the how-dumb-deid o the cauld hairst nicht   201
I toke hyr heid atween my hondes   95
I've a wee little loon, O ! ye ne'er saw his like   72
I've poached a pickle paitricks when the leaves were turnin' sere   141
I wuldna gae near thon tunnel gin I was you   299
If Edward Thomas or Rupert Brooke   177
If it must be ; if it must be, O God !   65
In a thrifty dress of an homely guise   54
In my eye I've no apple ; every object   259
In simmer, whan aa sorts foregether   253
In the great cause of Art I rose   31
In the high places lo ! there is no light   144
In the highlands, in the country places   81
Inexorable on ye stride   292
Into the grave, into the grave with him   184
Is it a god that thunders like a sea   199
It is a thousand sunsets since I lay   150
It is not in the sorrow of the deep   161
It is not yours, O mother, to complain   76
It's dowie in the hint o' hairst   6
It's no the resurrection day   230
It's no the sax month gane   51
It was but yestreen I had oot my bit claith, man   17
It will be plowtan syne : the lift   243

JUST gie us a griddle, a guid Culross griddle   123
Just one faint whimper below, but the mare's ears quiver   247

LADY of the lovely thighs   133
Lassie, can ye say whaur ye ha been   276
Lassie wi the creel, can ye loe a cadger   33
Last heiress she of many a rood   40
Last mercy to see, in our mortal failing   306
Launched three windy neptunes high from a gargoyle scree   296
Lay me low, my work is done   55
Let us praise the humble fish   190
Lighten, Lord, my load   260
Listen ! for a lost warld maunners here   228
Little sea house, when I found you   238
Lo, thus, as prostrate, ' In the dust I write   56

Long ago in a lonely land   200
Long blue shadow of salmon lying   240
Lord, if thou art not present, where shall I   134
Lord, Thou hast made this world below the shadow of a dream   129
Lyin' on a hillside   195

MINE is that delightful villa   30
My dainty lass, lay you the blame   120
My een are nae on Calvary   273
My heart is yearning to thee, O Skye !   43
My name is Tammie Treddlefeet   2
My word ! but ye seem nae sheep-shank   3

NAE man wha loves the lawland tongue   229
No man outlives the grief of war   233
Not because your body is lovely or your hair   298
Now in the none the prowde pavone, his ryall rone   150
Now is the yaird kail boiled and hashed   308
Now range up the carriages, feed up the fires !   8
Now the ice lays its smooth claws on the sill   177

O' a' da sangs I'm ever sung   111
O' a' the strokes that's in the game   107
O for a day at the Hint o' Hairst   125
O I remember you so lithe and gay   193
O is there a God in the Heavens ?   110
O Jean, my Jean, when the bell ca's the congregation   120
O leaf that blowest westward, where the sighing   138
O Louis ! you that like them maist   67
O luely, luely, cam she in   227
O Merlin in your crystal cave   185
O Rab an' Dave an' rantin' Jim   118
O ragin' wind   170
O Truth's a braw collady-stane   192
O wad this braw hie-heapit toun   148
O wae's me for the station-master's dochter !   187
O weel I mind the bonnie morn   94
O winter wind, lat grievin be   198
Och, gin ye come to our toun   240
Ochan, aonarain na cille   286
Of a' the ills that flesh can fear   79
Of speckled eggs the birdie sings   75
Oh, never revisit ! The burn that I thought was a Spey   196
Oh ! The King's gane gyte   200
Oh, what a glister's to the wintry night !   280
Oidhche de 'n dà bhliadhna   272
Once only by the garden gate   81
' Others had parents, you had only me   199
Our shadowy congregation rested still   59
Out of this ugliness may come   244
Outpouring from an earth   197

INDEX OF FIRST LINES

Over my nose and mouth a cold, hard cone   223
Overburdened, out you clear   135

RANSOMED from darkness and released in Time   185
Red granite and black diorite, with the blue   206

SAE lang has Sorrow tenanted   172
Saftly, saftly, throu the mirk   228
Said the auld spaewife to me   245
Scant are the few green acres that I till   235
Scotland, when it is given to me   205
See the leaves are falling faster   133
She has given all her beauty to the water   239
She's weel respeckit i the kirk   250
She was skilled in music and the dance   136
She was the lassie to redd the house   262
Shon Campbell went to College   92
Sing, Poet, 'tis a merry world   46
Sittin spinnin, sittin spinnin   37
Smile through thy tears, like the blush moss-rose   5
Smooth on the aftermath came an iron law   290
So here hath been dawning   10
So on we marched.   That awful loneliness   217
So you were David's father   215
Soldiers and guns, soldiers and guns   236
Sometimes the whisky-balanced miner sings   296
Spawn he was in the steamy mire   92
Stay me with mosses, comfort me with lichens   209
Sweet Saint Eloi, bend a convenient ear   188

T. 99 would gladly hear   70
Tell me not the good and wise   66
Tell me the auld, auld story   206
'Tha iad ann an grunnd na mara   284
Tha 'n iarmailt ciùin, 'san Loch-a-Tuath   284
Thar na sìorruidheachd, thar a sneachda   270
That all should change to ghost and glance and gleam   178
That old lonely lovely way of living   275
The auld days are gane   242
The auld wife sat ayont her man   170
The bens are nae ayebydan.   Frost and sun   277
The boat sits stuck in light, the water   257
The breakers white and sorrowful   248
The church is bright with candlelight   191
The clever and angry confident on benches   226
The day's impatient, but you sit still   259
The Firm of Glendale & Co.   83
The first cold doubts of new experience   222
The flowers are fled : they say that I am mad   305
The gaslicht flichtered on the stair   294
The gude auld Kirk o' Scotland   36

The hinmost whaup has quat his eerie skirl 91
The hurlygush and hallyoch o the watter 299
The last week of the year's no time 258
The loch o the North i the quaet air 285
The Lord took a staw at mankind 163
The man that mates wi' Poverty 171
The Minister said it wald dee 274
The mirk shaws teeth o steel-cauld ice 306
The nicht's duin wi daunce, the citie's wabbit oot 256
The posters show my country blonde and green 279
The rest of us enjoy the earth 134
The rider Victory reins his horse 182
The room was shrouded from the sun 236
The Rose of all the world is not for me 215
The sunlicht still on me, you row'd in clood 202
The tank had grund him to the yirth 280
The train ! The twelve o'clock for Paradise 160
The veteran Greeks came home 180
The whins are blythesome on the knowe 243
The win' blaws oot o' Orkney 162
The winter's awa : and yonder's the spring 227
There aince was a very pawky duke 111
There are clear moments when we truly know 232
There are so many deaths that go 258
There cometh a time in the life of man 53
There's a puckle lairds in the auld house 230
There's a reid lowe in yer cheek 248
There's nane o' my ain to care 196
There was an ironmaster 62
These chill pillars of fluted stone 276
They all were looking for a king 39
They call Him the Good Shepherd and the Lamb 145
They come ! they come in a glorious march ! 51
They move forward into nomans-land 302
They're wearin' by, the guid auld lives 73
This is our native land 179
Thon nicht the three pit the sails ty her 288
' Thonder they ligg on the grund o the sea 285
Thou doitert, donnert, deil's invention 250
Though buds still speak in hints 169
Though our eyes turn ever waveward 106
Through countless wanderings 186
Time that has dinged doun castels and hie toures 149
'Tis sweet, when smiling Summer flings 34
'Tis thought Odysseus, when the strife was o'er 69
To fight for loyalty outworn 109
To love, and more to love 297
To my true king I offer'd free from stain 13
To the wedding of Shon Maclean 67
To thriftless England we have lent 109
Twa sarious men ae simmer nicht 241

INDEX OF FIRST LINES

Twa traivlers gaed ance to the Hielans awa   90
'Twas a bonnie day—and a day o' dule   127

Under an arch o' bramble   173
Uttermost isle of Europe   24

Wae for the lanely kirkyaird fowk   287
Waement the deid I never did   304
Wauken be nicht, and bydand on some boon   149
We foucht the Prussian Guairds   128
We'll meet nae mair at sunset, when the weary day is dune   27
We swing ungirded hips   221
We were in the frenzied mob, you and I   246
We zealots made up of stiff clay   14
Wee Willie Winkie runs through the toon   25
Westward I watch the low green hills of Wales   68
What ails you, you puir auld body?   168
What blast of Fate, melodious mocker! say   88
What mind is not made whole   233
What shall we do, my soul, to please the King?   143
What tho his grave hauds naething mair   225
Whaur yon broken brig hings owre   234
Wheesht, Joyce, wheesht, and let me hear   203
When Bess was badly and lain doun sae quait   238
When first I saw you in the curious street   158
When from the dark the day is born   232
When Norman knights came trampling from the south   244
When our loud days are chronicles   231
When straight and still the body lies   155
When the shadows o' the e'enin' mingle wi' the summer gloamin'   93
When the warld is aa brunt duin   249
When youthful faith hath fled   7
Where shall he come from, the poet, whose fire   71
Where will I return? To the bell-tower town?   307
While I still lingered on that river-walk   58
Whiles, when frae the far clachan ayont the hill   246
Whit care I for the leagues o sand   291
Whit wey does the engine say *Toot-toot*?   140
Who are you that so strangely woke   154
Who goes there on an evil night?   269
Who in his heart broke churches and burnt fugues   300
Why should your face so please me   181
Wi meal in the girnel   229
Will *Burns*' late frien' and bosom cronie   1
Within the confines of this room   281

Ye were the dawn on the hills o the Coolin   265
Yird him, yird snod the muckle nyaff o him   262
You are a cousin of mine   212
You are blind like us. Your hurt no man designed   221

363

PRINTED IN GREAT BRITAIN AT
THE PRESS OF THE PUBLISHERS